OUR FATHER FORSAKEN

OUR FATHER FORSAKEN

THE ABANDONMENT OF THE GOD OF THE OLD AND NEW TESTAMENTS

H. J. SEAN MOON

BEAUFORT
BOOKS

For inquiries about volume orders, please contact:
Beaufort Books
27 West 20th Street, Suite 1102
New York, NY 10011
sales@beaufortbooks.com

Published in the United States by Beaufort Books www.beaufortbooks.com
Distributed by Midpoint Trade Books, a division of Independent Book Publishers
www.midpointtrade.com
www.ipgbook.com

ISBN: 9780825309311
Ebook: 9780825308147

Cover Design by Misha Panzer
Interior design by Mark Karis

All Biblical quotes are from either the King James Bible or the International Standard. The Holy Bible, King James Version. Cambridge Edition: 1769; King James Bible Online, 2019. www.kingjamesbibleonline.org

Scriptures taken from the Holy Bible, New International Version®, NIV®. Copyright © 1973, 1978, 1984, 2011 by Biblica, Inc.™ Used by permission of Zondervan. All rights reserved worldwide. www.zondervan.com The "NIV" and "New International Version" are trademarks registered in the United States Patent and Trademark Office by Biblica, Inc.™

Printed in the United States of America

This book could not have been written without the talents, hard work, and dedication of Gregg Noll, Richard A. Panzer, Jim Stephens, Lourdes Swarts, and Kerry Williams. Special thanks goes to Dr. Paul Williams for his extensive research and commitment to this book.

CONTENTS

You can enter God's Kingdom only through the narrow gate. The highway to hell is broad, and its gate is wide for the many who choose that way. But the gateway to life is very narrow and the road is difficult, and only a few ever find it.

Beware of false prophets who come disguised as harmless sheep but are really vicious wolves. You can identify them by their fruit, that is, by the way they act. Can you pick grapes from thorn bushes, or figs from thistles? A good tree produces good fruit, and a bad tree produces bad fruit. A good tree can't produce bad fruit, and a bad tree can't produce good fruit. So, every tree that does not produce good fruit is chopped down and thrown into the fire. Yes, just as you can identify a tree by its fruit, so you can identify people by their actions.

Not everyone who calls out to me, "Lord! Lord!" will enter the Kingdom of Heaven. Only those who actually do the will of my Father in heaven will enter. On judgment day many will say to me, "Lord! Lord! We prophesied in your name and cast out demons in your name and performed many miracles in your name." But I will reply, "I never knew you. Get away from me, you who break God's laws."

MATTHEW 7:13-23

INTRODUCTION

A CALL TO ARMS

THIS BOOK REPRESENTS not only an historical-critical analysis of the abandonment of the God of the Old and New Testament in contemporary Christianity, but also a theological defense of the Second Amendment. As such, it merits the attention of freedom-loving people throughout the world.

In the modern church, the Old Testament injunctions regarding self-defense are no longer topics of discussion. The Torah's insistence upon the *lex talionis* has been condemned as barbaric. This law states: "Thus you shall not show pity: life for life, eye for eye, tooth for tooth, hand for hand, foot for foot" (Deut. 19:21). But this injunction does not represent vindictive cruelty. It rather represents the first formal enunciation of the principle of equal justice for all and the end of the pre-Mosaic practice of exacting heavier punishments from the lower classes.

Similarly, the misinterpretation of the sixth commandment, "Thou shalt not kill" has prompted liberal and progressive clerics to call a ban on firearms and the termination of defense spending. Such misinterpretation has caused Quakers in Russia to refuse to kill lice but rather "to put them somewhere else." But the word for kill in this commandment is *ratsakh*, the Hebrew word for premeditated murder or manslaughter. It is never used for legal killing, such as the administration of capital punishment or for the killing of an enemy combatant in war.

The claim that *ratsakh* applies only to intentional murder is buttressed by the fact that God Himself orders the killing of people throughout the Old Testament. Indeed, in approximately one thousand verses, God is depicted as the direct executioner of violent punishments.

What's more, God of Moses proscribes a list of moral offenses that must be balanced by capital punishment. The list includes murder, physically assaulting one's father or mother, kidnapping for purpose of selling the victim into slavery, adultery, incest, homosexuality, and bestiality.

The demand for such punishment gives the impression that the ancient Hebrews were constantly involved in performing acts of capital punishment. But, in truth, this was not the case, as this book shows. Indeed, it was difficult for anyone to receive a death penalty in ancient Israel. First of all, circumstantial evidence wouldn't cut it. One needed two impeccable witnesses who had observed the person transgressing a law that was punishable by death. Next, these two witnesses had to have warned the accused of the capital punishment he could receive by committing the prohibited act, even if he already knew. Finally, the subject must have committed the transgression in direct defiance of the warning. Any hesitation by the perpetrator meant that the death penalty could not be applied to his offense.

Still and all, in this day and age of gay rights and same sex marriage, it strikes the vast majority of believers that the death penalty for practicing homosexuals is outrageous and barbaric. But such reasoning fails to take into account the fact that the prohibition against homosexuality, as Pastor Moon argues, stems from the very essence of Judaism, and this injunction within the Torah:

> See, I set before you today life and prosperity, death and destruction.
> For I command you today to love the Lord your God, to walk in
> obedience to him, and to keep his commands, decrees and laws; then
> you will live and increase, and the Lord your God will bless you in
> the land you are entering to possess.

But if your heart turns away and you are not obedient, and if you are drawn away to bow down to other gods and worship them, I declare to you this day that you will certainly be destroyed. You will not live long in the land you are crossing the Jordan to enter and possess.

This day I call the heavens and the earth as witnesses against you that I have set before you life and death, blessings and curses. Now choose life, so that you and your children may live and that you may love the Lord your God, listen to his voice, and hold fast to him. For the Lord is your life, and he will give you many years in the land he swore to give to your fathers, Abraham, Isaac and Jacob (Deuteronomy 30:15-20).

A primary reason for the abandonment and condemned of the God of Moses by contemporary Jews and Christians is lodged in the fact that the Old Testament contains accounts of genocide instigated in God's name. According to the sixth chapter of the Book of Joshua, the ancient Hebrews were commanded by God to invade the land of Canaan and to kill everyone they encountered—men, women, and children. According to Joshua, they obeyed this command and the desert ran red with blood. Reacting to this Biblical passage, Richard Dawkins has labeled the God of the Old Testament "the most unpleasant character in all fiction." Dawkins made this remark even though he is keenly aware that the Old Testament was not written as a work of fiction and that much of it has been verified by the spade work of thousands of archaeologists. Still and all, modern ministers and priests, by and large, agree with Dawkins and, for the most part, refuse to address the passages in the Bible which condone violence. Those who accept to issue an apologetic dismiss such passages as hyperbole, treat the acts of genocide as a misunderstanding of God's real purpose, or relegate the Book of Joshua, along with the Torah, as a reflection of a primitive mindset and a primitive understanding of the divine being.

But, as this book argues, the acts of genocide were necessary. The harshness of these desert areas forced the Canaanite tribes continuously to seek for water and arable land. Wars were incessant and incredibly violent. The Scythian men were ferocious, bearded giants who lived on wagons, fought to live and lived to fight, drank the blood of their enemies, and used scalps as napkins. The Scythian women, as long as they were virgins, rode, shot arrows, and threw their javelins while mounted. They did not lay aside their virginity until they had killed three of their enemies. The right breasts of these women were hacked off and cauterized so that all of their strength would be diverted to their right shoulder and right arm. The Hittites were equally violent. They ruled over the source of the Tigris and Euphrates Rivers as a military caste. They mined iron from the mountains near Armenia and forged iron weapons that made them fierce foes. The men that they captured were forced to work the mines, while the women, if attractive, were sold as concubines. The old and the infirm were put to death.

In addition, the Canaanite people sacrificed children to their savage gods. The Bible makes it clear that child sacrifice was a regular feature of the religion of the Canaanites and the surrounding nations: ". . . they do for their gods every detestable thing that Jehovah hates, even burning their sons and their daughters in the fire to their gods" (Deuteronomy 12:31). The failure to eradicate all of the Canaanite tribes, as God commanded, allowed these practices to seep into Israelite culture and religion in later centuries.

Along with genocide came the notion of "holy war." The Ark of the Covenant was carried into battle by the priests so that God could participate in the defeat of His enemies. Before the conflict commenced, a priest was obliged to address the Hebrew army as follows: "Hear, Israel: Today you are going into battle against your enemies. Do not be fainthearted or afraid; do not panic or be terrified by them. For the Lord your God is the one who goes with you to fight for you against your enemies to give you victory" (Deuteronomy 20:2-4).

Upholders of the second amendment should take much of this to heart. The God of Moses condoned the use of weapons for self-defense, demanded capital punishment, and sanctioned just warfare.

But what of the New Testament?

Many modern priests and ministers maintain that gun ownership, even for the purpose of self-defense, is un-Christian. Jesus, they insist, was a pacifist who said: "Blessed are the peacemakers for they shall be called children of God" (Matt. 5:9) and rebuked all acts of violence by saying: "those who live by the sword shall die by the sword" (Matt. 26:52). They argue, in the manner of Marcion, that Jesus brought a new understanding of God to man, an understanding that included a dispensation from the Mosaic Law. They inevitably verify this claim by turning to this passage from the Sermon on the Mount: "You have heard that it was said, 'An eye for an eye and a tooth for a tooth.' But I say to you, Do not resist an evildoer. But if anyone strikes you on the right cheek, turn the other also" (Matthew 5: 38-39).

But such presentations of Jesus, as this book explains, are historically and scripturally inaccurate. Jesus employed a whip to drive the moneychangers from the temple, condemned the religious leaders of His day with vituperative language, and proclaimed to His followers: "I have not come to bring peace but a sword" (Matthew 10:34). What's more, the depiction of Jesus as a modern milquetoast is completely undermined by this passage from the Gospel of Luke:

> Jesus asked them, "When I sent you without purse, bag or sandals, did you lack anything?"
>
> "Nothing," they answered.
>
> He said to them, "But now if you have a purse, take it, and also a bag; and if you don't have a sword, sell your cloak and buy one. It is written: 'And he was numbered with the transgressors'; and I tell you that this must be fulfilled in me. Yes, what is written about me is reaching its fulfillment."
>
> The disciples said, "See, Lord, here are two swords."
>
> "That's enough!" he replied (22: 35-38).

Similarly, those who argue that Jesus granted His followers a dispensation from the laws of Moses are obliged to edit the gospels with a carving knife—cutting off vast portions of the Lord's teachings, including these words from the Sermon on the Mount:

> Do not think that I have come to abolish the Law or the Prophets;
> I have not come to abolish them but to fulfill them. For truly I tell
> you, until heaven and earth disappear, not the smallest letter, not
> the least stroke of a pen, will by any means disappear from the Law
> until everything is accomplished. Therefore anyone who sets aside
> one of the least of these commands and teaches others accordingly
> will be called least in the kingdom of heaven, but whoever practices
> and teaches these commands will be called great in the kingdom of
> heaven. For I tell you that unless your righteousness surpasses that of
> the Pharisees and the teachers of the law, you will certainly not enter
> the kingdom of heaven (Matthew 5: 17-20).

Modern proponents of gun control also ignore two thousand years
of such teaching in support of bearing arms and just warfare. This tradition explains the pivotal role of Christian clerics during the American
Revolution. In 1776, Reverend John Peter Muhlenberg threw off his
clerical garb at the end of his sermon to his Woodstock, Virginia congregation to reveal his military uniform, proclaiming, "There is a time
to pray and a time to fight, and that time has now come!" Muhlenberg
took part in the fighting at Charleston, Brandywine, Stony Point, and
Yorktown, as well as in the winter at Valley Forge. Jonathan Mayhew, the
pastor of the West Church in Boston, gave moral sanction to taking up
arms against the British occupiers by preaching that opposition to tyrants
was a "glorious" Christian duty. James Caldwell, a Presbyterian minister,
helped the American rebels win the Battle of Springfield in 1780. Upon
noticing that his fellow rebels had run out of wadding, the paper used to
hold the powder in the barrel of their muskets and long rifles, Caldwell
ran to a nearby church and returned with a pile of hymnals for the job.
After the war, the Militia Act of 1792 made gun ownership and militia
membership a legal obligation rather than a voluntary option.

The Second Amendment remains firmly rooted in the Old and New
Testament and two thousand years of Christian tradition.

Bearing arms for self-defense or to protect the lives not only of family, friends, and loved ones, but also fellow human beings is a moral and religious duty.

It is not merely a matter of a civil right or a political privilege.

Proof of this contention resides within the pages of this book.

LARRY PRATT

Lawrence D. Pratt is the executive director emeritus of Gun Owners of America, a United States-based firearm lobbying group, and a former member of the Virginia House of Delegates.

Pro iis qui quaerunt veritatem

For those who seek the truth

PART ONE

THE HERESY

1

THE FIRST HERETIC

Marcion explained the Old Testament in its literal sense and rejected every allegorical interpretation. He recognized it as the revelation of the creator of the world and the god of the Jews, but placed it, just on that account, in sharpest contrast to the Gospel. He demonstrated the contradictions between the Old Testament and the Gospel in a voluminous work (The Antithesis). In the god of the former book he saw a being whose character was stern justice, and therefore anger, contentiousness and unmercifulness. The law which rules nature and man appeared to him to accord with the characteristics of this god and the kind of law revealed by him, and therefore it seemed credible to him that this god is the creator and lord of the world (kosmokratos). As the law which governs the world is inflexible, and yet, on the other hand, full of contradictions, just and again brutal, and as the law of the Old Testament exhibits the same features, so the god of creation was to Marcion a being who united in himself the whole gradations of attributes from justice to malevolence, from obstinacy to inconsistency.

ADOLF VON HARNACK, *HISTORY OF DOGMA*, VOLUME I

FIFTY YEARS AFTER THE DEATH OF ST. PAUL, a charismatic preacher named Marcion appeared in Rome to proclaim the "hidden" meaning of the teachings of Jesus. His interpretation relied heavily upon the mystery religions that had spread throughout the Roman Empire during the early Christian era and the teachings of the Neo-Platonists. It centered on the concept of *gnosis*—the knowledge required for a soul to transcend the confines of matter.

According to Marcion, the exacting and wrathful deity of the Old Testament, whom he called the "Demiurge," was not the God of the New Testament. Jesus, he insisted, bore witness to the unknown Supreme Being of Acts 17:23.[1] This higher God was a Being of pure light, the giver of eternity, and a fount of infinite mercy and goodness.

To establish his case, Marcion pointed to contradictions between the Old and New Testaments. Joshua, he argued, had the sun stopped in its tracks in order to prolong a battle against the Hebrew people, while Christ, through St. Paul, said: "Let not the sun go down on your wrath." Elisha had commanded bears to attack children, while Jesus said: "Let the little children come unto me." The Demiurge demanded an eye for an eye, and a tooth for a tooth," while Jesus said: "Do not resist an evil person. If someone strikes you on the right cheek, turn to him the other also."[2]

Surely, Marcion maintained, there is a cleft between the two testaments that cannot be breached. Since the God of Jesus is a God of pure light and perfect love, the entire Old Testament, which sanctions violence for the defense of home and hearth, must be discarded from the Christian canon.

Concerning Marcionism, St. Justin Martyr in his *First Apology* wrote: "And, as we said before, the devils put forward Marcion of Pontus, who is even now teaching men to deny that God is the maker of all things in heaven and on earth, and that the Christ predicted by the prophets is His Son, and preaches another god besides the Creator of all, and likewise another son. And this man many have believed, as if he alone knew the truth, and laugh at us, though they have no proof of what they say, but are carried away irrationally as lambs by a wolf,

---

1   W. H. C. Frend, *The Early Church* (Philadelphia: J. B. Lippincott, 1966), p. 67.

2   Ibid.

and become the prey of atheistic doctrines, and of devils."[3]

The theology of Marcion was rooted in Gnosticism, a blend of Neo-Platonism and the various mystery religions, including the cults of Mithras, Isis, and Osiris/Dionysus that had spread throughout the Greco-Roman world. Many of these mystery religions bore a striking resemblance to the depictions of Jesus in the four canonical gospels. The cult of Osiris/Dionysus concerns a Son of God who is born of a virgin in a humble cowshed, transforms water into wine at a wedding ceremony, suffered a sacrificial death, descended into hell, vowed to return as the judge of mankind during the Last Days, and instructed his disciples to celebrate his death and resurrection by a ritual meal which consisted of bread and wine.[4] Such parallelism caused many pagans to confuse Christ with a mystery deity.

The core of Gnosticism was the claim that a divine spark (soul) remained entrapped in the matter (body) of every human being. This spark could be freed through gnosis (knowledge) of the Highest God who was the source of all light and the passwords necessary for souls to return to their true celestial home. The various manifestations of Gnosticism shared the following beliefs in common: (1) All matter, including every fleshly desire, is evil, and the non-material, spirit-realm is good. (2) From the essence of the Highest God had emanated Aeons, lesser deific beings, who inhabit various levels of the universe. (3) The Creator of the (material) universe is not the Highest God, but an inferior spirit, known as the Demiurge. (4) The true Gnostic is the individual who understands his own divine nature. (5) To achieve salvation requires knowledge of the passwords so that the Aeons, who inhabit the seven planets of the universe, will allow the soul to ascend to

---

3   St. Justin Martyr, "Dialogue with Trypho," 35, excerpted from *Ante-Nicene Fathers*, Volume 1, edited by Alexander Roberts & James Donaldson. 1885. Online Edition, https://en.wikisource. org/wiki/Ante-Nicene_Fathers/Volume_I/Dialogue_with_Trypho

4   Timothy Freke and Peter Gandy, *The Jesus Mysteries: Was the "Original Jesus" a Pagan God?* (New York: Three Rivers Press, 1999), p. 5.

the highest heaven, and the possession of amulets, which would weaken the monstrous powers that the Aeons wielded over their various realms.[5]

THE MARCION CANON

The gospels of Matthew, Mark, and John were also unacceptable to Marcion since they displayed the ties between Jesus and the Hebrew tradition. The only primitive Christian documents acceptable to him were the Gospel of Luke and the epistles of St. Paul.[6]

Marcion's teachings were condemned by the leaders of the primitive Christian communities. The great church fathers, including Tertullian, labeled him "the son of Satan." But the movement of the first heretic of Christianity spread throughout the Mediterranean world. More Gnostic Christians, including Valentinus, appeared to claim that Jesus had come to save mankind from the evil reign of the God of the Jews.

THE DOCETIC JESUS

Valentinus appeared in Rome shortly after Marcion's departure to set up his own school of Gnostic thought. Christ, he maintained, was not born of Mary but only assumed a physical body. This disguise was necessary since the real presence of Christ, who was constituted of pure light, would have blinded anyone who beheld him. This Jesus did not eat or defecate. He never died on the cross since spirit cannot suffer. On Good Friday, he had merely engaged in divine playacting.[7]

According to Valentinus, mankind was divided into three categories: (1) the elect, who knew of their divine nature; (2) the psychics, who possessed a spark of light within them that could be rekindled; and (3) the vast majority of mankind, who ate, drank, married, and died eternally.[8]

---

5   Stephan A. Hoeller, "The Gnostic World View," The Gnostic Archive, n. d., http://gnosis.org/gnintro.htm

6   Tertullian, *Against Marcion*, Book IV, in *New Advent*, http://www.newadvent.org/fathers/03124.htm

7   Henry Chadwick, *The Early Church* (Baltimore, Maryland: Penguin Books, 1969), p. 37.

8   Frend, *The Early Church*, p. 65.

THE GOSPEL OF TRUTH

Valentinus maintained that he had received the truth about Jesus from Theudas, who had been a member of St. Paul's inner circle. The "secret wisdom" that Theudas had received from the great apostle constituted the crux of *The Gospel of Truth*, a work that Valentinus put to paper. This work is not an account of the life of Jesus but rather a homily for a gathering of Gnostics. In it, Valentinus maintains that mankind remains enslaved to Error, which he identifies as the Demiurge, who created the material world, and his fellow Aeons. Man's ignorance of the Father God of boundless light over the centuries has coalesced into a fog that permeates the earth. Valentinus described the work of Christ as follows:

> He [Jesus] appeared, informing them of the Father, the illimitable one. He inspired them with that which is in the mind, while doing his will. Many received the light and turned towards him. But material men were alien to him and did not discern his appearance nor recognize him. For he came in the likeness of flesh and nothing blocked his way because it was incorruptible and unrestrainable. Moreover, while saying new things, speaking about what is in the heart of the Father, he proclaimed the faultless word. Light spoke through his mouth, and his voice brought forth life. He gave them thought and understanding and mercy and salvation and the Spirit of strength derived from the limitlessness of the Father and sweetness. He caused punishments and scourgings to cease, for it was they which caused many in need of mercy to astray from him in error and in chains—and he mightily destroyed them and derided them with knowledge. He became a path for those who went astray and knowledge to those who were ignorant, a discovery for those who sought, and a support for those who tremble, a purity for those who were defiled.[9]

---

9   Valentinus, *The Gospel of Truth*, translated by Robert M. Grant, The Nag Hammadi Library, http://gnosis.org/naghamm/got.html

The Gospel of Truth upholds the doctrine of predestination. The message of salvation can only be understood by those who possess a remembrance of their true spiritual home. These fortunate few are the Elect whose names have been uttered by the Highest God. Those whose names have not been spoken are destined to live and die in total ignorance.[10]

Regarding this work, St. Irenaeus of Lyons wrote:

> But the followers of Valentinus, putting away all fear, bring forward their own compositions and boast that they have more Gospels than really exist. Indeed, their audacity has gone so far that they entitle their recent composition the Gospel of Truth, though it agrees in nothing with the Gospels of the apostles, and so no Gospel of theirs is free from blasphemy. For if what they produce is the Gospel of Truth, and is different from those the apostles handed down to us, those who care to can learn how it can be shown from the Scriptures themselves that [then] what is handed down from the apostles is not the Gospel of Truth.[11]

A GLUT OF GOSPELS

Throughout the second century, a host of other Gnostic gospels appeared, including *Secret Teachings of John*, *The Gospel of the Twelve*, *The Gospel of Thomas*, and *The Gospel according to the Egyptians*. These works were so widely circulated that it became imperative for Christians to establish an orthodox canon of scripture.

To accomplish this task, Irenaeus argued that believers should look to the Church of Rome, since that ". . . most great and universally known church. . . had been founded and established by the glorious

---

10   Ibid.

11   Irenaeus, *Against Heresies*, Book III, Chapter 3, in *Ante-Nicene Fathers, Volume 1*, edited by Alexander Roberts, et alia (Buffalo, NY: Christian Literature Publishing Company, 1885), p. 198.

Apostles Peter and Paul. . . ."[12] By heeding this advice, two objectives were met: (1) a central authority—the Church of Rome—was established, and (2) four gospels—Matthew, Mark, Luke, and John—were sanctioned as the oldest and most reliable.[13]

MARCIONISM TRANSMOGRIFIES

But even the establishment the New Testament canon failed to put an end to the movement of Marcion. It assumed the form of the Paulicians, who emerged in Syria during the 8th Century. It formed the crux of the teachings of the Bogomils who appeared in Bulgaria in the 9th Century. And it animated the thought of the Cathars who came into being in the Languedoc region of France during the 11th Century.[14]

Marcionism eventually crystallized into the clandestine society of Freemasonry that was established in 1716 at the Goose and Gridiron Ale House in London.[15] The freemasons saw themselves as emissaries of the highest God, a being of immeasurable light.[16] Knowledge of the spark of the Monad that is implanted in every human being, they came to believe, can only be obtained by members of Freemasonry through a series of gradual steps or "degrees" until they are worthy of entering the *arcanum arcanorum* (the fraternity within the fraternity) and to receive

---

12   Ibid.

13   Richard M. Grant, *The Early Christian Doctrine of God* (Charlottesville: The University of Virginia Press, 1966), pp. 94-98.

14   "Medieval Gnosticism," in *The Gnostic Jesus*, http://www.gnostic-jesus.com/gnostic-jesus/Medieval-gnosticism.html

15   Sanford Holst, "Founding of the Grand Lodge of England in 1717," *Masonic Sourcebook*, n. d., http://www.masonicsourcebook.com/grand_lodge_of_england.htm See also Albert Gallatin Mackey, *The History of Masonry*, Volume 2, Chapters XXIA-XXXI, 1898, available online at Petre-Stones Review of Freemasonry, http://www.freemasons-freemasonry.com/mackeyhi08.html

16   W. H. C. Frend, *The Early Church* (Philadelphia: J. P. Lippincott Company, 1966), pp. 60-68.

"the Truth which it calls Light."[17] Albert G. Mackey in his *Encyclopedia of Freemasonry* wrote: "The religion of Freemasonry is not sectarian. It admits men of every creed within its hospitable bosom, rejecting none and approving none for his particular faith. It is not Judaism . . . it is not Christianity. It does not meddle with sectarian creeds or doctrines, but teaches fundamental truth. At its altar, men of all religions may kneel; to its creed, disciples of every faith may subscribe."[18]

The Masonic movement quickly spread to South Africa, India, Ireland, Germany, the Netherlands, Russia, Spain, and France, where it helped to spark the French Revolution. In the United States, the list of freemasons came to include George Washington, Benjamin Franklin, John Jay, Ethan Allen, Patrick Henry, Paul Revere, John Brown, John Paul Jones, John Hancock, John Marshall, Thomas Paine, William Randolph, and Roger Sherman.

ENDING THE OLD TESTAMENT

By the middle of the 18th Century, leading "Christian" theologians throughout the world began to openly espouse the ancient heresy. In Germany, the prominent Lutheran theologian and Freemason Johann Salomo Semler (1725-91) wrote: "As a general rule, Christians cannot come to a knowledge of God through the books of the Old Testament but only through the perfect doctrine of Christ and His disciples."[19]

One hundred years later, another Freemason, German theologian Adolf von Harnack (1851-1930), in a book dedicated to Marcion, wrote: "Rejecting the Old Testament in the second century was an error that the Church rightly avoided. Keeping it in the sixteenth century was

---

17   Albert Pike, *Morals and Dogma* (Charleston, South Carolina: Supreme Council of the Thirty-Third Degree of the Scottish Rite, 1871), p. 105.

18   Albert G. Mackey, *An Encyclopedia of Freemasonry*, Volume 1, (Chicago: Masonic History Company, 1924), p. 641.

19   Johann Salomo Semler, *Institutio as Doctrinam Christianam Liberaltier Discendam* (Regensburg, Germany: Halae Magdeburgicae, 1774), p. 79.

a fate that even the Reformation could not escape. But to preserve it in the nineteenth century as a canonical document at the heart of Protestantism is a result of religious and ecclesiastical paralysis."[20]

A SYMBOL OF ALIENATION

The Gnosticism of Marcion has formed the theological basis of Freemasonry and influenced the thought of such influential writers and philosophers as Arthur Schopenhauer, Karl Jung, Thomas Mann, Herman Hesse, and Helena Petrovna Blavatsky.[21] It also constitutes the core of mainstream contemporary Christianity, which has managed to dismiss the God of the Old Testament as a product of a primitive and barbaric people, while upholding Jesus as a harbinger of theological enlightenment and religious indifferentism.

Rudolf Bultmann, the leading New Testament scholar of the 20th Century, maintained that the commandments of God in the Old Testament serve to make human beings aware of the consequences of living under the Law, while the Gospel frees them from this subjection. The Old Testament, for Bultmann, represents a mere symbol of the alienated relationship between God and mankind.[22]

THE NAG HAMMADI DISCOVERY

The rise of Gnosticism in the 20th Century was fueled by the discovery of an entire library of ancient Gnostic texts, including Valentinus's *The Gospel of Truth*, within a cave in the upper Egyptian town of Nag Hammadi. James Robinson, the editor of these texts and a Presbyterian minister, declared his attraction to the spirituality of the Gnostics by

---

20   Adolf von Harnack, *Marcion. Das Evangelium vom Fremden Gott,* Second Edition (Leipzig, Germany: J. C. Hinrichs, 1924), p. 217.

21   Kirsten J. Grimstad, *The Modern Revival of Gnosticism and Thomas Mann's Doktor Faustus* (Rochester, New York: Camden House, 2002), p. 49.

22   Rudolf Bultmann, "Die Bedeutung des Alten Testaments fur den Christlichen Glauben," in *Glauben und Verstehen* I, Seventh Edition (Tubingen: J. C. B. Mohr, 1972), pp. 313-336.

writing: "The focus of this [Gnostic] library has much in common with primitive Christianity, with eastern religions, and with holy men of all times, as well as with the more secular equivalents of today, such as the counter-culture movements coming from the 1960's."[23] In Robinson's view, Gnosticism, no less than Orthodoxy, was a "valid trajectory" of primitive Christianity.[24]

---

23   James Robinson, quoted in Peter Jones, "Gnosticism in the Mainline," *Truthxchange,* May 2008, https://truthxchange.com/2008/05/gnosticism-in-the-mainline/

24   Ibid.

2

THE NEW GNOSTICISM

Gnosticism can bring us such truths with a high authority, for it speaks with the voice of the highest part of the human—the spirit. Of this spirit, it has been said, "it bloweth where it listeth." This then is the reason why the Gnostic worldview could not be extirpated in spite of many centuries of persecution.

The Gnostic worldview has always been timely, for it always responded best to the "knowledge of the heart" that is true Gnosis. Yet today, its timeliness is increasing, for the end of the second millennium has seen the radical deterioration of many ideologies which evaded the great questions and answers addressed by Gnosticism. The clarity, frankness, and authenticity of the Gnostic answer to the questions of the human predicament cannot fail to impress and (in time) to convince.

STEPHAN HOELLER, "THE GNOSTIC WORLDVIEW," 2018

THE RECIRCULATION OF THE GNOSTIC GOSPELS prompted pro-gressive Christian scholars to maintain that a "new form" of Christianity had been discovered for a "new generation." Episcopalian Bishop John Spong proclaimed that Christians finally had arrived at "the end of an era [where]. . . most traditional Christian doctrine. . . [has] become obsolete," and called upon the Church to abandon its "theistic definition of God."[1]

---

1   Bishop John Spong, quoted in Ibid.

In keeping with the resurgence of Gnostic Christianity, Timothy Freke and Peter Gandy wrote *The Jesus Mysteries: Was the "Original Jesus" a Pagan God?* In the book, the two authors, like Valentinus, denied that Jesus was a flesh and blood person. Explaining the impact of the newly discovered Gnostic texts on their work, Freke said: "What it's done is completely transform our understanding of Christianity. Its message is not tied to belief in a historical event, so that you either believe it happened, or you don't—and if you believe it, you're saved, and if not, you're damned. What we've discovered is that the message of original Christianity was far deeper than that. It was about, for the original Christians, becoming a Christ oneself."[2] *The Jesus Mysteries* was remarkably well-received, reaching bestseller status in the United Kingdom, and garnering a "Book of the Year" award.[3]

Imbued with the Gnostic notion of a spiritual Christ unsullied by matter, Bill Phipps, the moderator of the United Church of Canada (Canada's largest denomination) denied the virgin birth, the bodily resurrection of Christ as well as the reality of heaven and hell. "People have to realize," Phipps explained, "that within our church there's a wide range of faith convictions."[4] The denomination's General Council, in support of this position, announced: "Rarely, if ever, do we use doctrinal standards to exclude anyone from the circle of belonging."[5] The church as "the circle of belonging," Peter Jones points out in "Gnosticism in the Mainline," has morphed into an all-inclusive circle of pagan monism where all religions and faith expressions are welcomed. All, that is, except historic orthodoxy.

Moreover, the Gnostic view of a god of highest light, who transcends

2   David Allen Dodson, "Raising a Holy Ruckus: The 'Jesus Mysteries' Open a Controversial Can of Worms," *CNN*, September 21, 2000, http://www.cnn.com/2000/books/news/09/21/jesus.mysteries/

3   Jones, "Gnosticism in the Mainline."

4   Bill Phipps, quoted in Ibid.

5   Ibid.

the God of the Bible, is openly promoted by the group Presbyterians for Lesbian and Gay Concerns. In their bi-monthly publication, *More Light*, they send a call for spiritual testimonies of various examples of "connection to The Source, the sacred, the realm of The Spirit . . . and all the other ways of describing It. . . . Dykes! Send us. . . profound mystical experiences, connection to The Source, the connection between sex and spirit. . . . How do you connect to The Source? Prayer? Art? Ritual? Magic? Trance? Dance? Mind-altering substances. . . spells, chants, charms. . . [for compiling an anthology of] writings by bi-sexual people of faith (Jews, Christians, Pagans, Quakers, Unitarian Universalists, and those following other spiritual paths."[6]

The new Gnostics delighted in the "death of God" theology which, they believed, celebrated the end of Judeo-Christian theology. In 1974, theologian David Miller proclaimed: ". . . the announcement of the death of God [is] the obituary of a useless single-minded and one-dimensional norm of a civilization that has been predominantly monotheistic, not only in its religion, but also in its politics, its history, its social order, its ethics, and its psychology. . . ." Miller went on to prophesy: "When released from the tyrannical imperialism of monotheism by the death of God, man has the opportunity of discovering new dimensions hidden in the depths of reality's history." At the funeral of the Biblical God, Miller announced the rebirth of the spirituality of gods and goddesses of ancient Greece and Rome, including the deities of the mystery religions and Gnosticism.[7]

MARCIONISM REDUX

Recently, the *United Methodist Insight*, the denomination's official publication, ran an article by Brian Snyder entitled "No Guns for Jesus Folk." Snyder condemned Christians who use arms to defend

---

6   Ibid.

7   David Miller, quoted in https://www.renewamerica.com/columns/kimball/181209

themselves, claiming that such self-defense is contrary to the teachings of Jesus. Upholding the teachings of the denomination, he wrote:

> There are no guns, at least not guns intended to be used for self-defense, in the hands of Christians who trust in God's love. If you own a gun for self-defense, it implies that you are so afraid to die that you would kill to save yourself and your family. It implies that you would ignore Jesus's teachings about turning the other cheek, about those who live by the sword, and about loving one's enemies. It implies that you would ignore the penultimate act of Jesus's ministry, his death at the hands of the Romans, his nonviolent resistance in the face of great evil. Using violence against evil is like using a blowtorch to light a birthday cake; it might work, but it is exceedingly dangerous to everyone involved. Instead, a much better tool is available. When John wrote "God is love," he argued that the essence of God is love. That suggests that love is profoundly powerful. Love—not guns or bombs or evil—is the most powerful force in the universe, so perhaps if we want to defeat evil, we might try using it.[8]

In keeping with this position, the United Methodist Church prohibited the National Rifle Association from sponsoring an information table at their 2016 General Conference.[9]

Certainly, the Supreme Being of the United Methodist Church is vastly different from the God of Moses, Joshua, and David, who called upon the ancient Israelites to rid the promised land of all the tribes who inhabited it.

A UNISEXUAL DEITY

In 2017, the United Church of Christ (UCC) upheld its faith in the

---

8   Brian Snyder, "No Guns for Jesus Folk," *United Methodist Insight*, November 6, 2017, http://um-insight.net/perspectives/no-guns-for-jesus-folk/

9   "United Methodist Church Displays Intolerance by Banning the NRA from General Conference," *Hacking Christianity*, February 4, 2016.

higher god of Gnosticism by issuing an Inclusive Language Covenant which read as follows:

> We will seek to include male, female, and genderneutral language and imagery for God, taking particular care to be expansive in the language and imagery chosen so that they do not inadvertently suggest that God is exclusively associated with one gender. (Examples: "God in God's wisdom" rather than "God in his wisdom"; "O God, who watches over us as a Father and nurtures us as a Mother" rather than "O God, who watches over us as a Father.")

> We will seek to include language that helps to avoid male only terms in pronouns and images of people. (Examples: "people" rather than "men"; "humankind" rather than "mankind;" "forebears" rather than "forefathers"; "when you become an adult" rather than "when you become a man.")

> We will seek to include language and imagery that are not pejorative regarding the different physical conditions and abilities of persons. (Examples: "People may stand" rather than "All stand"; "Persons with leprosy" rather than "lepers.")

There remains scant similarity between the unisexual deity whom the UCC venerates and the God of the Torah: "The Lord is a warrior. The Lord is His name" (Exodus 15:3), let alone the mighty God of the Hebrew prophets: "The Lord will go forth like a warrior, He will arouse His zeal like a man of war He will utter a shout, yes, He will raise a war cry He will prevail against His enemies" (Isaiah 14:13).

The God of the Old Testament, unlike the he/she being of the UCC, is masculine. All the verbal forms that the Old Testament uses to describe the actions of God are masculine.[10] Moses speaks to God face to face "as one would speak man to man" (Exodus 33:1). And over fifty

---

10   Thomas Romer, *Dark God: Cruelty, Sex, and Violence in the Old Testament* (New York: Paulist Press, 2013), p. 25.

Old Testament texts present God as a king. Psalm 93, for example, says:

The Lord is king! He is robed in majesty.

Indeed, the Lord is robed in majesty and armed with strength.

THE SOLE SOURCE OF TRUTH

The dogmatic integrity of the Roman Catholic Church resided in its claim of spiritual exclusivity—an adamant insistence that it alone possessed the absolute, universal, and univocal truth. Any religious body that deviated from the doctrines of the Church was in error. The first expression of this teaching came from the following passage from St. Cyprian's "On the Unity of the Catholic Faith" (AD 240):

> The Spouse of Christ cannot become wanton. She is a virgin and chaste. She knows one house, and guards the sanctity of one bridal chamber with chaste reserve. She keeps us for God. She appoints to the Kingdom the sons to whom she has given life. Whoever has been separated from the Church is yoked with an adulteress, is separated from the promises made to the Church. Nor shall he who leaves Christ's Church arrive, at Christ's rewards. He is a stranger; he is sacrilegious; he is an enemy. Who has not the Church for mother cannot have God for his father. If anyone outside the ark of Noah could escape, then may he also escape who shall be outside the Church.[11]

Extra Ecclesiam nulla salus ("Outside the Church, there is no salvation") was affirmed by the great canonical doctors, including St. Ambrose, St. Jerome, St. Augustine, and St. Thomas Aquinas, and upheld by the Fourth Lateran Council. The Council of Florence in 1431 proclaimed:

---

11   St. Cyprian, "On the Unity of the Church," New Advent, Church Fathers Series, http://www.newadvent.org/fathers/050701.htm

The most Holy Roman Church firmly believes, professes, and proclaims that those not living within the Catholic Church, not only pagans, but also Jews and heretics and schismatics cannot become participants in eternal life, but will depart "into everlasting fire which was prepared for the devil and his angels" (Matt. 25:41), unless before the end of life the same have been added to the flock; and that the unity of the ecclesiastical body is so strong that only to those remaining in it are the sacraments of the Church of benefit for salvation, and do fastings, almsgiving, and other functions of piety and exercises of Christian service produce eternal reward, and that no one, whatever almsgiving he has practiced, even if he has shed blood for the name of Christ, can be saved, unless he has remained in the bosom and unity of the Catholic Church.[12]

In his encyclical *Singulari quidem*, issued on March 17, 1856, Pius IX maintained: "There is only one true, holy, Catholic Church, which is the Apostolic Roman Church. There is only one See founded on Peter by the word of the Lord (St. Cyprian, Epistle 43), outside of which we cannot find either true faith or eternal salvation. He who does not have the Church for a mother cannot have God for a father."[13]

Five years before the convocation of Vatican II, Pius XII in his Allocution to the Gregorian University (October 17, 1953) said: "By divine mandate the interpreter and guardian of the Scriptures, and the depository of Sacred Tradition living within her, the Church alone is the entrance to salvation: She alone, by herself, and under the protection and guidance of the Holy Spirit, is the source of truth." [14]

---

12 The Ecumenical Council of Florence," *Cantatate Domino*, 1441, https://www.ewtn.com/library/ COUNCILS/FLORENCE.HTM

13 Pius IX, *"Singulari Quidem,"* March 17, 1856, http://www.papalencyclicals.net/Pius09/p9singul. htm

14 Pius XII, "Allocution to the Gregorian University, October 17, 1953, quoted in *Extra Ecclesiam Nulla Solus*, Apostolic Apologetics, n.d., https://sites.google.com/site/apostolicapologetics/extra- ecclesiam-nulla-salus

FALSE AND TRUE ECUMENISM

Because Catholicism represented the one true and apostolic faith, Pope Pius XI in his encyclical *Mortalium animos* (1928) drew a distinction between false and true ecumenism. The encyclical stated:

> These pan-Christians who turn their minds to uniting the churches seem, indeed, to pursue the noblest of ideas in promoting charity among all Christians: nevertheless, how does it happen that this charity tends to injure faith? Everyone knows that John himself, the Apostle of love, who seems to reveal in his Gospel the secrets of the Sacred Heart of Jesus, and who never ceased to impress on the memories of his followers the new commandment "Love one another," altogether forbade any intercourse with those who professed a mutilated and corrupt version of Christ's teaching: "If any man come to you and bring not this doctrine, receive him not into the house nor say to him: God speed you." For which reason, since charity is based on a complete and sincere faith, the disciples of Christ must be united principally by the bond of one faith. Who then can conceive a Christian Federation, the members of which retain each his own opinions and private judgment, even in matters which concern the object of faith, even though they be repugnant to the opinions of the rest? And in what manner, we ask, can men who follow contrary opinions, belong to one and the same Federation of the faithful?
>
> How so great a variety of opinions can make the way clear to affect the unity of the Church We know not; that unity can only arise from one teaching authority, one law of belief and one faith of Christians. But We do know that from this it is an easy step to the neglect of religion or indifferentism and to modernism, as they call it. Those, who are unhappily infected with these errors, hold that dogmatic truth is not absolute but relative, that is, it agrees with the varying necessities of time and place and with the varying tendencies

of the mind, since it is not contained in immutable revelation, but is capable of being accommodated to human life.[15]

CATHOLIC GNOSTICISM

This position crumbled in the wake of Vatican II and the discovery of the Gnostic gospels. The spirit of religious indifferentism entered the Church and began to erode its cherished claims. It became evident in *Nostra aetate,* a decree which Pope Paul VI issued on October 28, 1965. "In Hinduism," the decree said, "men contemplate the divine mystery and express it through an inexhaustible abundance of myths and through searching philosophical inquiry. They seek freedom from the anguish of our human condition either through ascetical practices or profound meditation or a flight to God with love and trust."[16] On August 22, 1969, he continued his praise of the Hindus by stating that Mahatma Gandhi was "ever conscious of God's presence."[17] Brahma, Vishnu, and Shiva, it appeared, had come to replace the Holy Trinity.

"Buddhism," Paul VI maintained in *Nostra Aetate,* "teaches a way by which men, in a devout and confident spirit, may be able either to acquire the state of perfect liberation, or attain, by their own efforts or through higher help, supreme illumination."[18] On September 30, 1973, he greeted the Dalai Lama by saying: "We are happy to welcome you today. You come from Asia, the cradle of ancient religions and human

---

15 Pius XI. *Motalium Animos,* January 6, 1928, http://www.papalencyclicals.net/Pius11/
    P11MORTA.HTM

16 Paul VI, *Nostra Aetate,* a decree promulgated on October 28, 1965, http://www.vatican.va/
    archive/hist_councils/ii_vatican_council/documents/vat-ii_decl_19651028_nostra-aetate_
    en.html

17 Paul VI, "To the President of India for the Centenary Celebrations of the Birth of Mahatma
    Gandhi," August 22, 1969, http://www.catholicnewsagency.com/document/to-the-president-of-
    india-for-the-centenary-celebrations-of-the-birth-of-mahatma-gandhi-517/

18 Paul VI, *Nostra Aetate.*

traditions which are rightly held in deep veneration."[19] But Asia was the cradle of neither Judaism nor Christianity and the faith that the pontiff now held "in deep veneration" denied the "revealed truths" of the Old and New Testaments and Catholic tradition.

Such statements of religious indifferentism caused Catholics to question the purpose of the Society of the Propagation of the Faith and the need for non-Catholics to convert from their native religions, and the purpose of Catholic missionaries. It was little surprise that Paul VI's statements regarding other religions produced a sharp decline in U.S. Catholic missionaries; their number dwindled from 9,655 in 1968 to 4,164 in 1996.[20]

THE WORSHIP OF MAN

In keeping with Gnosticism, Pope Paul VI spoke of the divinity of man and of the rise of a new form of humanism. Addressing the last general meeting of Vatican II, he said: "The attention of our Council has been absorbed by the discovery of human needs. But we call upon those who term themselves modern humanists, and who have renounced the transcendent value of the highest realities, to give the Council credit at least for one quality and to recognize our own new type of humanism: We, too, in fact, We more than any others, honor mankind; we have the cult of man."[21] In 1971, he issued this press statement to commemorate the success of the Apollo mission: "Man is the king of the earth and the prince of heaven. Honor to man, honor to thought, to science, to technology, to labor, to the synthesis of scientific and organizational activity of man."[22]

---

19   "Pope Greets the Dalai Lama," *L'Osservatore Romano*, October 11, 1973.

20   "Mission Inventory," *U.S. Catholic Mission Handbook* (Washington, D.C.: U.S. Catholic Mission Association, 2008), p. 21.

21   Paul VI, "Address during the Last General Meeting of the Second Vatican Council," December 7, 1965, http://www.ewtn.com/library/papaldoc/p6tolast.htm

22   Paul VI, quoted in "Pope Paul Hails Apollo Mission," *The Lewiston Daily Sun*, February 8, 1971.

THE GATHERINGS AT ASSISI

Pope John Paul II continued to propagate the Gnosticism of Paul VI. On October 27, 1986, he invited leaders of various religions throughout the world to unite with him in a celebration of prayer and worship at the Basilica of St. Francis in Assisi, Italy. The gathering was attended by rabbis, Islamic muftis and mullahs, Buddhist monks, Jains, ministers from mainstream Protestant denominations, African and Native American Animists, Hindus, and Zoroastrians, who came forward before the altar which housed the remains of St. Francis to offer prayers for peace and religious unity. The Dalai Lama, before offering his prayer, placed a statue of Buddha on the sacred tabernacle and lit candles of incense, while the Holy Father bowed his head to it in a gesture of reverence.[23]

On January 24, 2004, John Paul II hosted another pan-Christian gathering at the Basilica of St. Francis of Assisi. In preparation of this event, all the crucifixes and trappings of traditional Catholicism were covered with drapes. Within the convent on the lower level of the basilica, Muslims were granted a room which faced Mecca; Zoroastrians were allocated a room with windows so that they could burn wooden chips; and the Jews were provided a room that had not been blessed in the name of Jesus Christ. A highlight of the gathering came when a voodoo priest ascended to the pulpit within the central sanctuary of the basilica to shake a rattle at all those in attendance, including the Holy Father, before placing them under a voodoo spell of tranquility.[24]

THE NEW CATHOLICISM

Reacting to the gathering, Robert Sungenis, in an article for *Catholic*

---

23 Roberto Suro, "12 Faiths Join Pope to Pray for Peace," *New York Times*, October 28, 1986, http://www.nytimes.com/1986/10/28/world/12-faiths-join-pope-to-pray-for-peace.html

24 "A Statement of Reservations concerning the Impending Beatification of Pope John Paul II," *The Remnant*, March 21, 2001, http://www.remnantnewspaper.com/2011-0331-statement-of-reservations-beatification.htm

Apologetics International, wrote: "If the pope believes a world religion can pray for physical and spiritual blessings as a mutual concern with Catholics, then it appears he must also believe that the pagan has an established, not just incidental, relationship with God, to the point where God would hear the prayers of a pagan the same as he would hear the prayers of any faithful Catholic. Moreover, it suggests that God is not the least bit disturbed by the pagan's worship of false gods and sinful lifestyle, nor the least bit disturbed that the Catholic is not discouraging the pagan from his false worship and lifestyle."[25]

Transforming the religious indifferentism of Marcion into new Catholic orthodoxy, Pope Francis permitted for the first time in history an imam to recite Muslim prayers and to read from the Koran within the confines of the Vatican. The prayer service was conducted on June 6, 2014, in conjunction with a visit to the Holy See by Palestinian president Mahmoud Abbas and Israeli president Shimon Peres. A beaming pope told the press: "It is my hope that the meeting will mark the beginning of a new journey that will unite so as to overcome the things that divide." Francis, unfortunately, was unaware that the imam's prayer, which was offered in Arabic, called for "victory over all infidels."[26] In another display of indifferentism, Pope Francis released a prayer video January 16, 2016 which featured Muslim prayer beads, but no rosary; a statue of Buddha but no statue of any Catholic saint, let alone the Virgin Mary; and a Menorah but no cross.[27]

The Lord God in the Book of Genesis made man "in His own image and likeness." This teaching has been turned upside down. The God of

25 Robert Sungenis, "A No, No to Assisi—Another Loyal Son Protests," *Catholic Apologetics International,* June 12, 2002, http://www.freerepublic.com/focus/religion/712755/posts

26 *"Islamfachmann: Koran-Rezitation bei Fridensgebeten Ist Legitim,"* Vatican Radio, June 11, 2014, http://de.radiovaticana.va/storico/2014/06/11/islamfachmann_koran-rezitation_bei_friedensgebeten_ist_legitim/ted-806221

27 Gregory Tomlin, "Pope Again Stresses 'Dialogue' with Other Religions as Video Depicts All as Equal," *Christian Examiner,* January 12, 2016, http://www.christianexaminer.com/article/pope-again-stresses-dialogue-with-other-religions-as-video-depicts-all-as-equal/50031.htm

many contemporary Christians has been made in the image and likeness of the progressive leaders of their denominations. Anyone who decries this transformation and dares to uphold the holiness and righteousness of God is depicted as "warped" and "unconscionable."

Luke 22:35-38 records the following:

> And He said to them, "When I sent you out with no moneybag or knapsack or sandals, did you lack anything?" They said, "Nothing." He said to them, "But now let the one who has a moneybag take it, and likewise a knapsack. And let the one who has no sword sell his cloak and buy one. For I tell you that this Scripture must be fulfilled in me: 'And he was numbered with the transgressors.' For what is written about me has its fulfillment." And they said, "Look, Lord, here are two swords." And He said to them, "It is enough."

Heeding such words and upholding the revealed truth of the Old Testament is unacceptable to many Christian clerics. The reason for this rejection of gospel truth resides in the fact that they have been indoctrinated in false belief by Marcionists, who preside over leading Protestant and Catholic seminaries.

3

A STAY IN SEMINARY

The historical-critical method is the indispensable method for the scientific study of the meaning of ancient texts. Holy Scripture, inasmuch as it is the "word of God in human language," has been composed by human authors in all its various parts and in all the sources that lie behind them. Because of this, its proper understanding not only admits the use of this method but actually requires it.

"THE INTERPRETATION OF THE BIBLE IN THE CHURCH,"
PONTIFICAL BIBLE COMMISSION, MARCH 18, 1994

SURELY, THE FAITH OF MANY CHRISTIANS will be challenged, if not shattered, if they enroll as students within any leading mainline Protestant or Catholic seminary. When they attend Old Testament classes, they will be exposed to contemporary Biblical criticism which will serve to convince them that the scriptures come from various, conflicting sources and cannot be used to uphold basic doctrine, including the concept of monotheism. They will be taught that the ancient Hebrews were composed of particularly violent and blood-thirsty nomadic tribes who engaged in human sacrifice and genocide.

In New Testament classes, the students will be informed that the gospels and epistles are rooted in mystery religions, including the cults of Isis and Mithras; that the account of the Virgin Birth is a result of religious syncretism; that the grandiose miracles of Jesus have no historical basis; and that the Resurrection of Jesus was a pious myth that arose from the fact that the body of Jesus was dragged away by some hungry jackals.

By the time they receive their diplomas, the seminarians will view the Bible as a hodge-podge of primitive myth and folklore that can be used to support any political or religious position. For this reason, they are apt to become candy-store clerics, selecting one passage of scripture as significant, while relegating another to the barbaric past. From this process of picking and choosing, a duality of deities has emerged: the savage God of Abraham and the compassionate God of the Psalms. *Ergo* comes the resurgence of the ancient heresy of Marcion in churches throughout the world.

THE FORMS OF BIBLICAL CRITICISM

Various forms of modern Biblical criticism and analysis are employed in mainline seminaries. Textual Criticism seeks to establish the most original and authoritative text. It is based on the presumption that, over the course of centuries, various scribes made additions and alterations to the original text. The critic, therefore, attempts to unearth and reconstruct the manuscript's transcription history.[1] Form Criticism classifies passages of scripture by their literary pattern and attempts to trace each

---

1   Graeme D. Bird, "Textual Criticism as Applied to Classical or Biblical Texts," Center for Hellenistic Studies. Harvard University, 2010, https://chs.harvard.edu/CHS/article/display/4742.1-textual-criticism-as-applied-to-biblical-and-classical-texts

passage to its period of oral transmission.[2] Redaction Criticism regards the authors of the Biblical stories as editors or redactors of the source material and focuses on the theological purpose or meaning they wished to illustrate in their presentation of the various stories.[3]

Regarding the Garden of Eden, students in America's leading seminaries are taught that the legend of Paradise appears in the folklore of Egypt, India, Tibet, Babylonia, Persia, Greece, and Mexico. Almost all of these Edens contained trees with forbidden fruit and serpents that stripped primordial man of his immortality. They also featured a woman who served as the lovely evil agent of the serpent.[4] The fact that no trace of an earthly Paradise has been found prompts Old Testament professors to dismiss the entire account as a mere flight of fancy.

THE FLAMING SWORD

At the conclusion of the story of the Fall, the Bible says that God, after driving Adam and Eve from the Garden of Eden, stationed cherubim (male militant angels) at the east side of the Garden to protect the tree of life (Genesis 3:24). The cherubim wielded fiery swords that served as assault weapons since they flashed back and forth to ward off all intruders.[5]

> The LORD God made garments of skin for Adam and his wife and clothed them. And the LORD God said, "The man has now become like one of us, knowing good and evil. He must not be allowed to reach out his hand and take also from the tree of life and eat, and live

---

2   "Form Criticism," Oxford Biblical Studies Online, n.d., http://www.oxfordbiblicalstudies.com/article/opr/t94/e693

3   "Redaction Criticism," Oxford Biblical Studies Online, n.d., http://www.oxfordbiblicalstudies.com/article/opr/t94/e1597

4   Will Durant, *Our Oriental Heritage*, Volume I, *The Story of Civilization* (New York: Simon and Schuster, 1954), pp. 329-330.

5   Michael Lichtenstein, "The Fearsome Sword of Genesis 3: 24," *Journal of Biblical Literature*, Volume 134, No. 1, Spring 2015, pp. 53-57.

forever." So the LORD God banished him from the Garden of Eden to work the ground from which he had been taken. After he drove the man out, he placed on the east side of the Garden of Eden cherubim and a flaming sword flashing back and forth to guard the way to the tree of life. (Genesis 3:22-24).

The significance of the story resides not in the possibility that it may have been a 6th Century BC redaction of a story from Hebrew folklore or any similarity of this account to other stories regarding the tree of life in ancient Near Eastern religions.[6] Its importance rather resides with the matter of the cherubim, who are militant angelic guards rather than inhabitants of Eden. They safeguard access to the fruit of the tree of life since the eating of such fruit would elevate man towards divinity.[7] The fact that these creatures wield swords displays the belief of the ancient Hebrews that the first weapons were forged not by Adam or Satan, but by God Himself. Arguments continue to flare up about the source of this story, its historicity, and the time in which it was written. But no one can question that the authors or redactors of Genesis 3 affirm that the supernatural beings dispatched by God bore arms.

THE CONFLICTING SOURCES

In the sixth chapter of Genesis, God destroys all of mankind, save for Noah and his family, because of "wickedness," including the sexual comingling of women with the Nephilim. The Nephilim, according to *Encyclopedia Judaica,* are "a race of giants said to have dwelled in pre-Israelite Canaan."[8]

---

6   Peter Thatcher Lanfer, *Remembering Eden: The Reception History of Genesis 3: 22-24* (New York: Oxford University Press, 2012), p. 13.

7   Anna Rozonoer, "The Invariable Variability of the Cherubim," Boston University, 2014, p. 19, https://open.bu.edu/bitstream/handle/2144/15153/Rozonoer_bu_0017E_10667.pdf

8   "Nephilim," *Encyclopedia Judaica*, Jewish Virtual Library, n. d., https://www.jewishvirtuallibrary.org/nephilim

When human beings began to increase in number on the earth and daughters were born to them, the sons of God saw that the daughters of humans were beautiful, and they married any of them they chose. Then the LORD said, "My Spirit will not contend with humans forever, for they are mortal; their days will be a hundred and twenty years." The Nephilim were on the earth in those days—and also afterward—when the sons of God went to the daughters of humans and had children by them. They were the heroes of old, men of renown. The LORD saw how great the wickedness of the human race had become on the earth, and that every inclination of the thoughts of the human heart was only evil all the time. The LORD regretted that he had made human beings on the earth, and his heart was deeply troubled. So the LORD said, "I will wipe from the face of the earth the human race I have created—and with them the animals, the birds and the creatures that move along the ground—for I regret that I have made them." (Genesis 6:1-7)

God brought forth this destruction by causing rain to fall forty days and forty nights so that every creature on the face of the earth, except for those on the Ark, was condemned to die in the deep.

Modern scholars insist that the story of Noah comes from two sources with different conceptions of God. "J" presents God as a demanding masculine Being who can only be appeased by "the sweet smell of sacrifice."[9] This oldest of Biblical sources is called "J" because it refers to God by the proper name of Jehovah.[10] The God of J is radically different from the God of "E," so-named because the source refers to God as "Elohim" or "Lord." Both sources date from 922 to 722 BC

---

9   Dennis Bratcher, "JEDP: Sources in the Pentateuch," *The Voice,* Christian Research Institute, 2013, http://www.crivoice.org/jedp.htm

10   Richard Elliott Friedman, *The Bible with Sources Revealed* (New York: HarperOne, 2009), pp. 7-8.

when Israel was divided into two kingdoms.[11] The God of E is a He/She Being who does not demand sacrifices but rather seeks to establish a loving relationship with mankind.[12] To prove the account of Noah comes from two different sources, Rabbi Dennis Bratcher contrasts Genesis 6:1-7 (cited on the previous page) with Genesis 6:11-13:

> Now the earth was corrupt in God's sight and was full of violence. God saw how corrupt the earth had become, for all the people on earth had corrupted their ways. So God said to Noah, "I am going to put an end to all people, for the earth is filled with violence because of them. I am surely going to destroy both them and the earth."

In the E account, God destroys the world because of man's inhumanity to man, and wishes to recreate it for the sake of a new beginning. On the basis of this view of the Flood account, the only means of sustaining a relevant exegesis is the Gnostic notion of two Gods: the demanding God of J and the loving God of E. Bratcher writes:

> In the *J* story, God wants to protect God's status vis-à-vis human beings and other creatures. It is in this story that the "divine beings" sleep with human women, provoking God's wrath. One expression of God's wrath is to limit the length of human life to one-hundred-and-twenty years, ensuring a clear distinction between humans and divine beings who live forever. It is in this story that God requires Noah to bring onto the ark seven of every pure animal, because it is in this story that God will demand animal sacrifices of Noah when he emerges from the ark. The God of the *J* story is appeased by the sweet smell of the sacrifices, because they are an expression of human subservience and obedience. All told, this is a God who demands a clearly superior position with relation to God's creation; the Supreme King to whom all creatures are radically subjects.

---

11   Ibid.

12   Ibid.

The God of the *E* story is portrayed very differently. The sin that this God sees is human violence; being concerned for human welfare, this God acts against that violence, but S/he never limits the length of human life (this God requires no such radical division between God and humans). This God requires only two of each species—male and female—to board the ark, because S/he will not demand sacrifices; the animals are needed only to perpetuate their species. Instead of demanding sacrifices upon Noah's exit from the ark, the God of the *E* story begins by blessing the humans, and then gives them laws. The most important of these laws is the one that protects human life.

Crucially, the God of *E* then goes on at length to express God's covenantal commitment to humanity, ensuring that flesh will never again be destroyed by a flood. The fact that this commitment is covenantal—the word covenant (*brit*) appears in this context (9:8-17) seven times is significant. A covenant is a contract, one in which two parties commit to one another by mutual agreement. The fact that this God can enter a covenant with humanity means that S/he views humanity as a worthy partner, not necessarily an equal but also not a radically submissive subject to be commanded and little more. These are two very different Gods, one jealous and superior, the other caring and available for relationship.[13]

Small wonder that students exposed to such an analysis of the Flood come to believe that it displays two radically different views of God and, therefore, two completely distinct divine beings.

ADDED CONFUSION

Naturally, the confusion for students is compounded by the claim of contemporary scholars that the story of the Flood is rooted in ancient legend. In *Voyages of the Pyramid Builders,* Robert Schoch writes: "Noah is but one tale in a worldwide collection of at least five hundred flood

---

13   Ibid.

myths, which are the most widespread of all ancient myths and, there-fore, can be considered among the oldest."[14]

THE TWO GODS OF ABRAHAM

This problem of the source material for the Genesis stories intensifies when one reaches the story of Abram, the patriarch of the Jewish race. The roots of this story are lodged in the time when the Hebrew people were known as the *Hapiru*—wandering tribes of Bedouins who were united in the worship of God and the care of a common sanctuary.[15] When the existence of one tribesman was threatened, the other tribes united in a holy war in which God Himself takes part in the military action.[16] Genesis 14:14-21 records the incident in which Lot, the nephew of Abram was taken captive by Chedorlaomer, a king of Elam in northern Samaria:

> When Abram heard that his kinsman had been taken captive, he led forth his trained men, born in his house, three hundred and eigh-teen of them, and went in pursuit as far as Dan. And he divided his forces against them by night, he and his servants, and routed them and pursued them to Hobah, north of Damascus. Then he brought back all the goods, and also brought back his kinsman Lot with his goods, and the women and the people. After his return from the defeat of Chedorlaomer and the kings who were with him, the king of Sodom went out to meet him at the Valley of Shaveh (that is, the King's Valley). And Melchizedek king of Salem brought out bread and wine; he was priest of God Most High. And he blessed him and said, "Blessed be Abram by God Most High, maker of heaven and earth;

14   Robert Schoch, *Voyages of the Pyramid Builders* (New York: Putnam, 2003), p. 249.

15   William F. Albright, "Abram the Hebrew: A New Archaeological Interpretation," *Bulletin of the American Schools of Oriental Research,* No. 163, 191, pp. 36-52.

16   Gerhard von Rad, *Old Testament Theology,* Volume I, *The Theology of Israel's Historical traditions* (translated by D. M. G. Stalker (New York: Harper and Row, 1962), p. 17.

and blessed be God Most High, who has delivered your enemies into your hand!" And Abram gave him a tenth of everything.

After his victory, Abram is welcomed and blessed by the priest-king Melchizedek, the King of Salem and "priest of God Most High," seen by Paul in Hebrews 7 as a "type" of Christ. Abram is careful to offer a tithe of ten percent of the wealth captured to Melchizedek. This is in keeping with the customs of the ancient Hebrews who believed that the spoils of war must be shared with their God, since He was present with His people in battle and evoked terror in the hearts of the enemies of His people.[17]

This story seems straightforward save for the contention that it comes from yet another source called D (the Deuteronomist). The writings of D, scholars maintain, are characterized by quasi-historical events that include the names of the primordial people of the Transjordan.[18] And D, who was writing in the post-exile era, possessed a different view of God from J and P (the priestly source). The deity of D is a Demiurge who possesses some of the barbarity of the God of J and a good measure of the kindness of the God of P.[19] But, unlike the anthropomorphic deity of J and P, this God remains an aloof and abstract figure who remains in heaven and only allows His name to dwell on earth.[20]Such are the findings of modern exegetes concerning the first chapters of the Bible.

17   Ibid. See also Bill Nourse, "Four Source Theory of the Torah," *Deacon page,* April 22, 2003, http://www.billnourse.com/4SOURCE.HTM

18   Janet Lamarche, "The Meaning of Genesis 14:11-24: A Syntactical and Redactiional Analysis," Concordia University, March 2009, http://citeseerx.ist.psu.edu/viewdoc/download?doi=10.1.1.6 33.3147&rep=rep1&type=pdf

19   Ibid.

20   Jonathan Kirch, *Moses: A Life* (New York: Ballantine Books, 1998, p. 338.

DOCUMENTARY HYPOTHESIS

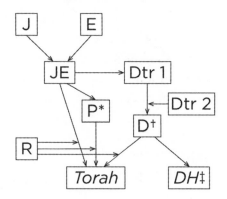

Diagram of the documentary hypothesis.[21] J: Jahwist source (7th century BC or later). E: Elohist source (late 9th century BC) Dtr1: early (7th century BC) Deuteronomist historian Dtr2: later (6th century BC) Deuteronomist historian P*: Priestly source (6th/5th century BC; includes most of Leviticus) D†: Deuteronomist source (includes most of Deuteronomy) R: redactor DH: Deuteronomistic history (books of Joshua, Judges, Samuel, Kings)

Invariably the painstaking effort to identify the source material for every verse within the Book of Genesis betrays the perspectivism of the scholars who embark upon this task. Their own religious views and preconceptions cause them to allocate one part of a story to the enlightened priests (D) and another to the unenlightened Jahwist (J). The Book of Genesis becomes the strange saga of two gods—one of which remains a figure to be shunned.

HISTORICAL CRITICISM AND MARCION

For this reason, it is not surprising to discover that Marcion, as Paul Johnson points out, used "historical and critical methods basically

---

21   Diagram of the Documentary Hypothesis. https://www.revolvy.com/page/Documentary-hypothesis, accessed May 20, 2019.

similar to those of modern scriptural scholars."[22] This allowed him to reject the Old Testament *in toto* since it displayed a God who was monstrous, evil-creating, bloody, and the patron of such ruffians as David—at odds with the God of Jesus. Marcion's textual analysis permitted him to compile a canon of scripture that had a unity, since he scrapped the Hebrew scriptures and all the Judaizing elements within the New Testament.[23]

FINDING THE TRUTH

How can anyone read the Old Testament, which was compiled from conflicting sources, and obtain any spiritual understanding? How can Christian faith be sustained in America's leading seminaries, where the scriptures are ripped apart verse by verse, chapter by chapter, and book by book for the sole purpose of fostering doubt and unbelief? Such efforts would seem hopeless save for fact that the Biblical stories were edited in their final form by a Redactor (known as R) and the message or truth that he sought to impart.[24] The truth of Genesis 3:22-24 is that God forged weapons to protect His spiritual and terrestrial domain. The truth of the story of Noah is that God destroyed the world because of man's sinfulness. The truth of Genesis 14:14-21 is that Abram assembled a militia to save the life of a clansman and, thereby, received God's blessing. These truths remain regardless of any contemporary hermeneutic (Biblical interpretation) that has been imposed upon them.

SMALL SOLACE

But abstract truth is not historical truth and Biblical scholars argue that passages from the same Old Testament chapter come from different sources with different conceptions of God. Some of these sources, the

---

22   Paul L. Johnson, *A History of Christianity* (New York: Simon and Schuster, 1976), p. 46.

23   Ibid.

24   Friedman, *The Bible with Sources Revealed*, p. 7.

scholars maintain, were polytheistic as evidenced by Genesis 1:26, which reads: "Then God said, 'Let us make man in our own image, in our own likeness. . .'"

Thus, within their first week in seminary, while studying the first book of the Bible, the new seminarians are taught to conclude that the Old Testament is far from a text of divine origin. It is rather a hodge-podge of ancient Bedouin beliefs strung together to form a single but far from coherent narrative. Within its pages, the seminarians come to believe, is nothing of real enlightenment, only tales of giants, sword-swinging angels, and incredibly old men who engage in incest, buggery, and harlotry.

The most industrious of new seminarians, in order to maintain their belief in the historicity of the Genesis stories, inevitably turn to the findings of archaeologists.

In this way they come upon some small solace.

ARCHAEOLOGICAL EVIDENCE

A case in point is the story of Sodom and Gomorrah. The cities, according to the Book of Genesis, were part of a metropolis located on the eastern bank of the Dead Sea, consisting of five "cities of the plain," each with its own king and the five kings under the dominion of eastern Mesopotamian overlords. Since there was no known route connecting the Dead Sea area with Mesopotamia, it seemed highly unlikely the Mesopotamians could have conquered it.

However, evidence of an ancient route between Mesopotamia and the Dead Sea area was uncovered in the 1920s. Forty years later, in the 1960s, a large cemetery on the eastern bank overseeing the Dead Sea was discovered that ultimately revealed about a half million bodies. Between 1973 and 1979 four more large "cities" were found, with more than 1.5 million bodies buried. Dating of the pottery of the grave goods in the first city revealed that it existed for about 1,000 years, but another, Numeira, existed for a short time period of less than 100 years. Was this Sodom, which the Talmud states existed for just 52 years?

> Then the LORD rained on Sodom and Gomorrah brimstone and fire
> from the LORD out of heaven; and he overthrew those cities, and all
> the valley, and all the inhabitants of the cities, and what grew on the
> ground. Genesis 19:24-25

What about the "fire and brimstone" which rained down on Sodom and Gomorrah? Bitumen/asphalt, a naturally occurring, very flammable substance is commonly found in the Dead Sea area. Archeologists have found that the entire areas of two of the discovered cities, Bab edh-Dhra and Numeira are covered with 4-20 inches of ash, residue from powerful, widespread fires.

Parallel to the five cities is a fault line where two large plates of earth exert tremendous pressure on each other, causing earthquakes in the area. The pressure can force subterranean material, such as magma, or bitumen, into the air. Did the earth spew flammable hydrocarbons into the atmosphere that were ignited by lightning and fell back to the earth, covering these two cities with asphyxiating "fire and brimstone," thus killing all of their inhabitants?[25] Archaeology has posited this possibility.[26] The story of Sodom and Gomorrah, much to the chagrin of modern Sodomites, appears to be anchored in historical fact.

This is not to say that archaeological evidence can be provided to substantiate every story within the Book of Genesis. Far from it. It is exceedingly difficult to support any aspect of ancient history by empirical evidence, including the existence of Socrates, Plato, and Aristotle and the entire matter of the Trojan, Messenian, and Lelantine Wars.

25   D. Neev & K.O. Emery, *The Destruction of Sodom, Gomorrah, and Jericho: Geological, Climatological, and Archaeological Background* (New York: Oxford University Press, 1995), pp. 13-14. Also, G.M. Harris & A.P. Beardow, "The Destruction of Sodom and Gomorrah: A Geological Perspective," *Quarterly Journal of Engineering Geology*, Vol. 28, https://qjegh.lyellcollection.org/content/28/4/349

26   Rabbi Leibel Reznick, "Biblical Archeology: Sodom and Gomorrah," April 5, 2008, http://www.aish.com/ci/sam/48931527.html.

REDACTION CRITICISM

Certainly, the significance of the story of the "Aqabah" or "Binding of Isaac" can be only truly discerned through the eyes of the Biblical redactor. In Genesis 22:2, God commands Abraham as follows: "Take your son, your only son Isaac, whom you love, and go to the land of Moriah, and offer him there as a burnt offering upon one of the mountains of which I shall tell you." Having confirmed that Abraham was absolutely committed, no matter what, to carry out His command, God stopped him from carrying out the sacrifice as Genesis records: "Do not lay your hand on the lad or do anything to him; for now I know that you fear God, seeing you have not withheld your son, your only son, from me." (22:12).

The redactor of the Genesis story makes it clear that God's plans and purposes are incomprehensible to mortal man. Biblical scholar Thomas Romer writes: ". . .the Aqedah narrative raises the issue of the personal image we have of God: we want a God who corresponds to the ideal of an enlightened human being, a just God and therefore a God who fits our conception of this enlightened human being. But such a 'politically correct' God risks becoming, to use the Biblical authors' own words, an idol who does nothing but legitimize merely human aspirations. . . ."[27]

Another lesson from the redactor is the importance of unconditional obedience to the word of God in a hostile world in which the welfare of the communal tribes remains all-important. Such obedience must supersede all personal concerns. Most Biblical scholars agree that the only human sacrifice demanded by God applies to this particular context: the testing of the first patriarch of the Hebrews. This lesson is supported by the codicil in which God Himself provides an animal for Abraham to sacrifice: "And Abraham looked up and saw a ram, caught in a thicket by its horns. Abraham went and took the ram and offered it up as a burnt offering instead of his son. So. Abraham called that place 'The LORD will provide' as it is said to this day, 'On the mount of the

---

27   Ibid.

LORD it shall be provided'" (Genesis 22:13-14).

The story, within its historical setting, remains remarkable. Among ancient Indo-European peoples, the sacrifice of children was commonplace and so the command that Abraham received would not have struck him as unprecedented or unusual. The Syrians and the Phoenicians on occasions of importance sacrificed their own children to Baal, whom they viewed as the sun-god. The priests came to the ceremony dressed for a festival, and the cries of the children burning in the lap of the god were muffled by the blaring of trumpets and the piping of flutes.[28] The story of the Aqedah stands in sharp contrast to such accounts and upholds the view of the ancient Hebrews that their God was merciful and "would provide" for His people. This message resounds throughout the Pentateuch (the first five books of the Bible) and remains the basis of the Hebrews' belief that they must abide by God's word regarding all matters.

EVISCERATED EXODUS

But redaction criticism cannot establish the *historical* truth of the Genesis accounts and the matter of conflicting sources within the Old Testament persists in the Book of Exodus. To make matters worse for the defenders of the Judeo-Christian faith, the scholars' attempt to "demythologize" the stories cannot be offset by ample archaeological evidence.

Biblical scholars point out that the divine name of God is revealed to Moses twice, in Exodus 3 and 6, and in each case, for the first time. These two revelations, the scholars contend, belong to E (the Elohist) and P (the Priestly source), respectively. These sources, the scholars are quick to point out, disagree about what happened to Moses when he ascended the mountain in the wilderness, and can't even agree on the name of the mountain. For J (the Jahwist) and P, it is called Sinai; for E, it is called Horeb. Many of these differences, the academics insist, occur "in ways that may seem almost unthinkable to those who know only the

---

28   Durant, *Our Oriental Heritage*, p. 297.

canonical text. . ."[29] For instance, the burning bush is known to only the J document. P has seven plagues, J has six, and E has none. In J the Israelites escape hastily at night; in P they walk out boldly during the day. E has no notion of manna. The Ten Commandments, the tablets, and the golden calf are completely unknown to J and P. The crossing of the sea is unknown to E. The Tent of Meeting is known only to E. There is no ark of the covenant in E. There is no Joshua in J. And Miriam is only known to E.[30]

The Book of Exodus also displays, according to Biblical scholars, three different views of Moses. For J, Moses was no worker of miracles, no military leader, and no founder of a religion, but simply an inspired shepherd whom God used to make His ways known to men.[31] For E, Moses was a more exalted and powerful figure, who could perform mighty miracles.[32] For D, Moses is the archetype of all prophets, since God speaks through him. In this account, there is no mention of Moses transforming history by miracles and only rarely is he depicted as a military leader giving strategic orders.[33] Such findings have led several scholars to conclude that Moses never existed.

MOSES AS MYTH

This conclusion is reinforced by the lack of archaeological evidence concerning Moses, the bondage of the Hebrews in Egypt, and the Exodus. The story of baby Moses in the bulrushes, scholars argue, has its roots in the birth legend of King Sargon, the founder of the Akkad dynasty in 2360 BC. Cuneiform tests contain the following statement:

---

29   Old Testament Department, "Book of Exodus, Session 1, Introduction," Yale Divinity School, https://divinity.yale.edu/sites/default/files/exodus-1-introduction_0.pdf

30   Ibid.

31   Von Rad, *Old Testament Theology*, p. 292.

32   Jonathan Kirch, *Moses: A Life* (New York: Ballantine Books, 1998), p. 354.

33   Von Rad, *Old Testament Theology*, p. 294.

"I am Saragon, the powerful king, the king of Akkad. My mother was an Enitu princes. I did not know my father. . . . My mother conceived me and bore me in secret. She put me in a little box made from reeds, sealing its lid with pitch. She put me in the river. . . . The river carried me away and brought me to Akki, the drawer of water. Akki, the drawer of water, adopted me and brought me up as his son. . . ."[34] Exodus 2:1-10 relates the following:

> Now a man of the tribe of Levi married a Levite woman, and she became pregnant and gave birth to a son. When she saw that he was a fine child, she hid him for three months. But when she could hide him no longer, she got a papyrus basket for him and coated it with tar and pitch. Then she placed the child in it and put it among the reeds along the bank of the Nile. His sister stood at a distance to see what would happen to him.
>
> Then Pharaoh's daughter went down to the Nile to bathe, and her attendants were walking along the riverbank. She saw the basket among the reeds and sent her female slave to get it. She opened it and saw the baby. He was crying, and she felt sorry for him. "This is one of the Hebrew babies," she said.
>
> Then his sister asked Pharaoh's daughter, "Shall I go and get one of the Hebrew women to nurse the baby for you?"
>
> "Yes, go," she answered. So the girl went and got the baby's mother. Pharaoh's daughter said to her, "Take this baby and nurse him for me, and I will pay you." So the woman took the baby and nursed him. When the child grew older, she took him to Pharaoh's daughter and he became her son. She named him Moses saying, "I drew him out of the water."

Similarly, the story of the breaking of the tablets after the incident of the Golden Calf is reminiscent of Akkadian legal terminology where

---

34   Werner Keller, *The Bible as History*, Second Revised Edition (New York: William Morrow and Company, 1981), p. 123.

"to break the tablet" means the nullification of an agreement. In Ugaritic myth, the deity Mot was destroyed by the goddess Anath by being pulverized, and scattered, in the same way that Moses burned, pulverized, and scattered the remains of the golden calf.[35]

> When Moses approached the camp and saw the calf and the dancing, his anger burned and he threw the tablets out of his hands, breaking them to pieces at the foot of the mountain. And he took the calf the people had made and burned it in the fire; then he ground it to powder, scattered it on the water and made the Israelites drink it (Ex. 32:19-20).

Indeed, the only non-Biblical reference to the story of the bondage of the Hebrews and their deliverance comes from Manetho, an Egyptian historian of the third century BC, who says that the Exodus was due to the desire of the Egyptians to protect themselves from a plague that had broken out among the destitute and enslaved Jews, and that Moses was an Egyptian priest who went among the Jewish lepers as a missionary, and gave them rules for cleanliness based upon those of the Egyptian clergy.[36]

A LACK OF EVIDENCE

It gets even worse.

Biblical scholars claim that since the prophets make no mention of Moses and the Exodus, the scriptural accounts must date from the time of Ezra, when the Jews returned to Jerusalem after the Babylonian captivity (circa 540 BC).[37] This late date means that the great kings of Israel, including David and Solomon, knew nothing of the deliverance of the Hebrew and their years of wandering in the wilderness.

---

35 Stephen Bourke, *The Middle East: The Cradle of Civilization Revealed*, (Birmingham, Alabama: Sweetwater Press, 2018), p. 156.

36 Durant, *Our Oriental Heritage*, pp. 301-302.

37 Ibid., pp. 328-329.

Regarding the lack of evidence for the Exodus story, Stephen Gabriel Rosenberg writes in *The Jerusalem Post:*

> The whole subject of the Exodus is embarrassing to archaeologists. The Exodus is so fundamental to us and our Jewish sources that it is embarrassing that there is no evidence outside of the Bible to support it. So we prefer not to talk about it, and hate to be asked about it. For the account in the Torah is the basis of our people's creation, it is the basis of our existence and it is the basis of our important Passover festival and the whole Haggada that we recite on the first evening of this festival of freedom. So that makes archaeologists reluctant to have to tell our brethren and ourselves that there is nothing in Egyptian records to support it. Nothing on the slavery of the Israelites, nothing on the plagues that persuaded Pharaoh to let them go, nothing on the miraculous crossing of the Red Sea, nothing.[38]

Nothing.

---

38   Stephen Gabriel Rosenberg, "The Exodus: Does Archaeology Have a Say?" *Jerusalem Post,* April 14, 2014, https://www.jpost.com/Opinion/Op-Ed-Contributors/The-Exodus-Does-archaeology-have-a-say-348464

4

THE SEEDS OF DOUBT

Can any section among us afford to concede to this professorial and imperial anti-Semitism and confess "for a truth we and our ancestors have sinned" we have lived on false pretenses and were the worst shams in the world? Forget not that we live in an historical age in which everybody must show his credentials from the past. The Bible is our patent of nobility granted to us by the Almighty God, and if we disown the Bible, leaving it to the tender mercies of a Wellhausen, Stade and Duhm, and other beautiful souls working away at diminishing the "nimbus of the Chosen People," the world will disown us. There is no room in it for spiritual parvenus. But this intellectual persecution can only be fought by intellectual weapons and unless we make an effort to recover our Bible and to think out our theology for ourselves, we are irrevocably lost from both worlds.

SOLOMON SCHECHTER, "HIGHER CRITICISM—
HIGHER ANTI-SEMITISM," MARCH 26, 1903

THE RESULTS OF SOME TWO CENTURIES of Biblical criticism have been almost completely negative. The Biblical books, according to many scholarly critics are not what they claim to be—and their contents of these books do not reflect actual events or real people. "A Biblical narrative reflects the historical context of its writing rather than the more distant past of its referent," writes Thomas L. Thompson, professor of theology at the University of Copenhagen.[1] The conclusions for believers are devastating. Nothing of the Pentateuch came from the hand of Moses; David and Solomon, assuming they ever existed, were minor tribal leaders of a small area around Jerusalem; and any of the oracles the prophets may have uttered were adapted, expanded, and edited centuries after they were spoken.[2] Consequently, the Hebrew Bible is a work of propaganda for a Judaism that arose in the Persian period or later—a work that has been stripped of its claim to be a source of divine revelation.

EXEGETICAL EMPTINESS

The Biblical critics remain intransigent in their claims. They dismiss the notion of divine revelation, and refuse to consider the evidence that refute their theories. In 1975, John van Seters published *Abraham in History and Tradition*, a book that has heavily influenced all subsequent studies of the Patriarchs and remains a standard text at many of America's leading seminaries. Van Seters argues that there is no basis for the belief that Abraham lived in ancient Canaan during the Middle Bronze Age (the early second millennium BC). For proof, he points to the rarity of references to tents in Canaanite documents from that period, while the documents of the next millennium contain abundant mention of tent dwellers.[3] He does not explain why he prefers a later date for the Genesis narratives simply based on the rarity of tent references. He merely opts to ignore the alternative explanations provided by

---

1   Thomas L. Thomas, *The Mythic Past: Biblical Archaeology and the Myth of Israel* (New York: Basic Books, 1999), p. 206.

2   Alan Millard, "Critical Biblical Scholarship: A Response," *Bible History Daily*, October 10, 2012, https://www.biblicalarchaeology.org/daily/archaeology-today/archaeologists-biblical-scholars-works/critical-biblical-scholarship-a-response/

3   John van Seters, *Abraham in History and Tradition* (New Haven: Yale University Pres, 1975), p. 14.

W. F. Albright and others.[4] Despite the fact that recent archaeological findings support the Biblical story of Abraham and the tent dwellers of his tribe,[5] the Van Seters book continues to be upheld as the definitive source on the patriarch of the Hebrew nation.

Similarly, evidence has been unearthed to support the Moses story by David Rohl and other Egyptologists.[6] Yet such findings remain ignored since they challenge the teachings of such venerated Biblical critics as Volkman Fritz and Robert Coote. And scholars such as Niels Peter Lemche of The University of Copenhagen continue to insist that "the David of the Bible is not a historical figure,"[7] although a broken Aramaic inscription was uncovered at Tel Dan in 1993 mentioning "the house of David."[8]

Whence comes modern Biblical scholarship and the deconstructive work of textual and form critics?

A GERMAN RATIONALIST

Julius Wellhausen and the other fathers of modern Biblical criticism were German rationalists who regarded human reason as the theological source and test of all knowledge—even spiritual knowledge. They denied the concept of *divine revelation*. The Bible, in their view, was merely a human book compiled from several and often conflicting sources (J, E, P, and D).[9]

---

4   Millard, "Critical Biblical Scholarship: A Response."

5   Cf. M. M. Homan, *To Your Tents, O Israel: The Terminology, Function, Form and Symbolism of Tents in the Hebrew Bible and the Ancient Near East* (Leiden: Brill, 2002).

6   Cf. David M. Rohl, *Exodus: Myth or History* (St. Louis, MN: Thinking Man Media, 2015).

7   Niels Peter Lemche, quoted in Kevin D. Miller, "Did the Exodus Never Happen?" *Christianity Today*, September 7, 1998, https://www.christianitytoday.com/ct/1998/september7/8ta044.html

8   Millard, "Critical Biblical Scholarship: A Response."

9   Dennis Leap, "Answering Bible Critics," *The Trumpet*, June 2005, https://www.thetrumpet.com/1460-answering-bible-critics

In 1875, Wellhausen published his *Prolegomena to the History of Ancient Israel*, which purported to be the *true* Biblical story. He maintained that the Torah was not written by Moses but rather represented the compilation of four documents. Each document had a distinctive character, both in content and in general outlook. Though they had been skillfully interwoven by an editor, the special characteristics of each document made it possible to isolate each source throughout the books of the first five books of the Bible. The earliest was the J document (J being the first letter of the Divine Name, which was used throughout this source and so became essential). It was followed soon after by the *Elohist Document—E*—in which God is designated as Elohim or "Lord." These two documents, according to Wellhausen, were composed in the early monarchical period, probably in the ninth or eighth century BC. The document of the Deuteronomist, D gave a narrative framework to Leviticus, Numbers, and Deuteronomy. Wellhausen dated the D document to the time of King Josiah in the seventh century BC. The Priestly Code (P), a universal history and extensive legal code, was chiefly concerned with matters of cult and was dominated by the priestly interest in prescribing the correct ritual for each ceremonial occasion. Wellhausen relegated this source of the Torah to the post-exilic age and connected it with the Law of Ezra in the fifth century BC.[10]

CHANGING WORDS

Wellhausen's method was doggedly straightforward. Every passage of the Old Testament that fits his theory was deemed by Wellhausen to be authentic. When Wellhausen encountered a passage that did not fit within his theory, he changed or expunged the Hebrew word and inserted what he called a "conjectural emendation."[11]

---

10   Rabbi Nathan Lopes Cordozo, "On Bible Criticism and Its Counterarguments," *Torat Emer*, 1995, http://www.aishdas.org/toratemet/en_cardozo.html#_edn6

11   Ibid.

SCRIPTURAL FORGERY

The passages of the Torah that complied with his analysis were deemed authentic, while the thousands of passages that did not fit were dismissed as "forgeries." The forgeries, he argued, had been inserted into the Bible after it had been redacted in the post-exile era. This mischievous figure worked with scissors and paste carving up the various documents—moving a half a sentence here and another there—chopping and stitching the four ancient documents until he fashioned a work to his peculiar liking.[12]

A JEWISH PROBLEM

In addition to wanting to strip the scriptures bare before the eyes of reason, Wellhausen was an anti-Semite, whose writings were peppered with venomous remarks against Judaism. In several of his letters, he confessed that he found the very survival of Judaism to be "lamentable."[13] He also said that there exists no explanation why the religious experience of the Hebrew nation has any functional value or significance for the world at large. "We cannot tell why Jehovah of Israel, rather than Chemosh, the god of Moab, became the patron of righteousness and the Creator of the Universe."[14]

Wellhausen also confessed that the inspiration for his scriptural analysis came from a 1773 essay by Johann Wolfgang von Goethe. In that work, Goethe wrote:

---

12   Ibid.

13   Julius Wellhausen, Letter to Ferdinand Justi (dated March 5, 1893); quoted in Friedemann Boschwitz, Julius Wellhausen: Motive und Mass-stäbe seiner Geschichtsschreibung (Darmstadt: Wissenschaftliche Buchgesellschaft, 1968), 56 . The letter reads: "Lieblich sind die alten Juden nicht, aber respektabel sind sie doch. Sic [sic] gehen doch ganz anders im Kampf gegen die Römer unter, als Athener und Spartaner, obwohl sie von militärischen Dingen absolut nichts verstehen und gar keine Disziplin kennen. Eigentlich sind sie überhaupt nicht untergegangen, sondern haben trotz allem über die Römer triumphiert. Man mag es bedauern, aber man muß es anerkennen."

14   Wellhausen, quoted in Wallis, "The Paradox of Biblical Criticism."

The Jewish people I regard as a wild, infertile stock that stood in a circle of wild and barren trees, upon which the eternal Gardener grafted the noble scion Jesus Christ, so that, by adhering to it, it ennobled the nature of the stock and from there slips were fetched to make all the remaining trees fertile. The history and teaching of this people, from its first shoots up to the grafting, is certainly particularistic, and the small amount of the universal [teaching] which may perhaps have been accorded it in anticipation of that future great deed is difficult and perhaps not even necessary to seek out. From the grafting on, the entire matter took a turn. Teaching and history became universal. And although each tree that was ennobled from it had its own special history and its own special teaching according to its circumstances, my opinion is nonetheless: Here [in the case of Christianity] there is as little particularistic to be suspected and interpreted as there is universal there [in the case of Judaism].[15]

WELLHAUSEN'S DISCIPLES

Wellhausen attracted hundreds of disciples who came to occupy prominent positions within the Biblical departments of Germany's leading universities. Friedrich Delitzsch, one of Wellhausen's most ardent admirers, delivered an address called "Babel und Bibel," in which he said that the Old Testament was devoid of any religious or moral value. Following the lecture, Kaiser Wilhelm congratulated Delitzch for helping "to dissipate the nimbus of the Chosen People."[16] Adolf Harnack, another Wellhausen disciple, argued that Protestants must

---

15   Johann Wolfgang von Goethe, "Zwo wichtige bisher unerörterte biblische Fragen," in *Der Junge Goethe* 22 1757-1775, ed. G. Sauder (München, 1987), 436-437, quoted and translated in Bernard M. Levinson, "Goethe's Analysis of Exodus 34 and Its Influence on Wellhausen: The Propfung of the Documentary Hypothesis," *Zeitschrift für die alttestamentliche Wissenschaft* 114 (2002), p. 216. See Rabbi Zev-Hayyim (William) Feyer, "Anti-Semetism in Wellhausen," Claremont, CA. December 2004, http://www.new-tzfat.com/publish/scholarly-papers/Anti-Semitism%20in%20Wellhausen.pdf

16   Cordozo, "On Bible Criticism and Its Counterarguments."

eliminate the Old Testament from the Bible.[17]

The thought of Wellhausen came to dominate Old Testament scholarship, not only in his own country but also in England and America. The most important histories of Israel and of Hebrew literature, such as the *International Critical Commentary on the Holy Scriptures* as well as a host of commentaries, including those edited by Wilhelm Nowack and Karl Marti and introductions, were based almost entirely on Wellhausen's contentions.[18]

UNIVERSAL ACCEPTANCE

Wellhausen and his school of thought received widespread acceptance because it mirrored the intellectual spirit of the late nineteenth century. The age was intoxicated with thought of Georg Wilhelm Friedrich Hegel (1770-1831), who had taught that all of human history represents a progression from a lower to a higher stage. Hegel's philosophy became buttressed by the findings of Charles Darwin that species undergo change during the course of many millennia, and the contention of Thomas Henry Huxley that man evolved from an apelike ancestor. Naturally, the same intellectuals were willing to believe that the Jewish religion developed from idolatry, and having passed through many intermediate stages, the earlier one of which was the Torah, reached the ultimate pure monotheism of Jesus.[19]

In *Critique of Religion and Philosophy,* Walter Kaufmann points out the glaring flaw in the Biblical analysis of Wellhausen and his school of thought as follows:

> Imagine a Higher Critic analyzing Goethe's Faust, which was written by a single human being in the course of sixty years. The scenes

---

17   Adolf von Harnack, *Marcion. Das Evangelium vom Fremden Gott,* Second Edition (Leipzig, Germany: J. C. Hinrichs, 1924), p. 217.

18   Cordozo, "On Bible Criticism and Its Counterarguments."

19   Ibid.

in which the heroine of Part One is called Gretchen would be relegated to one author; the conflicting conceptions of the role of Mephistopheles would be taken to call for further divisions, and the Prologue in Heaven would be ascribed to a later editor, while the prelude on the stage would be referred to yet a different author. Our critic would have no doubt whatsoever that Part Two belongs to a different age and must be assigned to a great many writers with widely different ideas. The end of Act IV, for example, points to an anti-Catholic author who lampoons the church, while the end of Act V was written by a man, we should be told, who, though probably no orthodox Catholic, was deeply sympathetic to Catholicism. Where do we find more inconsistencies in style and thought and plan: in Goethe's Faust or in the Five Books of Moses?[20]

Despite this criticism and the findings of famous archaeologists, such as William F. Albright, the school of Wellhausen continues to possess a stranglehold on leading Christian seminaries.

Why?

The answer resides in the fact that if the seminaries abandon the higher criticism of Wellhausen, they will lose a substantial amount of their funding.

---

20   Walter Kaufmann, *Critique of Religion and Philosophy* (Princeton, NJ: Princeton University Press, 1978), p. 377.

5

THIRTY PIECES OF SILVER

The power of the foundation is not that of dictating what will be studied. Its power consists in defining professional and intellectual parameters, in determining who will receive support to study what subjects in what settings. And the foundation's power resides in suggesting certain types of activities it favors and is willing to support. As [political theorist and economist Harold] Laski noted, "The foundations do not control, simply because, in the direct and simple sense of the word, there is no need for them to do so. They have only to indicate the immediate direction of their minds for the whole university world to discover that it always meant to gravitate to that angle of the intellectual compass."

ROBERT ARNOVE, PHILANTHROPY AND CULTURAL IMPERIALISM, 1980

WITHIN THE UNITED STATES, the Biblical criticism of Wellhausen and his disciples received the financial support of John D. Rockefeller, Jr. An avowed internationalist, Rockefeller during World War I became enamored with the concept of a one-world religion that would unite mankind under a global government. The young Rockefeller had fallen under the influence of Andrew Carnegie, a fellow financial tycoon.

After Carnegie sold his steel company to J. P. Morgan for $480 million (the highest price ever paid for a business at the time), he shelled out the funding ($40,000,000 in today's money) for the construction of the Peace Palace at The Hague to house a "permanent court of arbitration."[1] The task of this court would be to settle disputes between nations and to bring about the "complete banishment of war."[2] The construction of the Peace Palace represented the first attempt to dissolve national sovereignty and national law under an institution with global jurisdiction. When the building was completed, Carnegie called it "the most holy building in the world."[3]

THE CARNEGIE FOUNDATION

Carnegie now embarked on a crusade to create a "League of Peace" or "League of Nations," which would comprise a combination of the leading imperial powers, complete with an international police force.[4] He even publicized his proposal in a short article entitled "A League of Nations," which appeared in the pages of *Outlook* magazine May 25, 1907.[5]

The creation of such an organization, Carnegie realized, would require control of America's educational and political institutions— control that could only be achieved by the expenditure of vast sums of cash from a charitable foundation. These institutions would become reliant on these benefactions for their continued existence, and the trustees of the foundation thereby would gain control over their operations. To accomplish this objective, the Carnegie Endowment

---

1   Ron Chernow, *The House of Morgan: An American Banking Dynasty and the Rise of Modern Finance* (New York: Grove Press, 2001), p, 84.

2   Nasaw, *Andrew Carnegie*, p. 650.

3   Andrew Carnegie, quoted in Samuel Bostaph, *Andrew Carnegie: An Economic Biography* (New York: Rowman and Littlefield, 2015), p. 111.

4   Andrew Carnegie, "A Look Ahead."

5   Peter Koss, *Carnegie* (New York: John Wiley and Sons, 2002), p. 474.

for International Peace (CEIP) set up in 1910 its headquarters in Washington, D.C.

CONTROLLING EDUCATION

Knowing the rise of global government required social engineering, the Carnegie Foundation for the Advancement of Teaching (CFAT), which was established in 1905, gained control of America's educational system. The original purpose of the foundation was "to provide retiring pensions for teachers of universities, colleges, and technical schools . . . without regard to race, sex, creed, or color."[6] The foundation also provided general endowments to institutions that complied with its prescribed scholastic standards and entrance requirements. By 1909, the CFAT had become the national unofficial accrediting agency for colleges and universities.[7] It possessed the power to create the curricula, to oversee the faculty, and to supervise the actions of the administration.

Since Carnegie was an avowed socialist, an agnostic, a globalist, and an associate of the Rhodes Society, universities throughout America began to reflect his ideology and beliefs. In *Foundations: Their Power and Influence*, Rene Wormser, special counsel to the Reece Committee, wrote:

> The growing radicalism which was beginning rapidly to permeate academic circles was no grass-roots movement. Mr. [Aaron] Sargent cited a statement by Professor Ludwig Von Mises that socialism does not spring from the masses but is instigated by intellectuals that form themselves into a clique and bore from within and operate that way. It is not a people's movement at all. It is a capitalization on the people's emotions and sympathies toward a point these people wish to reach.[8]

---

6   David Nasaw, *Andrew Carnegie* (New York: Penguin Press, 2006), p. 671.

7   Joseph Frazier Wall, *Andrew Carnegie* (Pittsburgh: The University of Pittsburgh Press, 1989), p, 877.

8   Rene Wormser, *Foundations: Their Power and Influence* (New York: Covenant House Books, 1993), p. 31.

THE SWORD OF DAMOCLES

Funding from the CFAT came to hang over the country's institutions of higher learning like the Sword of Damocles. Those who complied with the dictates of the Foundation's trustees received massive benefactions; those who failed to comply did not. New subjects became mandatory college courses, including anthropology, comparative religions, and social science—all of which served to stress the relativity of cultural practices and ideals. The need to introduce such subjects had been brought on by the advent of the global conflict. Students had to be conditioned to abandon the isolationist stance of their father and forefathers before they could be expected to engage in a war on European soil.

The effects of the Carnegie Foundation on America's religious colleges were decried as follows in a speech delivered by Thomas W. Churchill, president of the New York Board of Education, on June 14, 1914:

> Mr. Carnegie's efforts are crushing individuality out of American colleges and lessening their contributions to public service. The Carnegie Foundation has deliberately and conspicuously made a mark of religious colleges—particularly of the small institutions which in their own field carried on a great Samaritan work with limited equipment but a splendid spirit. One after another many religious colleges have been seduced by great wealth to give up the independence that should have been found in a college if nowhere else, and to forsake the faith of their founders. It makes me boil with shame to think that in this generation and in this Republic any body of men would so blazingly employ the tremendous power of great wealth as to permit it to buy the abandonment of religion.[9]

BATHING IN A SEA OF MILLIONS

At the same time, Ernest Victor Hollis, the Chief of College

---

9   Thomas W. Churchill, "The Carnegie Attitude to the Religious College," *The Evening Post* (New York), June 17, 1914.

Administration in the U. S. Department of Education, also voiced his objection to the "sinister" influence of CFAT. The method used by the endowment, he said, was one of indirection—"indirectly through general and non-controversial purposes." "For instance," Hollis elaborated, "there is little connection between giving a pension to a college professor or giving a sum to the general endowment of his college, and reforming entrance requirements, the financial practices, and the scholastic standards of his institution." Yet, he insisted, the one was bound to the other. It was a case of conform, or no grant! When to conform meant bathing in a stream of millions, Hollis concluded, college and university administrators and their faculties were inclined to conform.[10]

THE ROCKEFELLER FOUNDATION

The Rockefeller Foundation was set up in 1913 by John D. Rockefeller, Jr. with an initial $100 million endowment "to promote the well-being of mankind throughout the world."[11] By this time, Junior had developed a close relationship with Carnegie, whom he held in avuncular affection. He spent several weeks every summer at Skibo and agreed with Carnegie that their foundations should direct their resources toward common global goals.[12] Carnegie's last public appearance was at a gathering of Junior's Bible Class at the Fifth Avenue Baptist Church in New York. The appearance was telling since Carnegie was instrumental in persuading Junior to shed his religious fundamentalism. Shortly after Carnegie addressed the Bible Class, Junior announced to the group his belief that anyone who manifested "the moral spirit" of Jesus merited entrance into the Kingdom of Heaven, even if he or she denied Christian doctrine.[13]

---

10   Ernest Victor Hollis, quoted in Rene Wormster, *Foundations*, p. 140.

11   Chernow, *Titan*, p. 564.

12   Nasaw, *Andrew Carnegie*, p. 615.

13   Chernow, *Titan*, pp. 639-640.

Junior's internationalism was further enhanced by his friendship with Raymond B. Fosdick, who became his lawyer and closest adviser. Fosdick had been appointed to serve as Under Secretary of the League of Nations by President Wilson.[14] In his fawning biography, *John D. Rockefeller, Jr.: A Portrait* (1956), Fosdick wrote: "More and more Mr. Rockefeller began to think in international terms. It is true that he had not favored the League of Nations when it was first proposed. Just as he had taken his church affiliations from his father, so his political loyalties were similarly inherited, and he had followed the Republican Party in its opposition to President Wilson. But his opinions were invariably marked by tolerance, and inflexibility was not part of his character."[15]

FOSDICK AND RAUSCHENBUSCH

Under the influence of the Reverend Harry Emerson Fosdick, Raymond's elder brother, Junior funded and spearheaded the Interchurch Movement (ICM) which sought to consolidate the Protestant churches into a corporate-like structure which would exercise control over their activities.[16] The ideology of the ICM sprang from the sermons of the Rev. Fosdick, who had become indoctrinated in the "higher criticism" of Wellhausen by Charles Briggs, his professor at Union Theological Seminary. Fosdick believed that Christianity should be "demythologized" and stripped of all "theological accretions," including the Virgin Birth, the miracles of Jesus, and the Resurrection, so that religions throughout the world would express no qualms about uniting.[17]

As a young pastor in lower Manhattan, Fosdick came upon the "social gospel" of Walter Rauschenbusch, who taught that Christianity

---

14 Ibid, p. 638.

15 Raymond E. Fosdick, *John D. Rockefeller, Jr.: A Portrait* (New York: Harper and Brothers, 1958), p. 216.

16 Chernow, *Titan*, p. 639.

17 Robert Moats Miller, *Harry Emerson Fosdick: Preacher, Pastor, Prophet* (New York: Oxford University Press, 1985), pp. 408-409.

is in its nature revolutionary; that Jesus did not perform an act of atonement on the cross; and that the Kingdom of Heaven "is not a matter of getting into heaven but of transforming life on earth into the harmony of heaven."[18] This was the message, Fosdick believed, that could unite all of mankind. The message struck a chord with Junior, who, in a 1917 speech at the Baptist Social Union, had said that a new, unified church "would pronounce ordinance, ritual, creed, as non-essential for admission into the Kingdom of God or His Church."[19]

"SHALL THE FUNDAMENTALISTS WIN?"

Harry Emerson Fosdick and Junior became bound together after Fosdick delivered a sermon called "Shall the Fundamentalists Win?" at the First Presbyterian Church in New York. In the sermon, the Rev. Fosdick denounced interpretations of the Bible which upheld the supernatural aspects of the life of Jesus as "intolerant."[20] When the congregation reacted to the sermon by demanding Fosdick's ouster as their pastor, Junior rallied to Fosdick's support and distributed copies of the sermons to ministers and seminarians throughout the country.[21] In addition, he arranged for Fosdick to be selected as the senior pastor of the Riverside Church in upper Manhattan, which had been constructed by the Rockefeller Foundation at a cost of $4 million.[22]

With the Fosdick brothers at his side, Junior initiated a policy of funding seminaries that complied with the dictates of higher criticism and the debunking of the Old and New Testaments. A new breed of

---

18   Walter Rauschenbusch, *A Theology of the Social Gospel* (New York: Abington Press, 1918), pp. 131-137.

19   John D. Rockefeller, Jr., quoted in Fosdick, *John D. Rockefeller: A Portrait*, p. 206.

20   Harry Emerson Fosdick, "Shall the Fundamentalists Win," a sermon delivered in 1922 at the First Presbyterian Church in New York City, http://historymatters.gmu.edu/d/5070/

21   James Perloff, "The War on Christianity, Part 1," jamesperloff.com, 2013, https://jamesperloff.com/tag/national-council-of-churches/

22   Ibid.

minister, who believed neither the account of the Resurrection nor the divinity of Jesus, was unleashed on the American people. The seeds of doubt and skepticism would be spread from sea to shining sea so that deeply held convictions would be surrendered for the sake of religious indifferentism

After sanctifying the de-bunking of the Old and New Testaments, Christian clerics no longer could uphold the deity of the Hebrews as an object of worship. And so, a new God was presented to modern man, a figure who was all-loving, all-caring, and all-forgiving, a deity who approved of all lifestyles and all means of religious expression, a divine being that sprang from the heresy of Marcion and the tradition of Freemasonry. Thus, Christians and Jews came to ignore what had been written in stone.

PART TWO

THE LAW

6

THE EVIDENCE FOR EXODUS

Fundamental changes to disciplines tend to come from outside. It is customary for students to be introduced to their fields of study gradually, as slowly unfolding mysteries, so that by the time they can see their subject as a whole they have been so thoroughly imbued with conventional preconceptions and patterns of thought that they are extremely unlikely to be able to question its basic premises. This incapacity is particularly evident in the disciplines concerned with ancient history.

MARTIN BERNAL, BLACK ATHENA, 1987

IF IT IS TRUE, as respected archeologists believe, that the Torah's account of Israelite enslavement in Egypt followed by a sudden exodus of hundreds of thousands of Hebrews to Canaan is a "pious fiction" that has not one shred of historical evidence, then the entire foundation of the Bible would be seriously undermined. The account of Moses receiving the Ten Commandments from God would also be discredited. If that is a fiction, then why should anyone believe the Ten Commandments are the truly authoritative instructions of God? The Bible would be a piece of literature, no more authoritative than, say, Harry Potter books. The Marcionites could rightly claim that since much of the Old Testament has no historical basis, men owe no allegiance to the God, Yahweh, of which it speaks. And since the New Testament repeatedly refers to events in the Old Testament, its credibility would be called into question as well.

So did the Israelite Exodus, as described in the Book of Exodus, really happen? Most scholars assume that the Exodus would have happened during the reign of Ramses II, the greatest builder king, in the 13th century BC. This is due to the text in Exodus 1:11. "Therefore they set taskmasters over them to afflict them with heavy burdens; and they built for Pharaoh store-cities, Pithom and Raamses."

Archeologists agree there is no archeological evidence for Semites living in the city of Ramses during the New Kingdom.[1] However, a number of archeologists, including Thomas Thompson and David Rohl,[2][3] believe that evidence of Semites living at that location several hundred years before the reign of Ramses II points to proof of the Hebrew enslavement.

At Tell El Daba in the town of Avaris, right below the southern sector of Ramses, archeologists found a "a much older city which was almost entirely populated by Asiatics from Canaan. That city—one of the largest in the ancient world—began life in the 12th Dynasty and expanded rapidly throughout the 13th Dynasty,"[4] The town, which enjoyed a special status, like a free zone, showed evidence of shepherds living there, which was not an Egyptian practice.

---

1   Thomas. Thompson, *The Bible in History* (London: Random House, 1999), p. xv.

2   David M. Rohl, *Exodus: Myth or History* (St. Louis Park, MN: Thinking Man Media, 2015), p. 20-21.

3   Also discussed in "Patterns of Evidence" book and movie. https://patternsofevidence.com/

4   David Rohl, *Exodus: Myth or History*, p. 21.

THE LUXOR MONUMENT

A monument called *Merenptah Stela* in Luxor created a few years after Ramses II's death by his son Merenptah undermines the belief of scholars who insist that the exodus of the Israelites took place during the New Kingdom reign of Ramses. The monument refers to an Israelite nation defeated by this Pharaoh. It read: "Israel is laid waste, his seed is no more."[5] If Ramses' army defeated an already existing Israelite nation living in Canaan, how could Ramses have also been the pharaoh who let the Israelite slaves depart from Egypt, before they even had a nation?

Another piece of evidence is the Berlin Pedestal at the State Museum in Berlin, Germany, dated around 1360 BC. This Egyptian document includes a reference to a bound enemy nation called Israel.[6] This serves to make the late date in the New Kingdom for the Exodus highly questionable.

THE MAN WITH RED HAIR

Also found in Avaris is a non-Egyptian, Syrian-style house that would have existed at the end of the 12th dynasty during the Middle Kingdom, many centuries before Ramses II. On top of the house was a palace built with 12 pillars and 12 tombs. One was a pyramid tomb, a high honor for an official, since pyramids were usually reserved solely for the Pharaoh himself.[7]

Inside the pyramid tomb archeologists found a "larger than life" statue of a man with red hair and yellow skin, indicating that he was a Semite (Syro-Palestinian "Asiatic") along with remains of paint

---

5   Margaret Drower, *Flinders Petrie: A life in Archeology* (Madison: University of Wisconsin Press, 1995), p. 221.

6   P. van der Veen, et al., "Israel in Canaan (Long) Before Pharaoh Merneptah? A Fresh Look at Berlin Statue Pedestal Relief 21687" *in the Journal of Ancient Egyptian Interconnections 2*, 2010, https://www.academia.edu/12078547/Israel_in_Canaan._Long_Before_Pharaoh_Merenptah_A_fresh_look_at_Berlin_statue_pedestal_relief_21687

7   David Rohl, *Exodus: Myth or History*, pp. 106-107.

indicating *a striped cloak,* possibly like the multi-color coat the book of Genesis says the patriarch Jacob gave to his favorite son. The Austrian archeological mission which discovered the statue comments that this man, although a non-Egyptian "Asiatic," "held a position of power," which was unusual since Egyptian Middle Kingdom images showing Asiatics "most commonly show these as conquered enemies."[8] [9] Could this have been Joseph, whom the book of Genesis describes as being elevated to the highest level of authority in Egypt, second only to the Pharaoh himself? Professor Charles Aling, an Egyptologist from the University of Northwestern, St. Paul, and archeologist Bryant Wood of the Association for Biblical Research believe it would have to refer to a Semite of the caliber that the Bible attributes to the person of Joseph.[10]

THE PHARAOH'S WORRY LINES

The Pharaoh of that time was Amenemhat, whose statue is depicted with worry lines.[11] This depiction indicates that Egypt during his leadership faced difficult times. Amenemhat's reign saw the end of influence of regional governors and centralization of power and wealth in the hands of the Pharaoh. [12] Such a centralization of power could surely have been prompted by the 7 years of plenty where the Pharaoh's government gathered vast stores of grain followed by 7 years of drought as described in Genesis 41:

---

8   Robert Schiestl, "The Cemeteries of F/I in the Strata d/2 (H) and d/l (G/4), late 12th Dynasty and early 13th Dynasty" at http://www.auaris.at/html/stratum_f1_d1_en.html

9   Robert Schiestl, "The Statue of an Asiatic Man from Tell El-Dab'a, Egypt" Ägypten Und Levante / Egypt and the Levant, vol. 16, 2006, pp. 173–185. JSTOR, www.jstor.org/stable/23790282.

10   Timothy P. Mahoney, "Patterns of Evidence: Exodus, A Filmmaker's Journey," (St. Louis Park, MN: Thinking Man Media, 2015).

11   David Rohl, *Exodus: Myth or History*, p. 90.

12   Ibid., p. 91.

Then Joseph said to Pharaoh, "The dream of Pharaoh is one; God has revealed to Pharaoh what he is about to do. The seven good cows are seven years, and the seven good ears are seven years; the dream is one. The seven lean and gaunt cows that came up after them are seven years, and the seven empty ears blighted by the east wind are also seven years of famine. It is as I told Pharaoh, God has shown to Pharaoh what he is about to do. There will come seven years of great plenty throughout all the land of Egypt, but after them there will arise seven years of famine, and all the plenty will be forgotten in the land of Egypt; the famine will consume the land, and the plenty will be unknown in the land by reason of that famine which will follow, for it will be very grievous. And the doubling of Pharaoh's dream means that the thing is fixed by God, and God will shortly bring it to pass. Now therefore let Pharaoh select a man discreet and wise, and set him over the land of Egypt. Let Pharaoh proceed to appoint overseers over the land, and take the fifth part of the produce of the land of Egypt during the seven plenteous years. And let them gather all the food of these good years that are coming, and lay up grain under the authority of Pharaoh for food in the cities, and let them keep it. That food shall be a reserve for the land against the seven years of famine which are to befall the land of Egypt, so that the land may not perish through the famine."

Joseph was thirty years old when he entered the service of Pharaoh king of Egypt. And Joseph went out from the presence of Pharaoh, and went through all the land of Egypt. During the seven plenteous years the earth brought forth abundantly, and he gathered up all the food of the seven years when there was plenty in the land of Egypt, and stored up food in the cities; he stored up in every city the food from the fields around it. And Joseph stored up grain in great abundance, like the sand of the sea, until he ceased to measure it, for it could not be measured.

The seven years of plenty that prevailed in the land of Egypt came to an end; and the seven years of famine began to come, as Joseph had said. There was famine in all lands; but in all the land of Egypt there was bread. When all the land of Egypt was famished, the people cried to Pharaoh for bread; and Pharaoh said to all the Egyptians, "Go to Joseph; what he says to you, do." So when the famine had spread over all the land, Joseph opened all the storehouses and sold to the Egyptians, for the famine was severe in the land of Egypt. Moreover, all the earth came to Egypt to Joseph to buy grain, because the famine was severe over all the earth.

Residents of the outlying areas would have had to sell their possessions, servants, lands, and even themselves during those harsh years in return for life-saving grain from the stores of the central government.

THE PYRAMID TOMB

Curiously, the pyramid tomb in Avaris is totally empty, including bones, which even grave-robbers would have no interest to take. Archaeologist Rohl believes a reasonable explanation would be that if the remains were of Joseph, they were removed from the tomb[13] and taken to Shechem in Canaan (Nablus of West Bank) when the Israelites left Egypt centuries later, as described in Joshua 24:32. There is also evidence of "exceeding great multiplication" of these Semitic sojourners, as described in Exodus 1:7, in the Egyptian delta including Avaris and other nearby towns.[14]

THE ENSLAVEMENT OF THE ISRAELITES

John Bimson, Professor of Old Testament at Trinity College, Bristol, England, explains that this extended period of prosperity during the reign of Amenemhat was followed by scarcity, where people were

---

13   Ibid., p. 112.

14   Ibid., p. 127.

dying in their 30s.[15] He also sees evidence of the killing of Hebrew boys. Excavations from Avaris indicate an "extremely high mortality rate of newborns." Fifty percent of those up to 10 years old died in the first 3 months of life.[16] Burial plots from that time show remains that are 60% female adults and 40% male adults.[17] Could the unnatural reduction in male adults be due to the murder of male infants, such as that described in the Bible?

A well-known document called the Brooklyn Papyrus from that time includes a list of domestic slaves in the residence of a wealthy Egyptian family. Seventy percent of the slaves listed are Semitic, including Israelite names such as Menahem, Issachar, and Asher as well as "Shiphrah,"[18] the same as the name of the Hebrew midwife who refused to kill male Hebrew babies spoken of in the beginning of the Exodus story. The evidence clearly shows a large presence of Hebrews in the 13th Egyptian Dynasty (Middle Kingdom), not the 19th Dynasty of the New Kingdom many centuries later.

PROOF OF THE PLAGUES

In the Leiden Museum in Holland is a papyrus written by an Egyptian scribe named Ipuwer known as "The Admonitions of an Egyptian Sage." This document describes a series of calamities such as the turning of "water into blood." It continues:

> Gone is the barley of abundance. Food supplies are running short. The nobles hunger and suffer. Those who had shelter are in the dark of the storm. Behold, plague sweeps the land, blood is everywhere,

---

15   E.M. Winkler & H. Wilfing: Tell el-Daba VI (Vienna, Untersuchungen der Zweigstelle Kairo des Osterreichischen Archäologischen Institutes, 1991), p. 82.

16   Ibid., p. 87.

17   Ibid., p. 140.

18   William Albright: "Northwest-Semitic Names in a List of Egyptian Slaves from the Eighteenth Century BC," Journal of the American Oriental Society, 74, no. 4 (1954), pp. 222-33.

with no shortage of the dead. Wailing is throughout the land, mingled with lamentations.[19]

Scholars discount the "Ipuwer Papyrus" because they cannot reconcile the description of want with poor people suddenly described as becoming rich and wearing fine clothes taken from the rich. "The slave takes what he finds. Gold, lapis lazuli, silver and turquoise are strung on the necks of the female slaves."[20] But this fantastic account exactly matches the biblical account in Exodus 12:35-36:

> The people of Israel had also done as Moses told them, for they had asked of the Egyptians jewelry of silver and of gold, and clothing; and the LORD had given the people favor in the sight of the Egyptians, so that they let them have what they asked. Thus, they despoiled the Egyptians.

Egyptologist Galit Dayan has uncovered another papyrus scroll that describes a "plague" that has spread ". . . throughout the land. Blood is everywhere—the river is blood, and the hail smote every herd of the field . . . the land is without light and there is a thick darkness throughout the land. . .the Lord smote all the firstborn in the land of Egypt—from the firstborn of Pharaoh that sat on his throne to the firstborn of the captive who was in prison. . . ."[21]

3 MAJOR PERIODS OF EGYPTIAN HISTORY		
Old Kingdom 2700–2200 B.C.E.	**Middle Kingdom** 2050–1800 B.C.E.	**New Kingdom** 1550–1100 B.C.E.

---

19 Alan H. Gardner, "The Admonitions of an Egyptian Sage, from a Hieratic Papyrus in Leiden," Leipzig: J. C. Hinrichs Buchhandlung, 1909.

20 Ibid.

21 Danielle Berrin, "Passover Proof Lies in Egyptian Hieroglyphs," *Jewish Journal,* March 24, 2010, http://jewishjournal.com/culture/religion/passover/77833/

The archeology of Avaris shows that after a couple of centuries, lasting from the late 12th Dynasty to the end of the 13th Dynasty, the original, highly Egyptianized Semitic population—the Israelite descendants of Jacob—abandoned Avaris and disappeared from the archeological record. But they left behind a scene of devastation. All over Avaris the Austrian archeologists found shallow pits in the ground containing bodies, simply thrown in without proper grave goods.[22] A virulent plague must have struck the city requiring the emergency burial of its victims. This, according to David Rohl, could well be evidence of the Tenth Plague, the death of the firstborn. Then, the Semitic quarter of the city was emptied; the people simply picked up their belongings and walked away, leaving the houses to crumble and decay.[23]

EVIDENCE OF EXODUS

While there remains no evidence of a catastrophe during the reigns of Ramses or his son, there are pits in the ground at Avaris and Kahun that were created centuries before the New Kingdom with mounds of bodies, evidence of emergency burials and the sudden disappearance of Semitic people who had been living there. Goods were found in the houses and streets indicating a sudden departure.

An Egyptian priest in the 3rd century BC called Manetho wrote a history of the reign of a king called Dudimose, one of the last kings of the 13th Middle Kingdom dynasty, stating that in his reign, "God smote the Egyptians."[24] Soon after the demise of Dudimose, Egypt was invaded by foreigners, a people of "obscure race" from the north and

---

22   Manfred Bietak: "Egypt and Canaan During the Middle Bronze Age," *American Schools of Oriental Research* 281 (1991), p. 38.

23   David Rohl, *Exodus: Myth or History*, p. 349.

24   *Manetho*, with English translation by W. G. Waddell, (Harvard University Press, Cambridge, MA, 1964). https://archive.org/stream/manethowithengli00maneuoft/manethowithengli00maneuoft_djvu.txt

they conquer the land, "without striking a blow."[25] Why? Because the Egyptians were already weakened and were unable to defend themselves. This is called the Hyksos period, when these foreign invaders enslaved the Egyptians. This was the only known collapse of Egyptian society during the Old, Middle, or New Kingdoms.[26]

THE CONQUEST OF CANAAN

According to 1 Kings 6:1, the Exodus took place 480 years before Solomon erected the Temple in the 4th year of his reign in 970 BC, which would have been 1450 BC. Mainstream scholars point out that there is no evidence of destruction in Jericho in the Late Bronze Age, which matches the New Kingdom in Egypt. But there *is* evidence of the walls falling before a vast fire that destroyed the city around 1550 BC (Middle Kingdom).[27] Archeologists also discovered jars full of grain in all of the houses, suggesting that the siege was very short, which would match the biblical account of the Israelites marching around the city for seven days followed by the collapse of the city's walls.[28]

Joshua 2:1-7 describes the actions of the harlot Rahab who hid the Israeli spies and aided their escape:

> And Joshua the son of Nun sent two men secretly from Shittim as spies, saying, "Go, view the land, especially Jericho." And they went, and came into the house of a harlot whose name was Rahab, and lodged there. And it was told the king of Jericho, "Behold, certain men of Israel have come here tonight to search out the land." Then the king of Jericho sent to Rahab, saying, "Bring forth the men that have come to you, who entered your house; for they have come to search out all the land." But the woman had taken the two men and

---

25   Ibid.

26   David Rohl, *Exodus: Myth or History*, p. 157.

27   K. Kenyon: *Excavations at Jericho*, Volume 3 (London, 1981), p. 110.

28   Ibid.

hidden them; and she said, "True, men came to me, but I did not know where they came from; and when the gate was to be closed, at dark, the men went out; where the men went I do not know; pursue them quickly, for you will overtake them." But she had brought them up to the roof, and hid them with the stalks of flax which she had laid in order on the roof. So the men pursued after them on the way to the Jordan as far as the fords; and as soon as the pursuers had gone out, the gate was shut.

Her home, described as being in the city walls, was spared because of her help to the invading chosen people. Archeologists found one part of the city wall that was not destroyed, with houses built in the wall,[29] as described in Joshua 2.

The scriptures also speak of Joshua killing the King of Hazor, who was named Jabin. Tablets unearthed from the remains of the palace in Hazor during the Middle Bronze Age make reference to this monarch.[30]

ARCHAEOLOGICAL REASSESSMENT

There is significant evidence of all of the 6 stages of the biblical account: (1) the arrival of the Israelites in Egypt, (2) the multiplication of the Hebrew tribes into hundreds of thousands; (3) the enslavement of the Hebrews, (4) the plagues that befell Egypt, (5) the Exodus/Sudden Departure, and (6) the conquest of City/States in Canaan. These events took place in the Middle Kingdom, not in the New Kingdom, as most archeologists expected. New research and a paradigm shift revealed what was hidden in plain sight, the reality of the Israelite presence in Egypt, their enslavement, their sudden departure after a series of catastrophic events, and the conquest of Jericho and other city-states, all as are indicated in the Pentateuch.

---

29   David Rohl, *Exodus: Myth or History* p. 281.

30   William Albright: *The Biblical Period from Abraham to Ezra* (New York: HarperCollins, 1963), p. 102.

This fortifies the central claim of the Jews that their God, unlike the deities of ancient Egypt, Greece, and Rome has revealed Himself in linear history and not mythological time and place, and these revelations, many of which are being supported by archaeological data, continue to confront skeptics, atheists, the despisers of religion, and contemporary Gnostics.

7

THE STONE TABLETS

The phrase "cut flower culture" is attributed to Will Herberg. This metaphor reminds that cut flowers are both attractive and destined to perish quickly. This is because cut flowers are separated from their roots. Without roots, the lovely cut flowers will perish. So by analogy, a culture cut from its roots is destined to perish regardless of how attractive the cultural values are that are being celebrated. This, then, describes where America is today with its secular culture that has uprooted our lives and institutions from the previous spiritual roots that caused us to "flourish." With the abandonment of the Ten Commandments in America by both secular and atheistic groups, and aided as well by Muslim immigration that insists that it owns no more than seven of the Ten Commandments, America is facing a time of cultural spiritual rootlessness.

PETER LILLBACK, "CAN CUT FLOWERS TAKE ROOT AGAIN? THE
FORSAKEN ROOTS OF OUR AMERICAN REPUBLIC," JANUARY 16, 2017

AS ENUMERATED IN EXODUS, Leviticus, Numbers, and Deuteronomy, the six hundred and thirteen laws of Moses represented a covenant between God and the Hebrew people. Those who obey them, as stated in Deuteronomy 28:3-14, would be richly rewarded:

You will be blessed in the city and blessed in the country.

The fruit of your womb will be blessed, and the crops of your land

and the young of your livestock—the calves of your herds and the lambs of your flocks.

Your basket and your kneading trough will be blessed.

You will be blessed when you come in and blessed when you go out.

The LORD will grant that the enemies who rise up against you will be defeated before you. They will come at you from one direction but flee from you in seven.

The LORD will send a blessing on your barns and on everything you put your hand to. The LORD your God will bless you in the land he is giving you.

The LORD will establish you as his holy people, as he promised you on oath, if you keep the commands of the LORD your God and walk in obedience to him. Then all the peoples on earth will see that you are called by the name of the LORD, and they will fear you.

The LORD will grant you abundant prosperity—in the fruit of your womb, the young of your livestock and the crops of your ground—in the land he swore to your ancestors to give you.

The LORD will open the heavens, the storehouse of his bounty, to send rain on your land in season and to bless all the work of your hands. You will lend to many nations but will borrow from none. The LORD will make you the head, not the tail. If you pay attention to the commands of the LORD your God that I give you this day and carefully follow them, you will always be at the top, never at the bottom. Do not turn aside from any of the commands I give you today, to the right or to the left, following other gods and serving them.

Conversely, according to Deuteronomy 28:15-29, those who disobey them would receive the full measure of God's wrath:

However, if you do not obey the LORD your God and do not carefully follow all his commands and decrees I am giving you today, all these curses will come on you and overtake you:

You will be cursed in the city and cursed in the country.

Your basket and your kneading trough will be cursed.

The fruit of your womb will be cursed, and the crops of your land, and the calves of your herds and the lambs of your flocks.

You will be cursed when you come in and cursed when you go out.

The LORD will send on you curses, confusion and rebuke in everything you put your hand to, until you are destroyed and come to sudden ruin because of the evil you have done in forsaking him.

The LORD will plague you with diseases until he has destroyed you from the land you are entering to possess.

The LORD will strike you with wasting disease, with fever and inflammation, with scorching heat and drought, with blight and mildew, which will plague you until you perish.

The sky over your head will be bronze, the ground beneath you iron.

The LORD will turn the rain of your country into dust and powder; it will come down from the skies until you are destroyed.

The LORD will cause you to be defeated before your enemies.

You will come at them from one direction but flee from them in seven, and you will become a thing of horror to all the kingdoms on earth.

Your carcasses will be food for all the birds and the wild animals, and there will be no one to frighten them away.

The LORD will afflict you with the boils of Egypt and with tumors, festering sores and the itch, from which you cannot be cured.

The LORD will afflict you with madness, blindness and confusion of mind. At midday you will grope about like a blind person in the dark.

You will be unsuccessful in everything you do; day after day you will be oppressed and robbed, with no one to rescue.

The laws governed every aspect of the lives of the ancient Hebrews: the manner in which they farmed, their sex lives, the food they ate and did not eat, and their personal hygiene. They proscribed the things that were forbidden, the punishment for violators of the ordinances, and the means of atonement. They established the compensation for accidental death, injury, and damage to property, and they set forth the rights and responsibilities of slaves and slave owners.[1] For example, Exodus 21:33-34 says: "If a man uncovers a pit or digs one and fails to cover it, and an ox or a donkey falls into it, the owner of the pit must pay for the loss; he must pay the owner, and the dead animal will be his."

THE HARSH AND THE HUMANE

The laws are straight-forward in their condemnation of homosexuality and cross-dressing. Leviticus 18:22 says: "You shall not lie with a male as with a woman; it is an abomination." And Deuteronomy 22:5 adds: "A woman must not wear men's clothing, nor a man wear women's clothing, for the LORD your God detests anyone who does this." No room within the sacral community was allowed for tolerance, let alone inclusivity.

Many of the laws are of surprising significance, including the distinction between clean and unclean animals. Leviticus 11 and Deuteronomy 14, for example, prohibit the eating of pigs, rabbits, and hyrax. Although these animals are of different species, they are all subject to tularemia, a dangerous disease which is contracted when a person skins and cleans a diseased animal. In addition, pigs are carriers of trichinosis, and the eating of rare or undercooked pork may result in death.[2]

---

1   William Albright, "The Law That Bound Israel," *Life*, Volume 57, Number 26, December 25, 1964, p. 55.

2   Ibid., p. 56.

Some of the laws appear to be harsh and unreasonable. Exodus 22:18 says: "You shall not allow a witch to live." Such passages, many believe, should be relegated to the desert of the distant past, save for the fact that black magic, including the casting of spells and mind-control, became the subject of a CIA operation called MK-Ultra during the 1950s and 1960s. This covert undertaking resulted in the deaths of thousands of innocent children in Quebec.[3]

LEX TALIONIS, THE LAW OF RETALIATION

The Torah's insistence upon the *lex talionis* has been misunderstood and condemned as barbaric. This law states: "Thus you shall not show pity: life for life, eye for eye, tooth for tooth, hand for hand, foot for foot" (Deut. 19:21). William Albright, the famed Biblical archaeologist, argues that this injunction does not represent vindictive cruelty. It rather stands, he maintains, as the first formal enunciation of the principle of equal justice for all and the end of the pre-Mosaic practice of exacting heavier punishments from the lower classes.[4] For Albright, the *lex talionis* has no more to do with revenge than the Hebrew concept of an "avenging God" has to do with vengeance in the modern sense. In Hebrew, avenge means "to champion, defend, or vindicate."[5]

The basic humanitarianism of the laws extended to the health of laborers and the care of widows, orphans, and the poor. Animals, even those belonging to enemies, were to be treated with kindness. "You shall not muzzle an ass when it treads out the grain" (Deut. 23:11). "If you meet your enemy's ox or his ass going astray, you shall bring it back to him. If you see the ass of one who hates you lying under its burden, you shall refrain from leaving him with it, you shall help him lift it up" (Exod. 23:4-5).

---

3   Christine Hahn, "The Worst of Times: How Psychiatry Used Quebec's Orphans as Guinea Pigs," *Freedom*, n. d., http://www.freedommag.org/english/canada/reports/page01.htm

4   Albright, "The Law That Bound Israel," p. 56.

5   Ibid.

THE TEMPORAL AND THE ETERNAL

The laws, according to archaeological findings, represent a treaty of alliance between God and the Hebrew people that were in accordance with the treaties forged between ancient Middle Eastern kings and the vassals, who ruled their lands. Such treaties began with an enumeration of the names, titles, and services of the "great king." "I am the Lord your God who has brought you out of the land of Egypt, out of the house of bondage" (Exod. 20:2). Vassals were forbidden to enter into any relationship with other kings. "You shall not have other gods before me" (Exod. 20:3). The imperious "you shall" and "you shall not" occur repeatedly throughout the treaties with vassals. One treaty with a vassal prescribes that "you shall not covet any territory of the land of the Hatti." In a similar way, the Mosaic law proscribes that "you shall not covet your neighbor's house" (Exod. 20:17).[6] Roland de Vaux, a leading Catholic scholar, discovered in a number of Hittite treaties with vassals the injunction that the text of the treaty was to be read out regularly in the presence of the king, the vassals, and their subjects. Similarly, Deuteronomy 31:10-13 proscribes: "At the end of every seven years, at the set time in the year of release, at the Feast of Booths, when all Israel comes to appear before the LORD your God at the place that he will choose, you shall read this law before all Israel in their hearing. Assemble the people, men, women, and little ones, and the sojourner within your towns, that they may hear and learn to fear the LORD your God, and be careful to do all the words of this law, and that their children, who have not known it, may hear and learn to fear the LORD your God, as long as you live in the land that you are going over the Jordan to possess." One must acknowledge such parallels while also remaining cognizant of the fact that these laws are not between a king and his vassal, but rather between the God of the Hebrews and His people.

---

6   Werner Keller, *The Bible as History*, translated from the German by William Neil, Second
     Edition (New York: William Morrow and Company, 1980), p. 139.

INSCRIBED BY GOD'S FINGER

Nothing was more sacred to the ancient Jews than the law, which was written by the "finger of God" on stone tablets. Rabbinical teaching throughout the ages has insisted that the commandments came from heaven and were written before the creation of the world.[7] Eleazar ben Shamma said: "Were it not for the Torah, heaven and earth would not continue to exist."[8] For thousands of years, any Jew who rejected this teaching, such as Spinoza, was condemned as a heretic and ostracized from the religious community.[9]

The heart of the law is the Decalogue as found in Exodus 20:1-7:

And God spoke all these words:

"I am the LORD your God, who brought you out of Egypt, out of the land of slavery.

"You shall have no other gods before me.

"You shall not make for yourself an image in the form of anything in heaven above or on the earth beneath or in the waters below. You shall not bow down to them or worship them; for I, the LORD your God, am a jealous God, punishing the children for the sin of the parents to the third and fourth generation of those who hate me, but showing love to a thousand generations of those who love me and keep my commandments.

"You shall not misuse the name of the LORD your God, for the LORD will not hold anyone guiltless who misuses his name.

"Remember the Sabbath day by keeping it holy. Six days you shall labor and do all your work, but the seventh day is a Sabbath to the

---

7   "Judaism: The Written Word—Torah," *Jewish Virtual Library*, n. d. https://www.jewishvirtuallibrary.org/the-written-law-torah

8   Eleazar ben Shamma, quoted in Ibid.

9   Ibid.

LORD your God. On it you shall not do any work, neither you, nor your son or daughter, nor your male or female servant, nor your animals, nor any foreigner residing in your towns. For in six days the LORD made the heavens and the earth, the sea, and all that is in them, but he rested on the seventh day. Therefore, the Lord blessed the Sabbath day and made it holy.

"Honor your father and your mother, so that you may live long in the land the LORD your God is giving you.

"You shall not murder.

"You shall not commit adultery.

"You shall not steal.

"You shall not give false testimony against your neighbor.

"You shall not covet your neighbor's house. You shall not covet your neighbor's wife, or his male or female servant, his ox or donkey, or anything that belongs to your neighbor."

THE ARK OF THE COVENANT

The stone tablets were kept within the Ark of the Covenant, a rectangular box (2½ cubits long, 1½ cubits broad, and 1½ cubits high) that was made of acacia wood.[10] The lid of the Ark was made of solid gold with two golden cherubim. This cover represented "the throne of God." Wherever it was placed, God was fully there. When it was raised, God, too, was raised to stand before the people of Israel. When it was lowered, God resumed his seat on the throne.[11] The Ark was fitted with handles so that it could be carried into battle (Numbers 10:35): "Rise up, O Lord, and let thine enemies be scattered." Members of the Levite tribe

---

10   Von Rad, *Old Testament Theology*, Volume I, p. 235.

11   Ibid., p. 237.

were charged with transporting the Ark, but even the Levites could not touch it or "to look upon it," lest they die (Num. 4:20).

Since the ancient Hebrews bore the Ark into battle, they were obliged to carry wooden paddles along with weapons of war so they could dig holes to bury their excrement.[12] "For the LORD your God moves about in your camp to protect you and to deliver your enemies to you. Your camp must be holy, so that he will not see among you anything indecent and turn away from you" (Deut. 23:14).

When David sought to make Jerusalem the religious center of Israel, he arranged to have the Ark brought to the city in an oxcart led by Uzzah, one of his soldiers, and Ahio, Uzzah's brother. When one of the oxen stumbled, Uzzah placed his hand on the Ark to steady it, but his good intentions did not spare him.[13] "When they came to the threshing floor of Nakon, Uzzah reached out and took hold of the ark of God, because the oxen stumbled. The LORD's anger burned against Uzzah because of his irreverent act; therefore God struck him down, and he died there beside the ark of God" (2 Sam. 6:6-7). Nothing was holier than the Ark that contained the law. It was finally placed behind a thick veil within the Temple of Solomon. The dark room in which it was kept represented "the Holy of Holies," a room (*debhir*) with walls of gold that could only be entered once a year by the high priest on the Day of Atonement.[14] To dismiss the transcendent importance of the law for the people of God is to abnegate the essence of the Torah.

THE GREATEST COMMANDMENT

The first *mitzvah*, which Jewish sages consider the greatest of the

---

12   Hirsch, *Moses*, p. 277.

13   Emil G. Hirsch and Schulim Ochser, "Uzza, Uzzah," *Jewish Encyclopedia*, 1906, http://www.jewishencyclopedia.com/articles/14621-uzza-uzzah

14   Joseph Telushkin, "The Temples (*Beit HaMikdah*): The First Temple—The Temple of Solomon," *Jewish Virtual Library*, 1991, https://www.jewishvirtuallibrary.org/the-first-temple-solomon-s-temple

commandments, states that the God of Moses, who brought the Hebrews "out of the land of slavery," is the only deity worthy of worship.[15] No other god, including Baal, Bethel, Dagon, Astarte, Anath, Asherah and the all-embracing Being of modern Marcionites, is to be placed above Him. This is the cornerstone of the covenant and the basis of Israel's monotheism. It binds Israel completely to one God, allowing no other deities any importance or authority.

This commandment laid the foundation for the new theocratic community, which was to rest not upon more civil law, but the laws that the ancient Hebrews believed had been given to them from heaven. Their God was the Invisible King who dictated every precept that was to be obeyed and every punishment that was to be meted out. The people of God were to be called *Israel,* meaning defenders of God.[16] Heresy or blasphemy was to be punished by death, even if the offender happened to be one's closest kin.[17] The first commandment serves to affirm the absolute holiness of God. This holiness, according to Biblical scholar Gerhard von Rad, was experienced by the Hebrews as a power, not something in repose, but rather as something "urgent" and "in every case incalculable."[18]

THE OFFENSE OF IDOLATRY

The offense of idolatry was so horrific that Moses smashed the stone tablets that He had received from God when he descended from the mountain and beheld the Hebrew people worshipping a golden calf.

> When Moses approached the camp and saw the calf and the dancing, his anger burned and he threw the tablets out of his hands, breaking them to pieces at the foot of the mountain. And he took the calf

---

15   Hirsch, *Moses,* p. 210.

16   Durant, *Our Oriental Heritage,* p. 331.

17   Ibid.

18   Von Rad, *Old Testament Theology,* p. 205.

the people had made and burned it in the fire; then he ground it to powder, scattered it on the water and made the Israelites drink it.

He said to Aaron, "What did these people do to you, that you led them into such great sin?"

"Do not be angry, my lord," Aaron answered. "You know how prone these people are to evil. They said to me, 'Make us gods who will go before us. As for this fellow Moses who brought us up out of Egypt, we don't know what has happened to him.' So I told them, 'Whoever has any gold jewelry, take it off.' Then they gave me the gold, and I threw it into the fire, and out came this calf!"

Moses saw that the people were running wild and that Aaron had let them get out of control and so become a laughingstock to their enemies. So he stood at the entrance to the camp and said, "Whoever is for the LORD, come to me." And all the Levites rallied to him.

Then he said to them, "This is what the LORD, the God of Israel, says: 'Each man strap a sword to his side. Go back and forth through the camp from one end to the other, each killing his brother and friend and neighbor.'" The Levites did as Moses commanded, and that day about three thousand of the people died. Then Moses said, "You have been set apart to the LORD today, for you were against your own sons and brothers, and he has blessed you this day."

The next day Moses said to the people, "You have committed a great sin. But now I will go up to the LORD; perhaps I can make atonement for your sin."

So, Moses went back to the LORD and said, "Oh, what a great sin these people have committed! They have made themselves gods of gold. But now, please forgive their sin—but if not, then blot me out of the book you have written."

The LORD replied to Moses, "Whoever has sinned against me I will blot out of my book. Now go, lead the people to the place I spoke of, and my angel will go before you. However, when the time comes for me to punish, I will punish them for their sin."

And the LORD struck the people with a plague because of what they did with the calf Aaron had made. (Ex. 32:19-35)

As a result of their sin, three thousand Hebrews were put to death, many of those who remained were struck with a plague, and the names of all those who worshipped the calf were blotted out of God's book of Life. Unfortunately, this lesson has been lost to modern Marcionites, who have forgotten the God of their fathers.

8

THE DEATH PENALTY

Perhaps you would give a couple of paragraphs to the misconception (and the mistranslation) of the Sixth Commandment [in Exodus 20:13], 'You shall not murder,' as 'You shall not kill.' The original Hebrew, lo tirtsah, is very clear, since the verb ratsakh means 'murder,' not 'kill.' If the commandment proscribed killing as such, it would position Judaism against capital punishment and make it pacifist even in wartime. These may be defensible or admirable views, but they're certainly not biblical.

BEREL LANG, PROFESSOR OF OLD TESTAMENT
THEOLOGY, TRINITY COLLEGE, 2004

RATSAKH!

Because of the misinterpretation of this Hebrew verb, people throughout the world have called for a ban on firearms and the termination of defense spending. Such misinterpretation has caused Quakers in Russia to refuse to kill lice but rather "to put them somewhere else."[1]

---

1   Bernard Canter, *The Quaker Bedside Book* (Liverpool, England: C. Tinling and Company, 1952), p. 48.

Ratsakh is the Hebrew word for premeditated murder or manslaughter. It is never used for legal killing, such as the administration of capital punishment or for the killing of an enemy combatant in war. For this reason, the King James' translation "Thou shalt not *kill,*" according to Jewish scholars, is too broad and misleading.[2] Adrian Ebens writes:

> There are two different Hebrew words (ratsakh, mut) and two Greek words (phoneuo, apokteino) for "murder" and "killing." One means "to put to death," and the other means "to murder." The latter one is the one prohibited by the Ten Commandments, not the former. In fact, ratsakh has a broader definition than the English word "murder." Ratsakh also covers deaths due to carelessness or neglect but is never used when describing killing during wartime. That is why most modern translations render the sixth commandment "You shall not murder" rather than "You shall not kill." However, a very large issue can arise depending on which translation one studies. The ever-popular King James Version renders the verse as "Thou shalt not kill," therefore opening the door to misinterpreting the verse altogether. If the intended meaning of "Thou shalt not kill" was just that—no killing—it would render all of the God-endorsed bloodletting done by the nation of Israel a violation of God's own commandment (Deuteronomy 20).[3]

GOD AS EXECUTIONER

The claim that ratsakh applies only to intentional murder is buttressed by the fact that God Himself orders the killing of people throughout the Old Testament. Swiss Jesuit theologian Raymond Schwager writes: "The passages are numerous where God explicitly commands someone to

---

2   "The Ten Commandments," Zola Levitt Ministries, n.d., https://www.levitt.com/hebrew/commandments.html

3   Adrian Ebens, "Thou Shalt Not Kill—Making the Muth Argument," Maranatha Media, February 12, 2017, http://maranathamedia.com/article/print/thou-shalt-not-kill-muting-the-muth-argument

kill. Aside from the approximately one thousand verses in which Yahweh himself appears as the direct executioner of violent punishments, and the many texts in which the Lord delivers the criminal to the punisher's sword, in over one hundred other passages Yahweh expressly gives the command to kill people. These passages do not have God himself do the killing; he keeps somewhat aloof. Yet it is he who gives the order to destroy human life."[4]

Key scriptural passages in which God directly orders killing are as follows:

> When the LORD your God brings you into the land you are entering to possess and drives out before you many nations...then you must destroy them totally. Make no treaty with them and show them no mercy. (Deuteronomy 7:1-2)

> ...Do not leave alive anything that breaths. Completely destroy them... as the LORD your God has commanded you. . . . (Deuteronomy 20:16)

> This is what the LORD Almighty says: "Now go and strike Amalek and devote to destruction all that they have. Do not spare them, but kill both man and woman, child and infant, ox and sheep, camel and donkey." (1 Samuel 15:3)

> Happy is he who repays you for what you have done to us—he who seizes your infants and dashes them against the rocks. (Psalm 137:9)

THE CAPITAL CRIMES

The *Exodus* chapter which follows the Ten Commandments mandates the death penalty for murder, physically assaulting one's father or mother, and for kidnapping for purpose of selling the victim into slavery:

---

4   Raymund Schwager, *Must There Be Scapegoats? Violence and Redemption in the Bible* (San Francisco: Harper, 1987), p. 60.

"Anyone who strikes a person with a fatal blow is to be put to death. However, if it is not done intentionally, but God lets it happen, they are to flee to a place I will designate. But if anyone schemes and kills someone deliberately, that person is to be taken from my altar and put to death. Anyone who attacks their father or mother is to be put to death. Anyone who kidnaps someone is to be put to death, whether the victim has been sold or is still in the kidnapper's possession" (Exodus 21:12-16).

In the Book of Leviticus (20:9-16), capital punishment was prescribed for a host of other acts, including cursing one's parents, adultery, incest, homosexuality, and bestiality:

> If anyone curses his father or mother, he must be put to death. He has cursed his father or his mother, and his blood shall be on his own head.

> If a man commits adultery with another man's wife—with the wife of his neighbor—both the adulterer and the adulteress are to be put to death.

> If a man has sexual relations with his father's wife, he has dishonored his father. Both the man and the woman are to be put to death; their blood will be on their own heads.

> If a man has sexual relations with his daughter-in-law, both of them are to be put to death. What they have done is a perversion; their blood will be on their own heads.

> If a man has sexual relations with a man as one does with a woman, both of them have done what is detestable. They are to be put to death; their blood will be on their own heads.

> If a man marries both a woman and her mother, it is wicked. Both he and they must be burned in the fire, so that no wickedness will be among you.

> If a man has sexual relations with an animal, he is to be put to death, and you must kill the animal.

If a woman approaches an animal to have sexual relations with it, kill both the woman and the animal. They are to be put to death; their blood will be on their own heads.

Leviticus 20:27 adds witches and mediums to the list: "A man or woman who is a medium or spiritualist among you must be put to death. You are to stone them; their blood will be on their own heads."

"AVENGERS OF BLOOD"

In the Book of Numbers, the family of a murder victim is granted the right to become "avengers of blood." "If anyone strikes someone a fatal blow with an iron object, that person is a murderer; the murderer is to be put to death. Or if anyone is holding a stone and strikes someone a fatal blow with it, that person is a murderer; the murderer is to be put to death. Or if anyone is holding a wooden object and strikes someone a fatal blow with it, that person is a murderer; the murderer is to be put to death. The avenger of blood shall put the murderer to death; when the avenger comes upon the murderer, the avenger shall put the murderer to death. If anyone with malice aforethought shoves another or throws something at them intentionally so that they die or if out of enmity one person hits another with their fist so that the other dies, that person is to be put to death; that person is a murderer. The avenger of blood shall put the murderer to death when they meet" (Numbers 35:16-21). But such vengeance, Numbers maintains, can only take place after the accused murderer is found guilty in a public trial (35:12).

Numbers also specifies that the death sentence requires corroborating evidence, since it can never be imposed upon the testimony of a single witness: "If anyone kills a person, the murderer shall be put to death on the evidence of witnesses. But no person shall be put to death on the testimony of one witness" (35:30).

A PROSCRIBED PROCEDURE

Contemporary Christians who rant against the harshness of the Mosaic law remain ill-informed about how difficult it was to receive a death penalty in ancient Israel. First of all, circumstantial evidence wouldn't cut it. One needed two impeccable witnesses who had observed the person transgressing a law that was punishable by death. Next, these two witnesses had to have warned the accused of the capital punishment he could receive by committing the prohibited act, even if he already knew. Finally, the subject must have committed the transgression in direct defiance of the warning. Any hesitation by the perpetrator meant that the death penalty could not be applied to his offense.[5]

HOMOSEXUALITY AND SCIENCE

Still and all, a law demanding the death sentence for gays and lesbians certainly smacks of barbarity and a primitive understanding of human sexuality. Many scientists now argue that being homosexual is neither a perversity nor a disease, as American psychiatrists had insisted until 1973.[6] A study by former Salk Institute researcher Simon LeVay concluded that the sexual orientation may be genetic, pointing to the differences in the hypothalamus portion of the brain in gay and straight men, and the presence in gays of a "thyroid stimulating hormone receptor" that gives them a tendency to be thin and to have a susceptibility to Graves' disease.[7]

Other scientists have critiqued LeVay's study for committing key methodological errors, including an assumption that the comparison group of "heterosexual" cadavers were all heterosexual, even though

---

5   Yehuda Shurpin, "Why Are Torah Punishments So Harsh?" *Chabad.org*, n.d., https://www. chabad.org/library/article_cdo/aid/1269629/jewish/Why-Are-Torah-Punishments-So-Harsh. htm

6   Allison Turner, "Today in 1973, the APA Removed Homosexuality from List of Mental Illnesses," *Human Rights Campaign*, December 15, 2015, https://www.hrc.org/blog/ flashbackfriday-today-in-1973-the-apa-removed-homosexuality-from-list-of-me

7   Simon Lavay, "A Difference in Hypothalamic Structure in Heterosexual and Homosexual Men," *Science*, August 20, 1991, pp. 1031-1037.

a number of these subjects had died of AIDS,[8] a disease that in the late 1980s and early 1990s especially was far more widespread among homosexual men. In fact, all of his homosexual subjects had died of AIDS. Their smaller brain clusters may have been caused by AIDS-related brain damage, not from their homosexuality.[9]

CONFLICTING STUDIES[10]

Another study reported that an area of the brain known as the anterior commissure (AC) "was larger in homosexual as opposed to heterosexual men, a finding that was interpreted as support for the hypothesis that sexual orientation reflects the sexually differentiated state of the brain."[11] Other researchers tried to replicate such findings in the cadavers of 120 individuals, but "found no variation in the size of the AC with age, HIV status, sex, or sexual orientation."[12]

Still another study points to psychological and environmental influences as well as early experiences. Psychiatrists Byne and Parsons, writing in *Archives of General Psychiatry*, state that "it seems reasonable to suggest that the stage for future sexual orientation may be set by experiences during early development, perhaps the first 4 years of life." The authors conclude: "The inadequacies of present psychosocial explanations do not justify turning to biology by default—especially when, at present, the biologic alternatives seem to have no greater explanatory value. In

---

8 Ibid.

9 William Byne and Bruce Parsons, "Human Sexual Orientation: The Biologic Theories Reappraised," *Archives of General Psychiatry*, 50: 235 (March 1993).

10 Following summary of research on homosexuality is drawn largely from Peter Sprigg and Timothy Dailey, Co-Editors, Getting It Straight: What the Research Shows about Homosexuality, Family Research Council, Washington, DC (2004).

11 L. S. Allen and R. A. Gorski (1991).

12 Mitchell S. Lasco, Theresa J. Jordan, Mark A. Edgar, Carol K. Petito, and William Byne, "A Lack of Dimorphism of Sex or Sexual Orientation in the Human Anterior Commissure, *Brain Research*, 936 (2002): 95.

fact, the current trend may be to underrate the explanatory power of extant psychosocial models."[13]

IS HOMOSEXUALITY A PSYCHOSIS?

As seen from these and other studies, the scientific evidence for a bio-logical/genetic cause for homosexuality is far from settled. As mentioned earlier, in 1973 the American Psychiatric Association removed homo-sexuality from its list of mental disorders. That decision did not come as a result of new research. Ronald Bayer, author of the most extensive review of that decision, has described what really happened as follows: "A furious egalitarianism that challenged every instance of authority had compelled psychiatric experts to negotiate the pathological status of homosexuality with homosexuals themselves. The result was not a conclusion based on approximation of the scientific truth as dictated by reason, but was instead an action demanded by the ideological temper of the times."[14]

In *Archives of Sexual Behavior,* Sigmund Freud (1916) described homosexuality as a mental disorder, caused by excessively loving mothers and retiring or absent fathers. Stekel (1930) noted it was caused by strong, dominant mothers and weak fathers. In 1936, Lewis Terman and Catherine Miles in their *Sex and Personality Studies* supported Freud by concluding that "the mothers of homosexuals were especially demonstrative, affectionate, and emotional, while the fathers were typically unsympathetic, autocratic, or frequently away from home."[15]

In support of the thesis that homosexuality represents a psychosis, researchers have found a strong link between child sexual abuse and

---

13 William Byne and Bruce Parsons, "Human Sexual Orientation: The Biologic Theories Reappraised," *Archives of General Psychiatry*, 50 (March 1993): 236.

14 Ronald Bayer, *Homosexuality and American Psychiatry: The Politics of Diagnosis* (Princeton, NJ: Princeton University Press, 1987), 3.

15 Marvin Siegelman, "Parental Background of Male Homosexuals and Heterosexuals," *Archives of Sexual Behavior*, 3 (1974): 3-4.

the development of homosexuality. A study in the *Journal of Sex & Marital Therapy* examined the past sexual experiences, sexual thoughts, and fantasies regarding the sexual contacts of 35 adult men who were sexually abused during their childhoods. The study found that among men, a history of homosexual child abuse was linked both to an adult homosexual orientation and to sexual attraction to children and upheld the following finding: "According to existing literature, gender identity confusion and gender preference are often cited as being affected by childhood sexual abuse. In this study, 46 percent of the abused men, as opposed to 12 percent of the non-abused men, defined their sexual orientation as either bisexual or homosexual, a nearly 400% difference. Therefore, these findings further validate previous research regarding the sexual orientation of children who have been sexually abused." The researchers concluded their study by saying: "Given these findings, it appears that being sexually abused as a child may affect the propensity of adult men to fantasize about young men."[16]

THE QUEER QUESTION

Is same-sex attraction an unchanging condition? According to the National Sex Survey, 9.1 percent of men report having had a sexual experience with another male in their lives, but nearly half (46%) of those men said they did so before the age of 18 and that they did not engage in homosexual activity in their adult lives.[17] Many teens who experience same-sex attraction and behaviors discontinue these behaviors as adults. Homosexual identity may not be as fixed as many would believe.

NO LEEWAY IN THE LAW

Still and all, several Biblical scholars have attempted to skirt the problem

---

16   James R. Bramblett, Jr., and Carol Anderson Darling, "Sexual Contacts: Experiences, Thoughts, and Fantasies of Adult Male Survivors of Child Sexual Abuse," *Journal of Sex & Marital Therapy*, 23 (4): 313 (Winter 1997).

17   Ibid. Table 8.1.

posed by Leviticus by insisting that the passage only condemns homo-sexual activity that is related to idolatry. In *Christianity and Crisis*, James Nelson writes: "In these passages, acts are condemned not because of some intrinsic aberration but because of their association with idolatry (particularly, in the sexual references, to Canaanite idolatry)."[18] But no evidence suggests that the Leviticus text limits the condemnation of homosexual acts to an idolatrous context. Leviticus speaks of homo-sexual acts in general:

But a comparison of texts from Deuteronomy 23:17 and Leviticus 20:13 shows that Deuteronomy is concerned with sacred sodomy, while Leviticus is concerned with civil sodomy. The technical terms for female [*qedeshah*] and male [*qadesh*] cultic prostitution are absent in the Leviticus condemnation. Instead, the text includes an unambiguous and generic description of the homosexual act: "You shall not lie with a male as with a woman."[19]

The argument that Leviticus 20:13 applies only to sacred sodomy leads to a logical impasse: If homosexuality is to be condemned only when practiced in an idolatrous context, then the same is true for the other prohibited behaviors listed in the immediate passage. As Michael Ukleja writes: "To hold to such a distinction, one would have to con-clude that adultery was not morally wrong (Leviticus18:20), child sac-rifice had no moral implications (18:21), and that nothing is inherently evil with bestiality (18:23)."[20]

HOMOSEXUALITY AS "ABOMINATION"

To make matters worse for "Christian inclusivity," homosexuality

---

18   James Nelson, quoted in Timothy J. Dailey, *The Bible, the Church, and Homosexuality* (Washington, DC: Family Research Council, 2014), p. 4.

19   Dennis Prager, "Why Judaism (and then Christianity) Rejected Homosexuality," *Crisis Magazine*, February 1, 2018, https://www.crisismagazine.com/2018/judaisms-sexual-revolution-judaism-christianity-rejected-homosexuality

20   Ibid.

is condemned by the Torah as an "abomination." Regarding the meaning of this term, David Greenberg, author of *The Construction of Homosexuality*, writes: "When the word *toevah* ('abomination') does appear in the Hebrew Bible, it is sometimes applied to idolatry, cult prostitution, magic, or divination, and is sometimes used more generally. *It always conveys great repugnance.*"[21]

The Biblical condemnation is of profound historical and religious importance since the ancient world made no little division between heterosexuality and homosexuality. Martha Nussbaum, professor of philosophy at Brown University, writes:

> Ancient categories of sexual experience differed considerably from our own. . . The central distinction in sexual morality was the distinction between active and passive roles. The gender of the object. . . is not in itself morally problematic. Boys and women are very often treated interchangeably as objects of [male] desire. What is socially important is to penetrate rather than to be penetrated. Sex is understood fundamentally not as interaction, but as a doing of something to someone...."[22]

Anal intercourse was freely depicted in figurative art in the ancient cities of Uruk, Assur, Babylon, and Susa; both Zimri-lin (king of Mari) and Hammurabi (king of Babylon) had male lovers; and *The Almanac of Incantations,* an ancient Assyrian text, contains prayers for divine blessings on homosexual relations.[23] The editors of *Reallexicon der Assyriologie*, a multi-language encyclopedia of the Ancient Near East, conclude: "Homosexuality in itself is thus nowhere condemned as

---

21   David Greenberg, *The Construction of Homosexuality* (Chicago: University of Chicago Press, 1988), p. 195.

22   Martha Nussbaum, quoted in Dennis Prager, "Why Judaism (and then Christianity Rejected Homosexuality."

23   Bruce L. Gerig, "Homosexuality in the Ancient Near East, beyond Egypt," *Homosexuality and the Bible,* Supplement, 2005, http://epistle.us/hbarticles/neareast.html

licentiousness, as immorality, as social disorder, or as transgressing any human or divine law. Anyone could practice it freely, just as anyone could visit a prostitute, provided it was done without violence and without compulsion, and preferably as far as taking the passive role was concerned, with specialists."[24]

THE ESSENCE OF JUDAISM

The prohibition against homosexuality stems from the essence of Judaism and the fact that God, in the Torah, issues the following injunction:

> See, I set before you today life and prosperity, death and destruction. For I command you today to love the LORD your God, to walk in obedience to him, and to keep his commands, decrees and laws; then you will live and increase, and the LORD your God will bless you in the land you are entering to possess.
>
> But if your heart turns away and you are not obedient, and if you are drawn away to bow down to other gods and worship them, I declare to you this day that you will certainly be destroyed. You will not live long in the land you are crossing the Jordan to enter and possess.
>
> This day I call the heavens and the earth as witnesses against you that I have set before you life and death, blessings and curses. Now choose life, so that you and your children may live and that you may love the LORD your God, listen to his voice, and hold fast to him. For the LORD is your life, and he will give you many years in the land he swore to give to your fathers, Abraham, Isaac and Jacob (Deuteronomy 30:15-20).

---

24   Gordon T. Wenham, "The Old Testament Attitude to Homosexuality," *Expository Times,* 1991, https://biblicalstudies.org.uk/article_attitude_wenham.html See Erich Ebelig and Bruno Meissner, *Reallexicon der Assyriologie* (Berlin: Walter de Gruyer, 1990), HTM edition, https://epub.ub.uni-muenchen.de/6819/1/6819.pdf

Judaism consistently affirms life over death. The Hebrew priests were forbidden to come into contact with the dead since such exposure would make them ceremonially unclean (Numbers 19:11). The concern with life over death forms the justification for the laws concerning the separation of meat (death) from milk (life), of menstruation (death) from sexual intercourse (life), and carnivorous beasts (death) from vegetarian animals (life). This accounts for the Torah's juxtaposition of child sacrifice with homosexuality. One deprives children of life; the other prevents their having life to begin with.[25]

In 2020, the Biblical injunction that practicing homosexuals represent such a threat to human society that they must be put to death represents the problem with Old Testament faith. It is a teaching that cannot be relegated to the distant past and deemed no longer binding for mankind. Moreover, it is a moral commandment. Not a theological suggestion. To condemn this injunction as barbaric and inhuman is to drag the God of Moses into a contemporary court of law, where He, in all likelihood, will be found guilty and sentenced to eternal silence, if not death.

---

25   Prager, "Why Judaism (and then Christianity) Rejected Homosexuality."

9

GENOCIDE

And it came to pass at the seventh time, when the priests blew with the trumpets, Joshua said unto the people, Shout; for the LORD hath given you the city. And the city shall be accursed, even it, and all that are therein, to the LORD: only Rahab the harlot shall live, she and all that are with her in the house, because she hid the messengers that we sent.

And ye, in any wise keep yourselves from the accursed thing, lest ye make yourselves accursed, when ye take of the accursed thing, and make the camp of Israel a curse, and trouble it. But all the silver, and gold, and vessels of brass and iron, are consecrated unto the LORD: they shall come into the treasury of the LORD.

So the people shouted when the priests blew with the trumpets: and it came to pass, when the people heard the sound of the trumpet, and the people shouted with a great shout, that the wall fell down flat, so that the people went up into the city, every man straight before him, and they took the city.

And they utterly destroyed all that was in the city, both man and woman, young and old, and ox, and sheep, and ass, with the edge of the sword.

JOSHUA 6:16-21

KILL THEM ALL.
   Kill the women and children.
   Kill the old and the infirm.
   Kill the widows and the orphans.
   Kill their livestock—every cow, lamb, goat, duck, and donkey.
   Let the hills run red with blood.
   This was the command delivered by the God of the Old Testament

to the ancient Hebrews as they were about to descend on the Land of Canaan.

And, according to the Biblical account, the Hebrews obeyed the command. They slaughtered almost everyone and everything they encountered—the Hittites, the Amorites, the Canaanites, the Perizzites, the Hivites, and the Jebusites. A few of the original inhabitants of the land were spared, including the harlot Rahab and the members of her household. This act of mercy later became a source of lamentation. The author of Psalm 106 writes:

> They did not destroy the peoples as the Lord had commanded them, but they mingled with the nations and adopted their customs. They worshiped their idols, which became a snare to them. They sacrificed their sons and their daughters to false gods. They shed innocent blood, the blood of their sons and daughters, whom they sacrificed to the idols of Canaan, and the land was desecrated by their blood. They defiled themselves by what they did; by their deeds they prostituted themselves.

"THE MOST UNPLEASANT CHARACTER IN ALL FICTION"

Responding to the accounts of genocide in the Old Testament, British biologist Richard Dawkins in *The God Delusion* writes: "The God of the Old Testament is arguably the most unpleasant character in all fiction: jealous and proud of it; a petty, unjust, unforgiving control-freak; a vindictive, bloodthirsty ethnic cleanser; a misogynistic, homophobic, racist, infanticidal, genocidal, filicidal, pestilential, megalomaniacal, sadomasochistic, capriciously malevolent bully."[1]

Similarly, Charles Templeton in *Farewell to God* maintains: "The God of the Old Testament is utterly unlike the God believed in by most practicing Christians. He is an all-too-human deity with the human failings, weaknesses, and practices of men—but on a grand scale. His

---

1   Richard Dawkins, *The God Delusion* (Boston: Houghton Mifflin, 2006), p. 51.

justice is often, by modern standards, outrageous, and his prejudices are deep-seated and inflexible. He is biased, querulous, vindictive, and jealous of his prerogatives."[2]

A PRIMITIVE TRIBAL GOD

Templeton says that his attempt to come to terms with the God of Moses and Joshua compelled him to abandon his ministry with Billy Graham and to assume the stance of an atheist. He writes: "A careful reading of the Old Testament only confirmed my doubts about the deity portrayed there. Wanting to believe, I found it impossible. The God revealed there is a primitive tribal god, created out of necessity to enable their [the Hebrew people's] leaders to mold a volatile and highly individualistic people into a cohesive group by uniting them about a central core of belief."[3]

At conservative and evangelical seminaries, Biblical professors, when asked about Old Testament genocide have been forced to argue that such passages are merely examples of the ancient Hebrew's use of "exaggerated rhetoric." Heath Thomas, professor of Old Testament at the Southeastern Baptist Theological Seminary, maintains that the passages meant that the original Canaanites were not "annihilated" but only "dispossessed."[4]

FALTERING FUNDAMENTALISTS

This argument is repeated in *The Lost World of the Israelite Conquest* by John H. Walton, Old Testament professor at Moody Bible Institute and now Wheaton College, Illinois, and his son, J. Harvey Walton, a

---

2   Charles Templeton, *Farewell to God: My Reason for Rejecting the Christian Faith* (Toronto: McClelland and Stewart, 1996), p. 117.

3   Ibid.

4   Richard Ostling, "In the Old Testament, Was God Guilty of Genocide?" *Patheos*, August 12, 2017, https://www.patheos.com/blogs/religionqanda/2017/08/old-testament-god-guilty-genocide/

graduate student at Scotland's University of St. Andrews. The Waltons insist that the war narratives in the Old Testament employ symbolism and hyperbole that ancient readers would have understood. These narratives, they maintain, should not be taken literally. They write:

> When we translate the event as holy war or jihad or genocide, or even conquest, we are not translating the event properly, because those words and ideas do not mean the same thing to us that the logic and imagery used to describe the conquest would have meant to the original audience, either in terms of their connotations or their objectives. When we hear words such as *genocide* we interpret them as 'a thing that should never be done.' But the text does not depict the conquest event in terms of a thing that should never be done. [5]

In response, Randal Rauser, a book critic, says:

> I'm sorry, but the reasoning here is stunningly bad. To begin with, Walton and Walton conflate a moral evaluation of the concept of genocide (i.e. it is "a thing that should never be done") with the concept of genocide itself. Furthermore, it should be *obvious* that the moral evaluation genocidaires provide for their own actions does not qualify in the assessment of whether those actions constitute genocide. No doubt the Nazis would justify their actions as a means to secure the purity of the German people just as the ancient Israelites would justify their actions as a means to secure the purity of their people. In neither case do we grant those apologetic defenses any merit in assessing whether the actions in question are genocide or not.[6]

---

5   John H. Walton and J. Harvey Walton, *The Lost World of the Israelite Conquest* (Downers Grove, Illinois: Inter-Varsity Press, 2017), p. 257.

6   Randal Rauser, "*The Lost World of the Israelite Conquest*; A Review," *The Tentative Apologist*, June 11, 2018, https://randalrauser.com/2018/06/the-lost-world-of-the-israelite-conquest-a-review/

LINGUISTIC AND LITERAL MISUNDERSTANDINGS

Even more quizzically, the Waltons dispute the usual translation of the key Hebrew term *herem* as a command to "utterly destroy" a population. The term, they contend, rather means "to remove a community identity from use, not to kill individual people."[7] Rauser responds by writing:

> The Israelites are *not* simply killing Canaanite people. Rather, they are seeking to destroy the Canaanite *identity*. Granted, killing persons may be required to destroy the identity, but the fact remains that the goal is to eliminate the identity rather than persons. And that means, so Walton and Walton believe, that the act is not genocide. Unfortunately, Walton and Walton have matters completely backwards. It is not the killing of persons which qualifies an event as genocide. Rather, it is the attempt to destroy an ethnic, cultural, or religious identity.[8]

In another attempt to explain away the genocide in the Old Testament, Catholic exegete Tommy Lane of Mount St. Mary's Seminary maintains that the ancient Israelites "misunderstood and misjudged" God.[9] In other words, the people of the Bible were unaware that the real God, the God revealed by Jesus, was far removed from the world of war and bloodshed.

THE OLD TESTAMENT AND ISLAM

Islamic apologists have pointed out that there exists a strong similarity between the Qur'an and the Old Testament on matters of jihad (holy war) and violence.[10] While the Old Testament God commands the

---

7   Walton and Walton, *The Lost World of the Israelite Conquest,* p. 190.

8   Rauser, "*The Lost World of the Israelite Conquest*: A Review."

9   Tommy Lane, quoted in Ostling, "In the Old Testament, Was God Guilty of Genocide?"

10   Philip Almond, "In Spite of Their Differences, Jews, Christians and Muslims Worship the Same God," *The Conversation*, September 5, 2017, https://theconversation.com/in-spite-of-their-differences-jews-christians-and-muslims-worship-the-same-god-83102

Hebrews to "utterly destroy" the inhabitants of Canaan (Deuteronomy 7:2), Allah exhorts his followers to "slay the unbelievers wherever you find them" (Qur'an 9:5) and to "make war on the unbeliever and the hypocrites and to deal rigorously with them" (Qur'an 9:73). Similarly, in the Book of Numbers, the God of Moses orders His people to "kill every male among the little ones, and kill every woman who has known a man intimately" (Numbers 31:17), and Allah says, "When ye meet the unbelievers in fight, smite at their necks; when ye have thoroughly subdued them, bind a bond firmly on them" (Qur'an 47:4).

But there is a difference between the two religions. The God of Moses commands the Hebrews to direct their actions against particular tribes at a particular place (the Hittites, Girgashites, Amorites, Canaanites, Perizzites, Hivites, and Jebusites in the areas of the Southern Levant), while Allah instructs his followers to kill unbelievers regardless of tribe or place. Robert Spencer writes:

> The Qur'an exhorts believers to fight unbelievers without specifying anywhere in the text that only certain unbelievers are to be fought, or only for a certain period of time, or some other distinction. Taking the texts at face value, the command to make war against unbelievers is open-ended and universal. The Old Testament, in contrast, records God's commands to the Israelites to make war against particular people only. This is jarring to modern sensibilities, to be sure, but it does not amount to the same thing. That's the one reason why Jews and Christians haven't formed terror groups around the world that quote these Scriptures to justify killing civilian non-combatants.[11]

THE NECESSITY OF KILLING

Behind and around the great ancient kingdoms of Egypt and Assyria, there existed a motley assortment of nomadic tribes. The people of

---

11 Robert Spencer, *The Politically Incorrect Guide to Islam and the Crusades* (Washington, DC: Regnery, 2005), pp. 29-31.

these tribes viewed themselves as the center of geography and history and would have been aghast at the supreme ignorance of a historian or writer who would relegate their importance to a mere paragraph.

The harshness of these desert areas forced them continuously to seek for water and arable land. Wars were incessant and incredibly violent. The Scythians, for example, were ferocious, bearded giants who lived on wagons, fought to live and lived to fight, drank the blood of their enemies, and used scalps as napkins.[12] Hippocrates says that the Scythian women, as long as they were virgins, rode, shot arrows, and threw their javelins while mounted. They did not lay aside their virginity until they had killed three of their enemies. The right breasts of these women were hacked off and cauterized so that all of their strength would be diverted to their right shoulder and right arm.[13]

The Hittites were equally violent. They ruled over the source of the Tigris and Euphrates Rivers as a military caste. They mined iron from the mountains near Armenia and forged iron weapons that made them fierce foes. The men that they captured were forced to work the mines, while the women, if attractive, were sold as concubines. The old and the infirm were put to death.[14]

THE CANAANITE RELIGION

The Canaanites worshipped a great number of gods, mostly representing forces of nature arranged in a complex hierarchy with El and Asherah as the reigning king and queen. Then there's Anat, the virgin goddess of war and strife, sister and putative mate of Ba'al Hadad. Attar is the god of the morning star who tried to take the place of the dead Baal and failed. Ba'al Hadad is the storm god. Baal Hammon is the god of fertility who renews all energies, and was worshipped in the Phoenician colonies

---

12 Will Durant, *Our Oriental Heritage* (New York: Simon and Schuster, 1954), p. 287.

13 Ibid.

14 Ibid., p. 286.

of the Western Mediterranean. Dagon, the father of Ba'al Hadad, is the god of crop fertility and grain. Eshmun is god of healing, or as Baalat Asclepius, the goddess of healing. Ishat is the goddess of fire, who was slain by Anat. Kothar-wa-Khasis is the skilled god of craftsmanship. Moloch is the god of fire. Resheph is the god of plague and of healing. Yam is the god of the sea and the river. Mot or Mawat is the god of death. Lotan is the twisting, seven-headed serpent ally of Yam.[15]

THE BAAL CYCLE

In the "Baal Cycle," a Ugaritic cycle of stories about the Canaanite god, Ba'al Hadad, the god of thunder, is challenged by and defeats Yam, the god of the sea, using two magical weapons (called "Driver" and "Chaser") made for him by Kothar-wa-Khasis, the god of craftsmanship. Afterward, with the help of Athirat, the queen god and Anat, the goddess of war, Ba'al persuades the head god El to allow him a palace. El approves, and the palace is built by Kothar-wa-Khasis. After the palace is constructed, Ba'al gives forth a thunderous roar out of the palace window and challenges Mot, the god of death. Mot enters through the window and swallows Ba'al, sending him to the Underworld. With no one to give rain, there is a terrible drought in Ba'al's absence. The other deities, especially El and Anat, are distraught that Ba'al has been taken to the Underworld. Anat goes to the Underworld, attacks Mot with a knife, grinds him up into pieces, and scatters him far and wide. With Mot defeated, Ba'al is able to return and refresh the Earth with rain.[16]

THE SACRIFICE OF CHILDREN

This is a story that depicts a drama about "gods" behind periods of lasting droughts, a life-and-death concern for the agricultural Canaanite

---

15   Michael D. Coogan and Mark S. Smith, editors and translators, *Stories from Ancient Canaan* (Louisville, KY: Westminster John Knox Press, 2012), pp. 173-180.

16   Philip Wilkinson, *Myths and Legends: An Illustrated Guide to Their Origins and Meanings* (New York: DK Publishing, 2009), pp. 154-159.

civilization.[17] By making offerings to the Canaanite gods, the people hoped to assuage and gain their favor. Such beliefs would be harmless if not for a certain "detail." According to the book of Jeremiah, the Canaanite gods demanded the sacrifice of children: "They built the high places of Baal in order to burn their sons in the fire as whole burnt offerings to Baal, something that I had not commanded or spoken of and that had never even come into my heart" (19:5).

Other passages in the Bible make it clear that child sacrifice was a regular feature of the religion of the Canaanites and the surrounding nations: ". . . they do for their gods every detestable thing that Jehovah hates, even burning their sons and their daughters in the fire to their gods" (Deuteronomy 12:31).

The failure to eradicate all of the Canaanite tribes allowed these practices to seep into Israelite culture and religion in later centuries. Centers of worship for Canaanite gods such as Molech and Baal were set up in Judah and Israel by apostate kings. As described in the Second Book of Kings, child sacrifice was even practiced in the Valley of Hinnom just outside of Jerusalem. Yet religious reformers such as King Josiah of Judah pulled down these places and rendered them unfit for use, as 2 Kings 23:10 records: "He also made unfit for worship Topheth, which is in the Valley of the Sons of Hinnom, so that no one could make his son or his daughter pass through the fire to Molech."

FROM CANAAN TO CARTHAGE

Although Canaanite civilization was largely driven out of the land of Israel, it emigrated elsewhere, founding colonies along the Mediterranean coast of North Africa, where it thrived for centuries.[18] Most notable among these was the colony of Carthage in modern-day Tunisia.

---

17   Michael D. Coogan and Mark S. Smith, editors and translators, *Stories from Ancient Canaan* (Louisville, KY: Westminster John Knox Press), 2012, p. 108.

18   Mark Cartwright, "Carthaginian Religion, Ancient History Encyclopedia, accessed on 1/25/2019. https://www.ancient.eu/Carthaginian_Religion/

That city-state became so powerful it at one time rivaled the Roman republic. Carthaginians spoke the Canaanite language and practiced the Canaanite religion. They also seemed to have brought with them their cruel predilection for child sacrifice as confirmed by archeological excavations since the 1920s.[19]

Writing in the 4th century BC, the Greek historian Cleitarchus said of the Carthaginian practice:

> There stands in their midst a bronze statue of Kronos (regional name for Baal Hammon, chief of Carthage's gods), its hands extended over a bronze brazier, the flames of which engulf the child. When the flames fall upon the body, the limbs contract and the open mouth seems almost to be laughing until the contracted body slips quietly into the brazier. Thus, it is that the 'grin' is known as 'sardonic laughter,' since they die laughing.[20]

Another Greek historian named Diodorus Siculus, writing less than a hundred years after the fall of Carthage affirms his countryman's account as follows: "There was in their city a bronze image of Cronus extending its hands, palms up and sloping toward the ground, so that each of the children when placed thereon rolled down and fell into a sort of gaping pit filled with fire."[21]

Around the same time the famous Greek historian Plutarch wrote:

> . . . with full knowledge and understanding they themselves offered up their own children, and those who had no children would buy

---

19   Dennis D. Hughes, *Human Sacrifice in Ancient Greece,* (London: Routledge, 1991), pp. 115 ff.

20   Paul G. Mosca, *Child Sacrifice in Canaanite and Israelite Religion,* quoted in Bennie H. Reynolds, "Molek: Dead or Alive?" in *Human Sacrifice in Jewish and Christian Tradition* (Leiden: Brill, 2007), pp. 122-150.

21   Paolo Xella, Valentina Melchiorri, and Peter van Dommelen, "Phoenician Bones of Contention," *Antiquity 87,* December 2013, https://www.academia.edu/5346788/Phoenician_Bones_of_Contention_Antiquity_2013_1199-1207_written_with_Paolo_Xella_Valentina_Melchiorri_and_Peter_van_Dommelen_

little ones from poor people and cut their throats as if they were so many lambs or young birds; meanwhile the mother stood by without a tear or moan; but should she utter a single moan or let fall a single tear, she had to forfeit the money, and her child was sacrificed nevertheless; and the whole area before the statue was filled with a loud noise of flutes and drums took the cries of wailing should not reach the ears of the people.[22]

As many as 300 Carthaginian children, usually from the lower classes, could be sacrificed in one day. In times of crisis, the upper classes, thinking the gods were offended by their failure to offer their own children, had hundreds of their sons and daughters slaughtered as well.[23]

SITES OF SACRIFICE

In 1921, excavations in ancient Carthage by French archeologists revealed graveyards with hundreds of grave markers. Underneath each one was a clay urn containing the cremated remains of human infants and animals (sometimes as many as seven urns were found one on top of another under a single marker). The soil was rich with olive wood charcoal indicating fires had been kept burning here for long periods of time. The archeologists dubbed this place a "Tophet," which is the Hebrew word for the place of child sacrifice near Jerusalem at Jeremiah 7:31. In time, many more Tophet cemeteries were discovered.[24] The largest contained the remains of approximately 20,000 infants in urns as well as some animals.[25]

---

22   The Complete Works of Plutarch, Delphi Classics, 2013, p. 2136.

23   Will Durant, *Caesar and Christ.* (New York: Simon and Schuster, 1944), p. 42.

24   P. XELLA , "Per un modello interpretativo del tofet: il tofet come necropoli infantile?", in G. BARTOLONI et al . (eds.), Tiro, Cartagine, Lixus: nuove acquisizioni. Atti del Convegno Internazionale in onore di Maria Giulia Amadasi Guzzo (Roma, 24-25 novembre 2008) (Quaderni di Vicino Oriente 4), Roma 2010, pp. 259-278.

25   "Did the Canaanites Really Sacrifice Their Children?" May 13, 2016. https://biblereadingarcheology.com/2016/05/13/did-the-canaanites-sacrifice-their-children/

Dr. Josephine Quinn of Oxford University's Faculty of Classics concluded in 2014, "It's becoming increasingly clear that the stories about Carthaginian child sacrifice are true… The archeological, literary, and documentary evidence for child sacrifice is overwhelming."[26]

RITUAL PROSTITUTION AND PEDOPHILIA

In the ancient Near East, the rhythm of nature was seen as a consequence of the periodic presence or absence of divine beings. Religious rites involving sexual symbolism were designed to secure divine blessings. Phallic statues were a part of festivals. When the god Osiris was being revived from the dead, as portrayed in the *Book of the Dead,* the goddess Isis is shown kneeling before him, her mouth around his sacred phallus. Other gods and goddesses appear as representations of human forms, endowed with sexual attributes.[27]

In Egypt, Sumer, and other ancient Near East societies, creation was imagined as a process of copulation and birth, with a supernatural primeval couple as the parents of all that exists. Since copulation was, at times, regarded as an act of worship, customs of ritual intercourse and sacred prostitution were major features of fertility cults.[28]

Sacred or temple prostitution involved male and female prostitutes, serving temporarily or permanently and performing heterosexual, homosexual, and bestial sexual activities, on behalf of a temple. The prostitute and the client, who gave an offering to the temple, acted as surrogates for the deities.[29]

It was considered a special honor for boys and girls as young as 10 or 11 to be sent to the temple of Ishtar, where they were trained to

---

26 Josephine Quinn, Paolo Xella, Valentina Melchiorri and Peter van Dommelen, "Phoenician Bones of Contention," *Antiquity* , Vol: 87, (2013), 1199-1207.

27 Sussman, N., *Sex and Sexuality in History* chapter in B. J. Sadock, H. I. Kaplan, & A. M. Freedman (Eds.), *The Sexual Experience* (Baltimore, MD: Williams & Wilkins, 1976), pp. 8-9.

28 Ibid.

29 Ibid.

serve the sexual needs of strangers. Gernot Wilhelm, an Orientalist at Julis Maximilian University in Würzburg, Germany discovered a fascinating legal document. It is about 3,300 years old, and it recounts how a man delivered his own daughter to the Temple of Ishtar to serve as a harimtu or "prostitute."[30] An Egyptian scroll addresses the topic of pre-pubescent priestesses. According to the text, girls worked as prostitutes in the temple until their first menstruation. After that, "they are cast out from their duties."[31]

A TRANSCENDENT GOD

The moral discourse between man and God seen in the Bible's accounts of Abraham and Moses was largely missing in the polytheistic religions of the ancient Near East. These were filled with enough drama, jealousy, and contention among the pantheon of male gods and female goddesses to fill a number of soap operas without much involvement by humans. Kings, however, got to play a role in certain religious ceremonies such as the *hieros gamos,* a symbolic ritual that re-enacts the marriage between a god and a goddess, engendering all that is.[32]

Genesis offers a radically different narrative of creation, in which God's intention expressed through His word has the power to bring the universe into existence (Genesis 1:1). The first thing Judaism did was to de-sexualize God: "In the beginning God created the heavens and the earth" by his will, not through any sexual behavior.

This was an utterly radical break with all other religions, and it alone changed human history. The gods of virtually all civilizations engaged in sexual relations. In the Near East, the Babylonian god Ishtar seduced

---

30   Mattias Schultz, "Did Prostitution Really Exist in the Temples of Antiquity?" Der Spiegel. March 26, 2010, 2. Accessed on 1/15/2019 from http://www.spiegel.de/international/zeitgeist/sex-in-the-service-of-aphrodite-did-prostitution-really-exist-in-the-temples-of-antiquity-a-685716-2.html

31   Ibid.

32   *Hieros gamos,* Encyclopedia Britannica, https://www.britannica.com/topic/hieros-gamos.

a man, Gilgamesh, the Babylonian hero.[33] In Egyptian religion, the god Osiris had sexual relations with his sister, the goddess Isis, and she conceived the god Horus.[34]

PERVERSE PAGAN DEITIES

In Canaan, El, the chief god, had sex with Asherah.[35] In Hindu belief, the god Krishna was sexually active, having had many wives and pursuing Radha; the god Samba, son of Krishna, seduced mortal women and men. In Greek beliefs, Zeus married Hera, chased women, abducted the beautiful young male, Ganymede, and masturbated at other times; Poseidon married Amphitrite, pursued Demeter, and raped Tantalus. In Rome, the gods sexually pursued both men and women.[36]

Given the sexual activity of the gods, it is not surprising that the religions themselves were replete with all forms of sexual activity. In the ancient Near East and elsewhere, virgins were deflowered by priests prior to engaging in relations with their husbands, and sacred or ritual prostitution was almost universal.[37]

Psychiatrist and sexual historian Norman Sussman describes the situation as follows: "Male and female prostitutes, serving temporarily or permanently and performing heterosexual, homosexual oral-genital, bestial, and other forms of sexual activities, dispense their favors in behalf of the temple."[38]

In ancient Egypt, Mesopotamia, and Canaan, annual ceremonial intercourse took place between the king and a priestess. Women

---

33 The Epic of Gilgamesh (Tablet 6), translated by Maureen Gallery Kovacs. Electronic edition by Wolf Carnahan, 1998.

34 Wilkinson, *Myths and Legends: An Illustrated Guide to Their Origins and Meanings,* p. 240.

35 Coogan and Smith, *Stories from Ancient Canaan,* p. 7.

36 Sussman, *Sex and Sexuality in History,* p. 11.

37 Ibid., p. 9.

38 Ibid., p. 9.

prostitutes had intercourse with male worshippers in the sanctuaries and temples of ancient Mesopotamia, Phoenicia, Cyprus, Corinth, Carthage, Sicily, Egypt, Libya, West Africa, and ancient and modern India.[39]

THE CHALLENGE OF JUDAISM

In ancient Israel itself, there were repeated attempts to re-introduce temple prostitution, resulting in repeated Jewish wars against cultic sex. The Bible records that the Judean king Asa "banished the male and female shrine prostitutes from the land" (1 Kings 15:12); that his successor, Jehosaphat "rid the land of the rest of the male shrine prostitutes who remained there even after the reign of his father Asa." (1 Kings 22:46); and that later, King Josiah, in his religious reforms, "tore down the quarters of the male shrine prostitutes that were in the temple of the Lord" (2 Kings 23:7).

Judaism placed limits on sexual activity so that it would no longer dominate religious and social life. Their god, Yahweh, had no sexual attributes and was not expected to participate in sexual rites, even symbolically.[40] Sex was to be sanctified—which in Hebrew means "separated"—from the world and placed in the home, in the bed of husband and wife. Judaism's restricting of sexual behavior was one of the essential elements that enabled society to progress.[41]

THE MORALITY OF GENOCIDE

Were the destruction of Sodom and Gomorrah, and later the Israelite eradication of the Canaanite tribes' moral acts? It is clear that God's intention was to eradicate the Canaanite culture and anyone complicit with it. How many innocent children in these cities were lost? Surely

39 Dennis Prager, "Judaism's Sexual Revolution: Why Judaism (and then Christianity) Rejected Homosexuality," *Crisis* 11, no. 8 (September 1993). http://www.orthodoxytoday.org/articles2/PragerHomosexuality.php_

40 Sussman, *Sex and Sexuality in History,* p. 10.

41 Prager, *Judaism's Sexual Revolution,* p. 9.

tens of thousands at least. Another question is how many children were *saved* in the ensuing centuries because child sacrifice and the state-sanctioned rape of pre-pubescent and adolescent youth as temple prostitutes would no longer be practiced? Tens of millions?

Can it be taken for granted that the modern world which arose out of the Judeo-Christian revelation rejects child sacrifice and ritual prostitution? Although it took centuries to accomplish, this rejection began with the acts of genocide that God commanded the Israelites to perform when they entered Canaan.

10

HOLY WAR

What, indeed is wrong with war? That people die who will eventually die anyway so that those who survive may be subdued in peace? A coward complains of this but it does not bother religious people. No, the true evils in warfare are the desire to inflict damage, the cruelty of revenge, disquiet and implacability of spirit, the savagery of rebellion, the lust for domination, and other such things. Indeed, often enough good men are, commanded by God or a lawful ruler to wage war precisely in order to punish these things in the face of violent resistance. In the course of human affairs, proper order sometimes forces the good either to command this sort of thing or rightly to obey such a command. Otherwise, when soldiers came to John to be baptized and asked him, "What should we do?" he would have told them: give up your weapons, leave the service, do not hit, wound, or disable anyone. He knew, however, that in doing these things in military service, they acted as enforcers of the law and defenders of public safety, not as murderers or avengers of private wrongs.

ST. AUGUSTINE, *DE CIVITAS DEI*

THROUGHOUT THE CENTURIES, Jews and Christians, like Muslims, have upheld the notion of "holy war." In the Old Testament, God conveyed His sanctioning of armed conflict through dreams (Judges 7:13-14), cleromancy, including the use of the Urim and Thummim as a means of divination (1 Sam. 28:6), and the proclamations of prophets (1 Kings 22:5-8). The military leaders would stand before the Ark of the Covenant, the "dwelling place" of God, and "enquire" if their plans for battle complied with His wishes. No answer implied a negative response (1 Sam. 14:36-37, 28:6), while a positive answer could include detailed instructions (2 Sam. 5:23-24).[1]

Once a "holy war" was declared, God sent down his *charisma* upon His chosen leader of the military campaign. The men, who rallied around the leader, were compelled to sanctify themselves, that is, to abstain from sexual intercourse until the enemy had been defeated.[2] After the war, they were obliged to assign to God a portion of the spoils as thanksgiving for His "divine terror."[3]

GOD'S PRESENCE IN BATTLE

The Ark was carried into battle by the priests so that God could participate in the defeat of His enemies. Before the conflict commenced, a priest was obliged to address the Hebrew army as follows: "Hear, Israel: Today you are going into battle against your enemies. Do not be fainthearted or afraid; do not panic or be terrified by them. For the Lord your God is the one who goes with you to fight for you against your enemies to give you victory" (Deuteronomy 20:2-4).

But God could not be coerced into providing the Israelites with victory. After the Israelites were routed by the Philistines at Ebenezer, a battle God had not sanctioned, they had the Ark brought from Shiloh and welcomed its arrival with great rejoicing. In the second battle the Israelites were again defeated, and the Philistines captured the Ark (1 Samuel 4:3-5, 10-11). The news of its capture was at once taken to Shiloh by a messenger "with his clothes rent, and with earth upon his head." The old priest, Eli, fell dead when he heard it; and his daughter-in-law, bearing a son at the time the news of the capture of the Ark was

---

1   Brian Truog, "A Study of Recent Research on the Concept of Holy War in the Old Testament" (1983). Master of Sacred Theology Thesis. 36. http://scholar.csl.edu/stm/36

2   Gerhard von Rad, *Old Testament Theology,* Volume I, *The Theology of Israel's Historical Traditions,* translated by D. M. G. Stalker (New York: Harper and Row, 1962), p. 17.

3   Ibid.

received, named him Ichabod, which means, "The glory of God is gone. (1 Samuel 4:12-22).[4]

CONSTANTINE AND THE CROSS

The notion of "holy war" persisted through the Christian era. In AD 312, Constantine became "God's anointed," according to Lactantius, when he routed his imperial rival at battle of the Milvian Bridge. His victory was attributed to Christ's intervention. Before the fateful battle, Constantine reportedly beheld a vision in the sky of the cross which bore this motto: *In hoc signo vinces* ("By this sign, you will conquer"). He inscribed the cross on the shields of his soldiers and marched against his foe to the glorious victory that reunited the Empire. No spokesman for the Church expressed alarm or outrage that the cross of Jesus Christ had become a banner for military bloodshed.[5]

JUST BLOODSHED

St. Augustine upheld the notion of "holy war" by writing:

> No one must ever question the rightness of a war which is waged on God's command, since not even that which is undertaken from human greed can cause any real harm either to the incorruptible God or to any of his holy ones. God commands war to drive out, to crush or to subjugate the pride of mortals. Suffering war exercises the patience of his saints, humbles them and helps them to accept his fatherly correction. No one has any power over them unless it is given from above. All power comes from God's command or permission. Thus, a just man may rightly fight for the order of civil peace even if he serves under the command of a ruler who is himself irreligious.

4   Morris Jastrow, Jr., Charles J. Mendelsohn, Marcus Jastrow, Issac Husik, Duncan B. McDonald, and George A. Barton, "The Ark of the Covenant," *Jewish Encyclopedia*, 1906, http://www.jewishencyclopedia.com/articles/1777-ark-of-the-covenant

5   Lactantius, *Liber de Mortibus Persecutorum*, XLIV, in *Early Church Texts,* https://earlychurchtexts.com/public/lactantius_constantine_heavenly_vision.htm

What he is commanded to do is either clearly not contrary or not clearly contrary to God's precept. The evil of giving the command might make the king guilty but the order of obedience would keep the soldier innocent. How much more innocently, therefore, might a person engage in war when he is commanded to fight by God, who can never command anything improperly, as anyone who serves him cannot fail to realize.[6]

This teaching was upheld by St. Thomas Aquinas, who, in his *Summa Theologiae* (1269-1272), listed three factors for a war to be just as follows:

First, the authority of the sovereign by whose command the war is to be waged. It is not the business of a private individual to declare war, because he can seek for redress of his rights from the tribunal of his superior. . .

Secondly, a just cause is required, namely that those who are attacked, should be attacked because they deserve it on account of some fault. . .

Thirdly, it is necessary that the belligerents should have a rightful intention, so that they intend the advancement of good, or the avoidance of evil. . .[7]

DEUS LO VOLT, GOD WILLS IT

In AD 637, the Byzantine Emperor Heraclitus preached the notion of holy war to his subjects when the Muslims first conquered the Holy Land. Heraclitus received the support of the Patriarch Sergius who placed the wealth of the Greek Church at his disposal. After a seven-year campaign, Heraclitus conquered the Muslim hordes and returned

---

6 "Augustine on War," in John Helgeland, et alia, *Christians in the Military: The Early Experience* (Minneapolis: Augsburg Fortress, 1985), p. 82.

7 St. Thomas Aquinas, *Summa Theologiae*, "War," *Seconda Secundae Partis*, Q. 40, http://www.newadvent.org/summa/3040.htm

in triumph to Constantinople.[8]

The idea of "holy war" came to full expression in AD 1095 when Pope Urban II proclaimed the need to recapture the Holy Land which had fallen into the hands of the Seljuk Turks. The Turks took Jerusalem from the Fatimids in AD 1070 and pious pilgrims began to bring to Rome terrifying accounts of the persecution of Christians and the desecration of the sacred shrines. Urban II spoke of such atrocities in a sermon he delivered to the Christian nobility at the Council of Clermont:

> Although, O sons of God, you have promised more firmly than ever to keep the peace among yourselves and to preserve the rights of the church, there remains still an important work for you to do. Freshly quickened by the divine correction, you must apply the strength of your righteousness to another matter which concerns you as well as God. For your brethren who live in the east are in urgent need of your help, and you must hasten to give them the aid which has often been promised them. For, as the most of you have heard, the Turks and Arabs have attacked them and have conquered the territory of Romania [the Greek empire] as far west as the shore of the Mediterranean and the Hellespont, which is called the Arm of St. George. They have occupied more and more of the lands of those Christians, and have overcome them in seven battles. They have killed and captured many, and have destroyed the churches and devastated the empire. If you permit them to continue thus for a while with impunity, the faithful of God will be much more widely attacked by them. On this account I, or rather the Lord, beseech you as Christ's heralds to publish this everywhere and to persuade all people of whatever rank, foot-soldiers and knights, poor and rich, to carry aid promptly to those Christians and to destroy that vile race from the lands of our friends. I say this to those who are present, it is meant also for those who are absent. Moreover, Christ commands it.[9]

---

8   Will Durant, *The Age of Faith* (New York: Simon and Schuster, 1950), p. 424.

9   Urban II, "Speech at the Council of Clermont, 1095," as recorded by Fulcher of Chartres, *Medieval Sourcebook*, Fordham University, https://sourcebooks.fordham.edu/source/urban2-5vers.asp

So forceful was Urban's plea that thousands of knights in attendance at Clermont thundered the response: "Deus lo volt" (*God wills it*). The knights and nobles sewed red crosses on their tunics and immediately laid plans for the great expedition.[10]

SANCTIFIED SOLDIERS

The expedition was to last 250 years and, to a great extent, accomplished the Pope's purpose. The feudal lords united with each other in a common cause. Jerusalem fell to the Crusaders on June 7, 1099 and a Christian Kingdom was established in the Middle East.[11] Moreover, by becoming transformed into soldiers of Christ, the medieval nobles and knights began to look upon the bearing of arms as a religious experience. Ceremonies surrounding initiation into knighthood assumed the aspects of a sacramental rite, with candidates expected to pray for divine guidance and favor the entire night before their dubbing. Priests bestowed blessings on men and arms alike, sermons were delivered on the nature of knightly virtue, and martial training came to include an emphasis on high standards of knightly conduct that regularized into precise and highly idealized codes. The Crusades had given rise to the age of chivalry.[12]

THE WARRIOR POPES

Since the spilling of blood could be just and holy, the Vicars of Christ often mounted their war horses and headed off to battle. One of the first warrior popes was the great reformer Leo IX (1048-1054). In 1052, the German Emperor Henry II donated the duchy of Benevento to the papacy. However, the resident Duke of Benevento, Pandulf by name, refused to recognize this gift. Pope Leo, in turn, asked the Emperor

---

10   Maurice Keen, *A History of Medieval Europe* (New York: Frederick A. Praeger, 1967), p. 97.

11   Durant, *The Age of Faith*, p. 592.

12   Charles T. Wood, *The Quest for Eternity: Medieval Manners and Morals* (Garden City, New York: Doubleday, 1971), p. 134.

to provide him with a German army in order to oust Pandulf and his Norman forces from the duchy. The Pope received from Henry a force of only seven hundred men. This shortage compelled Leo to round up hundreds of untrained Italians to join in the military undertaking. The campaign was a miserable failure. Pope Leo's forces were quickly routed by the Normans, who captured the Pope only to fall on their knees to beg pardon for killing his men.[13]

The most famous of the warrior popes was Julius II, the patron of Raphael and Michelangelo. When he ascended to the papal throne, Julius found that the Papal States remained in the hands of local dictators. Summoning forces from France, Germany, and Spain, the pope rode at the head of a formidable army. After regaining Perugia, the papal forces launched an attack on Bologna, an attack Pope Julius fortified with a bull of excommunication against anyone who resisted his army and an offer of a plenary indulgence to any man who killed any of his opponents.[14] This was a new brand of warfare and his enemies quickly raised the white flag. The same tactics worked in Venice, which surrendered to the Pope in 1510.[15]

Pope Julius II spent the remaining three years of his pontificate battling the French, who refused to abandon the Italian territories they had seized under the papal flag.[16]

THE GREAT WAR

The notion of holy war persisted into the 20th Century. In *The Great and Holy War*, historian Philip Jenkins writes: "The First World War was a thoroughly religious event, in the sense that overwhelmingly Christian nations fought each other in what many viewed as a holy war, a spiritual

---

13   Durant, *The Age of Faith*, p. 543.

14   Will Durant, *The Renaissance* (New York: Simon and Schuster, 1955), p. 443.

15   Ibid.

16   Ibid.

conflict. Religion is essential to understanding the war, to understanding why people went to war, what they hoped to achieve through war, and why they stayed at war. Not in medieval or Reformation times but in the age of aircraft and machine guns, the majority of the world's Christians were indeed engaged in a holy war that claimed more than ten million lives."[17]

At the onset of World War I, German preachers debated whether they should see the national mood in terms of Transfiguration or of a New Pentecost. Thuringian minister Adam Ritzhaupt asked, "When did peacetime ever offer us the heavenly exaltation that we are feeling in war?"[18] All the main combatants deployed Holy War language, particularly the monarchies with long traditions of state establishment—the Russians, Germans, British, Austro-Hungarians, and Ottoman Turks—but also those nationally secular republics: France and Italy.

"IT IS GOD'S WAR WE ARE FIGHTING"

When America entered the conflict in 1917, Randolph McKim, Episcopal rector of Washington's Church of the Epiphany, proclaimed: "It is God who has summoned us to this war. It is God's war we are fighting. . . . This conflict is indeed a crusade. The greatest in history—the holiest. It is in the profoundest and truest sense a Holy War. . . . Yes, it is Christ, the King of Righteousness, who calls us to grapple in deadly strife with this unholy and blasphemous power [Germany]."[19]

During the war, angels supposedly intervened to save beleaguered British troops; the Virgin Mary appeared to Russians at Augustovo; and the Germans claimed to follow the Archangel Michael.[20] Those

---

17 Philip Jenkins, *The Great and Holy War: How World War I Became a Religious Crusade* (New York: Harper One, 2014), pp. 4-5.

18 Ibid., p. 12.

19 Randolph McKim, quoted in Ibid., p. 10.

20 Ibid., p. 15.

stories circulated in the first days of the war, and they persisted through the whole struggle, long after we might expect the armies to be wholly focused on the grim realities of front-line life.

When the Germans launched their last great offensive in 1918, it was called Operation Michael. For the Allies, religious and apocalyptic hopes crested in 1917 and 1918, with the great symbolic victories in the Middle East. Most evocative were the capture of Jerusalem from the Turks, and the decisive British victory at Megiddo, the site of Armageddon.[21]

GAUDIUM ET SPES (THE JOY AND HOPE)

In accordance with the teachings of the Church Fathers, Vatican II's *Gaudium et Spes*, which was promulgated by Pope Paul VI on December 7, 1965, offered a weak affirmation of the doctrine of "just war." The papal constitution maintained that armed conflict can be just under the following conditions: (1) when a state is morally certain that its rights are being violated and that it is faced with certain and imminent danger; (2) when the cause of war is in proportion to the evils that are part of every war; (3) when every peaceful method had been ineffective; and (4) when there is a well-grounded hope of bettering the human condition by the conflict.[22] The document concluded as follows:

> It is our clear duty, therefore, to strain every muscle in working for the time when all war can be completely outlawed by international consent. This goal undoubtedly requires the establishment of some universal public authority acknowledged as such by all and endowed with the power to safeguard on the behalf of all, security, regard for justice, and respect for rights. But before this hoped for authority

---

21　Philip Jenkins, "Was the Great War a Holy War?" *On Faith*, 2014, https://www.onfaith.co/onfaith/2014/04/29/philip-jenkins-was-the-great-war-a-holy-war/31867

22　*Gaudium et Spes*, as promulgated by Pope Paul VI, 79. December 7, 1965, http://www.vatican.va/archive/hist_councils/ii_vatican_council/documents/vat-ii_const_19651207_gaudium-et-spes_en.html

can be set up, the highest existing international centers must devote themselves vigorously to the pursuit of better means for obtaining common security. Since peace must be born of mutual trust between nations and not be imposed on them through a fear of the available weapons, everyone must labor to put an end at last to the arms race, and to make a true beginning of disarmament, not unilaterally indeed, but proceeding at an equal pace according to agreement, and backed up by true and workable safeguards.[23]

In recent years, Catholic organizations have issued statements calling for the abandonment of the just war doctrine and the issuance of a new official papal document that affirms an unequivocal affirmation of pacifism and a total rejection of war under all circumstances. A Vatican Conference on Peace issued the following statement:

> Clearly, the Word of God, the witness of Jesus, should never be used to justify violence, injustice or war. We confess that the people of God have betrayed this central message of the Gospel many times, participating in wars, persecution, oppression, exploitation, and discrimination.
>
> We believe that there is no "just war." Too often the "just war theory" has been used to endorse rather than prevent or limit war. Suggesting that a "just war" is possible also undermines the moral imperative to develop tools and capacities for nonviolent transformation of conflict.
>
> We propose that the Catholic Church develop and consider shifting to a Just Peace approach based on Gospel nonviolence. We call on the Church we love to no longer use or teach "just war theory."[24]

---

23 Ibid., 82.

24 Vatican Conference on Peace, quoted in Ronald Conte, "Dangerous Distortions of Doctrine on Just War," *ronconte.com*, March 9, 2012, https://ronconte.com/2012/03/09/dangerous-distortions-of-doctrine-on-just-war/

FRANCIS CONDEMNS CATHOLIC TRADITION

In keeping with the Committee's suggestion, Pope Francis, on February 5, 2019, issued the following condemnation of the concept of a just and holy war:

> . . . we resolutely declare that religions must never incite war, hateful attitudes, hostility and extremism, nor must they incite violence or the shedding of blood. These tragic realities are the consequence of a deviation from religious teachings. They result from a political manipulation of religions and from interpretations made by religious groups who, in the course of history, have taken advantage of the power of religious sentiment in the hearts of men and women in order to make them act in a way that has nothing to do with the truth of religion. This is done for the purpose of achieving objectives that are political, economic, worldly and short-sighted. We thus call upon all concerned to stop using religions to incite hatred, violence, extremism and blind fanaticism, and to refrain from using the name of God to justify acts of murder, exile, terrorism and oppression. We ask this on the basis of our common belief in God who did not create men and women to be killed or to fight one another, nor to be tortured or humiliated in their lives and circumstances. God, the Almighty, has no need to be defended by anyone and does not want His name to be used to terrorize people.[25]

And so it had come to pass that a "Vicar of Christ" proclaimed that the commandments of God in the Old Testament, the actions of his papal predecessors, and the sacrifice of the lives of millions of soldiers who died in conflicts they believed were holy and just, should be deemed un-Christian and contrary to the will of the Supreme Being.

---

25   Pope Francis, "A Document on Human Fraternity for World Peace and Living Together," Apostolic Journey to the United Arab Emirates, February 5, 2019, http://w2.vatican.va/content/francesco/en/travels/2019/outside/documents/papa-francesco_20190204_documento-fratellanza-umana.html

PROTESTANT PABLUM

Mainline Protestant denominations also denounced the doctrine of just war. In 2015, the fifteenth General Synod of the United Church of Christ issued an unequivocal denunciation of war, even for self-defense, and the pronouncement of a "just peace" doctrine. "It is imperative," the synod leaders said, "to move beyond Just War thinking to the Theology of a Just Peace."[26] Nonviolent conflict, they continued, is a "healthy reflection of diversity." Demanding that war must be eliminated, the leaders affirmed their support of strengthening the United Nations to develop the following:

- more authority in disputes among countries;

- peacekeeping forces, including a permanent force of at least 5000, able to police border disputes and intervene when called to do so by the U.N.;

- peacemaking teams, trained in mediation, conflict intervention, and conflict resolution;

- support for international peace academies;

- a global satellite surveillance system to provide military intelligence to the common community;

- international agreements to limit military establishments and the international arms trade;

- an international ban on the development, testing, use, and possession of nuclear and biochemical weapons of mass destruction; and

- an international ban on all weapons in space and all national development of space-based defense systems and Strategic Defense Initiatives.[27]

26　"General Synod Pronouncement and Proposal for Action on the United Church of Christ as a 'Just Peace Church,'" United Church of Christ, 2015, http://www.ucc.org/beliefs_theology_general-synod-pronouncement

27　Ibid.

The denomination made no reference to the fact that the God of the Hebrews was "a man of war" (Exodus 15:3), who had led His people into battle and delivered them from their enemies. No mention was made of David who said: "Praise be to the LORD my Rock, who trains my hands for war, my fingers for battle." No acknowledgment of the military victories of Moses, Joshua, and Saul. No reference to the Torah and the laws that God had inscribed in stone with His own finger. For all intents of the UCC, this God did not exist.

11

NATURAL LAW

God created man in his own image, in the image of God he created him; male and female he created them.

GENESIS 1:27

The Torah clearly states its views about the act of homosexuality. The act of homosexuality, i.e. two men having sexual relations, is prohibited. The act is twice called a Toaivaan abomination and it is such a severe sin, that it merits the death penalty in a Jewish court system. If not for the fact that homosexuality is prevalent in Western Society today, there would be little controversy about this Torah sin. It is clearly forbidden and never condoned anywhere in the Torah.

RABBI DR. NACHUM AMSEL, "HOMOSEXUALITY IN ORTHODOX JUDAISM"

THE GENESIS STORY of Adam and Eve stresses that woman was made to serve as man's companion and sexual partner. The two anatomies were designed by God to unite for the sake of procreation:

"So God created mankind in his own image, in the image of God he created them; male and female he created them. God blessed them and said to them, 'Be fruitful and increase in number; fill the earth and subdue it. Rule over the fish in the sea and the birds in the sky and over every living creature that moves on the ground'" (1:27-28).

All sexual relations within ancient Judaism were prohibited that did not fit within the context of procreation.[1] And such relations are confined to married couples. Josephus, the first-century Jewish historian, wrote: "The Law recognizes no sexual connections, except the natural union of husband and wife."[2]

In order to safeguard the integrity of the family unit, which represented the basis of Jewish society, it was essential to ensure that the offspring of a woman were those of her husband. Hence the harsh penalty for those who violate the sanctity of marriage (If a man commits adultery with another man's wife—with the wife of his neighbor—both the adulterer and the adulteress are to be put to death (Leviticus 20:10).[3] Similarly, for the sake of a family's integrity, children are prohibited from cursing their parents. ("If anyone curses his father or mother, he must be put to death" Lev. 20:9).

PLATO AND ST. PAUL

The Mosaic laws governing sex were mirrored by the philosophical conception of natural law, the belief that sexual activity must be guided by the ends indicated for it by nature. Plato espoused this concept when he wrote in his *Laws*: ". . . we must not forget that this [sexual] pleasure is held to have been granted by nature to male and female when conjoined for the work of procreation; the crime of male with male, or female with female, is an outrage on nature and a capital surrender to lust of pleasure. . ."[4] This same teaching was advanced by Stoic philosophers from Chrysippus to Cicero.

---

1   Thomas Romer, *Dark God: Cruelty, Sex, and Violence in the Old Testament* (New York: Paulist Press, 2013), p. 103.

2   Josephus, quoted in Reay Tannahill, *Sex in History* (New York: Stein and Day, 1981), p. 70.

3   Romer, *Dark God*, p. 100.

4   Plato, *The Laws* (636), translated by A. E. Taylor, (Dutton, New York: Everyman's Library 1969), p. 13.

In the New Testament, St. Paul in his Letter to the Romans also condemned homosexuality as unnatural:

> Therefore, God gave them over in the sinful desires of their hearts to sexual impurity for the degrading of their bodies with one another.
>
> They exchanged the truth about God for a lie, and worshiped and served created things rather than the Creator—who is forever praised. Amen.
>
> Because of this, God gave them over to shameful lusts. Even their women exchanged natural sexual relations for unnatural ones. In the same way the men also abandoned natural relations with women and were inflamed with lust for one another. Men committed shameful acts with other men, and received in themselves the due penalty for their error (Romans 1:24-27).

In an even more explicit passage, St. Paul says: "Or do you not know that wrongdoers will not inherit the kingdom of God? Do not be deceived: Neither the sexually immoral nor idolaters nor adulterers nor men who have sex with men nor thieves nor the greedy nor drunkards nor slanderers nor swindlers will inherit the kingdom of God" (1 Corinthians 9-10). Being shunned from the Kingdom of Heaven for early Christians was a penalty infinitely worse than death.

"NOTHING MORE MAD OR DAMAGING"

After Christianity became the official religion of the Roman Empire in AD 380, homosexuals were not only excluded from the sacraments but also subjected to capital punishment.[5] In his Homily on the Epistle to the Romans (circa 390), Saint John Chrysostom maintained that homosexuals were worse than murderers:

---

5   David F. Greenberg and Marcia Bystryn, "Christian Intolerance of Homosexuality," *American Journal of Sociology*, Vol. 88, No. 3, https://www.journals.uchicago.edu/doi/abs/10.1086/227706

All passions are dishonorable, for the soul is even more prejudiced and degraded by sin than is the body by disease; but the worst of all passions is lust between men," he told his congregation. He continued by adding: "The sins against nature are more difficult and less rewarding, since true pleasure is only the one according to nature. But when God abandons a man, everything is turned upside down! Therefore, not only are their passions [of the homosexuals] satanic, but their lives are diabolic. . . . So, I say to you that these are even worse than murderers, and that it would be better to die than to live in such dishonor. A murderer only separates the soul from the body, whereas these destroy the soul inside the body. . . . There is nothing, absolutely nothing more mad or damaging than this perversity.[6]

Similarly, St. Augustine in his *Confessions* (circa 400) wrote:

Therefore those offenses which be contrary to nature are everywhere and at all times to be held in detestation and punished; such were those of the Sodomites, which should all nations commit, they should all be held guilty of the same crime by the divine law, which has not so made men that they should in that way abuse one another. For even that fellowship which should be between God and us is violated, when that same nature of which He is author is polluted by the perversity of lust."[7]

"WHENCE COMETH THIS PERVERSITY?"

Matters for gays were not improved by the Reformation. Martin Luther, in his condemnation of sodomy, upheld the concept of natural law, writing:

---

6   St. John Chrysostom, "Homilies on the Epistle to the Romans," Homily IV, http://www.documentacatholicaomnia.eu/03d/0345-0407,_Iohannes_Chrysostomus,_Homilies_on_The_Epistle_To_The_Romans,_EN.pdf

7   St. Augustine, *Confessions,* translated by Frank Sheed, (Indianapolis, IN: Hawkett Publishing, 2006, p. 47.

The heinous conduct of the people of Sodom is extraordinary, inasmuch as they departed from the natural passion and longing of the male for the female, which is implanted into nature by God, and desired what is altogether contrary to nature. Whence cometh this perversity? Undoubtedly from Satan, who after people have once turned away from the fear of God, so powerfully suppresses nature that he blots out the natural desire and stirs up a desire that is contrary to nature.[8]

Luther's pronouncements on homosexuality were upheld by other reformers, including Calvin, Zwingli, Know, William Farel, and Martin Bucher.

THE ENGLISH LAW

Under Henry VIII, the founder of the Church of England, the first English statute against homosexuality was placed in the books by Parliament in 1533. In accordance with this law, a capital penalty was meted out for any person that committed "the detestable and abominable vice of buggery with mankind or a beast." The wording of the law shows that it was based upon the Old Testament teaching. The theological expression "buggery" was derived from the "Bulgarian heresy." This law was reinstated by Elizabeth I in 1563 and remained unchanged throughout Great Britain until 1861, when the death penalty was replaced by a sentence of life in prison.[9]

HARSH LAWS IN AMERICA

In America, practicing homosexuals throughout the 17th and 18th centuries were rounded up and sent to the gallows. The Bay Colony, which

---

8   Martin Luther, quoted in Ewald Martin Plass, *What Luther Says*, Volume 1, (St. Louis, MO: Concordia Publishing, 2006), p. 134.

9   Louis Crompton, "Homosexuals and the Death Penalty in Colonial America," University of Nebraska, Lincoln, Faculty Publications, 1976, https://pdfs.semanticscholar.org/a787/62527be1 32f4e7f264274e311d0f38ad7772.pdf

adopted its Body of Laws and Liberties in 1641, set forth sodomy as a capital crime to keep their laws in complete conformity with the Mosaic Law. Section 8 of the 1641 laws represents a word-for-word translation of Leviticus 20:13. It reads: "If any man lyeth with mankinde as he lyeth with a woman, both of them have committed abomination, they both shall surely be put to death." This statute with the same phraseology remained on the books of the state of Connecticut until 1822.[10]

Nowhere was the identification of the Puritans with the ancient Hebrews more apparent than in the opening lines of the preamble to Connecticut's Laws of 1672, which proclaimed that "the Serious Consideration of the Necessity of the Establishment of wholesome LAWES for the Regulating of each Body Politik; Hath enclined us mainly in Obedience unto JEHOVAH the Great Law-giver: Who hath been pleased to set down a Divine Platforme, not only of the Morall, but also of Judicial LAWES, suitable for the people of Israel."[11]

In 1697, the Massachusetts legislature passed "An Act for the Punishment of Buggery," which read:

> For avoiding of the detestable and abominable Sin of Buggery with Mankind or Beast, which is contrary to the very Light of Nature; Be it Enacted and Declared by the Lieutenant Governor, Council, and Representatives, in General Court assembled: and by the authority of the same it is Enacted, That the same Offence be adjudged Felony, and such Order and Form of Process therein be used against the Offenders, as in Cases of Felony: And that every Man, being duly convicted of lying with Mankind, as he lieth with a Woman: and every Man or Woman, that shall have carnal Copulation with any Beast or Brute Creature, the Offender and Offenders, in either of the Cases before mentioned, shall suffer the Pains of Death, and the Beast shall be slain and burnt.

---

10 Ibid.

11 Ibid.

After the Revolution, this law was re-enacted as "An Act against Sodomy" (1785), which removed the English legal phraseology but retained the formula from Leviticus. This law remained in effect until 1822.[12] Colin Talley argues that the sodomy statutes in the colonies during the 17th century were seldom enforced since male to male intimacy did not threaten the social structure, or challenge the patriarchal ownership of wealth.[13]

JEFFERSON PRESCRIBES CASTRATION

Thomas Jefferson, filled with the spirit of the Enlightenment, worked to reform the criminal code of Virginia. In his outline for a "Bill Proportioning Crimes and Punishments," Jefferson said that poisoners should be poisoned, maimers maimed, and sodomites castrated.[14] His view prevailed with the committee, who published a report on June 18, 1779 that stated: "Whosoever shall be guilty of Rape, Polygamy, or Sodomy, with man or woman, shall be punished, if a man, with castration, if a woman, by cutting through the cartilage of her nose a hole of one half inch diameter at the least."[15] This suggestion proved to be too lenient for the Virginia legislature, which ruled on December 10, 1792 that sodomites should be put to death "without benefit of clergy."[16] These laws, however, were often unenforced. George Washington's staff included gay men, who were also numbered among leaders of the new republic.[17]

---

12   Ibid.

13   Colin L. Talley, "Gender and Male Same-Sex Erotic Behavior in British North America in the Seventeenth Century," *Journal of the History of Sexuality*, 1966, file:///C:/Users/15709/AppData/Local/Packages/Microsoft.MicrosoftEdge_8wekyb3d8bbwe/TempState/Downloads/18868-Article%20Text-44764-1-10-20130129%20(1).pdf

14   Thomas Jefferson, *The Papers of Thomas Jefferson*, Volume 2, edited by J. P. Boyd (Princeton: Princeton University Press, 1950), p. 664.

15   Ibid., 497.

16   Crompton, "Homosexuals and the Death Penalty in Colonial America."

17   William E Benemann, *Male-Male Intimacy in Early America: Beyond Romantic Friendships* (2006).

A MOVEMENT OF MODERATION

By the 19th Century, the laws governing homosexuality were changed so that the death penalty was no longer mandatory. In 1800, Virginia repealed its sodomy statute of 1792 by decreeing that anyone found guilty of "buggery" should henceforth be confined to prison for a period of "not less than one nor more than ten years." However, slaves who engaged in homosexual activity remained liable to execution. In 1805, the Massachusetts "Act against Sodomy and Bestiality" adjusted the punishment of these crimes to imprisonment "not exceeding ten years." Maryland and New Hampshire made the penalty 1 to 10 years in 1809 and 1812, respectively, but the Georgia's Penal Code of 1816 called for life imprisonment.[18] Delaware's Code of 1826 set the punishment for sodomy at "solitary confinement" for three years, and a public whipping "with sixty lashes on the bare back well laid on." The death penalty for homosexuals remained in effect in North Carolina until 1869, when the punishment was changed to 5 to 60 years' imprisonment.[19] In 1873, South Carolina became the last state to drop the death penalty, altering the punishment to a stay of five years in a state slammer.[20]

A TRUCE AND A COUNTER-ATTACK

Decriminalization of sodomy began in Italy and France in the late 18th century and in most of continental Europe by act of the Napoleonic Penal Code in 1810 and more than a century later in the United Kingdom in 1957. In 1962, Illinois became the first state to remove consensual sodomy from its list of crimes. In the following decades most states repealed their sodomy laws. Those that did not repeal the laws enacted legislation reducing the penalty for such acts. By the time of the 2003 Supreme Court decision in *Lawrence v. Texas*, which struck down the Texas same-sex sodomy law and hence the laws for the

---

18   Ibid.

19   *Laws of the State of Delaware*, Revised Edition (Wilmington, DE: R. Porter, 1829), p. 139.

20   Crompton, "Homosexuals and the Death Penalty in Colonial America."

whole country, the laws in most states were no longer enforced or were enforced very selectively.[21]

Most Americans and many Christians in the 21st century would view this as a victory for tolerance and individual choice. A consensus has emerged that the government should not regulate private behavior between consenting adults. Let individuals freely make their own decisions about sexual identity or morality based on their own faith perspective/values and keep the government "out of the bedroom."

FREE WILL V. DETERMINISM

If only it were that simple. What if someone involved in a homosexual lifestyle wants to see if it's possible to change? A concerted effort to outlaw counseling of any kind to help those with same-sex attractions seeking to affirm a traditional heterosexual identity is underway in dozens of states around the country.[22] It seems that government toleration should now only go in one direction, i.e., in favor of those who believe that gay identity is inborn and against those with Biblical or simply more traditional values.

In 2018, bills were introduced in 24 states making therapy against the law for minors and even adults who wish to see if it's possible to change same-sex attractions. Based on highly questionable studies alleging that homosexual orientation is inborn from birth, i,e., "genetic" and therefore unchangeable, previously discussed in chapter 8, the state is back in the bedroom, or at least the counseling room, this time on the side of gays who want to use the law to impose their views on the rest of the population, even against fellow gays or bisexuals who want to explore their heterosexual options or claim they have already successfully returned to a heterosexual orientation.[23]

---

21 Margot Canaday, "We Colonials: Sodomy Laws in America," *The Nation.* September 3, 2008, https://www.thenation.com/article/we-colonials-sodomy-laws-america/

22 Susan Miller, " 'Being LGBTQ is not an illness': Record number of states banning conversion therapy," USA Today, April 17, 2018.

23 Laurie Higgins, "Homosexuals Admit "Sexual Orientation" Can and Does Change," Illinois Family Institute, 2/24/2015.

CONSUMER FRAUD?

In 2018, California State Rep. Evan Low introduced a bill to prohibit advertising, offering, or engaging "sexual orientation change efforts with an individual (for adults of any age, since it is already banned for those under age 18)," treating such acts as a form of consumer fraud. The bill prohibited "any practices that seek to change an individual's sexual orientation" and "efforts to change behaviors or gender expressions, or to eliminate or reduce sexual or romantic attractions or feelings toward individuals of the same sex."[24]

This ban on free speech and religious liberty (since some views may be religiously based) regarding such issues, *even for adults*, was rejected, for now. However, it is clear that there is a vocal lobby against the idea that the free market should decide what kinds of therapy citizens can seek out. In states where there are bans on counseling that could assist minors with same-sex attractions who want to change, it is clear that youth and their parents cannot be trusted to seek out appropriate guidance on their own. The power of the state once punished homosexuality. Now it is mobilized to promote it.

GOVERNMENT'S ASSAULT ON NATURAL LAW

On May 13, 2016 the U.S. Department of Health and Human Services took steps to revoke natural law when it issued a new transgender mandate insisting that Title IX prohibitions against discrimination on the basis of sex would henceforth be interpreted to no longer apply to biological males or females, but rather to bar discrimination on the basis of "gender identity." Medical professionals and health care organizations which, based on faith, moral conviction, or their professional judgment, affirmed that maleness and femaleness are biological realities to be respected, not defects to be corrected, and therefore decline to

---

24   Conor Friedersdorf, "Conversion Therapy for Gays Is Awful, But So Is California's Bill to Ban It," *Los Angeles Times*, April 27, 2018, https://www.latimes.com/opinion/op-ed/la-oe-friedersdorf-gay-conversion-20180427-story.html

perform sex reassignment procedures, would be penalized for violations of federal law.[25]

That same day the departments of Justice and Education sent a "Dear Colleague" letter to the nation's schools setting forth policy on gender identity, defined as "an individual's internal sense of gender." The accompanying press release instructed schools to allow students "to participate in sex-segregated activities and access sex-segregated facilities consistent with their gender identity," because these federal agencies would now "treat a student's gender identity as the student's sex for purposes of enforcing Title IX."[26]

GOING TO THE BATHROOM

Originally passed in 1972, Title IX of the Education Amendments was intended to ensure that women and girls had equal opportunities in education, but the Obama administration's new interpretation required schools to allow boys unrestricted access to girl's bathrooms, locker rooms, dorm rooms, hotel rooms, and showers, if they claim to identify as girls. Anything less than full access to the sex-specific intimate facility of one's choice would be deemed a "transphobic" denial of civil rights and equality.[27] In addition, Section 1557 of the Affordable Care Act (Obamacare) was reinterpreted to mandate that all health-care plans provide transgender reassignment treatments.[28]

While Obama's nationwide transgender mandates were put on hold in February 2017 by the incoming Trump administration, government-enforced marginalization of those who hold to traditional and Biblical

---

25 Ryan T. Anderson, *When Harry Became Sally: Responding to the Transgender Moment.* New York: Encounter Books, 2018, p. 175.

26 U.S. Departments of Justice, Office of Public Affairs, "U.S. Departments of Justice and Education Release Joint Guidance to Help Schools Ensure the Civil Rights of Transgender Students," May 13, 2016.

27 Ryan Anderson, *When Harry Became Sally,* p. 175.

28 Ibid., p. 192.

beliefs that there are two sexes and that society should protect the modesty of children is in full swing in many parts of the United States. In August 2018, an Oregon judge ruled that "high school students do not have a fundamental privacy right to not share school restrooms, lockers, and showers with transgender students whose biological sex is different from theirs."[29]

According to U.S. District Judge Marco Hernandez, students who are unwillingly subjected to seeing students of the opposite sex naked are not having their rights violated.[30] Americans have a right to privacy in their bedrooms, but girls who do not want to undress or take a shower next to a student whose penis is in full display have no rights to privacy. It seems that such "micro-aggressions" are of no concern if they take place in a high school bathroom, locker room, or shower.

MY PRINCESS BOY

Gender identity policies are not just about allowing those who identify as transgender to live as they wish, but about forcing others to go along with a radical ideology. This process of indoctrination can start as early as kindergarten. In late 2015, administrators of the Nova Classical Academy, a public charter school in Minnesota, informed parents that an incoming student was "gender non-conforming" and that the school would be supporting the kindergartener's gender identity by requiring all K-5 students to read *My Princess Boy,* a book about "a boy who expresses his true self by dressing up and enjoying traditional girl things." The school adopted a "gender inclusion" policy, allowing students to choose their own gender at will. Students could demand to be addressed by a "preferred name" and pronouns, and would be entitled to use bathrooms and locker rooms of the opposite sex, as well

---

29   Ibid.

30   Claire Chretien, "Judge Upholds Transgender Bathrooms: Female 'Students Do Not Have a Fundamental Privacy Right,'" Life Site News, August 7, 2018, https://www.lifesitenews.com/news/judge-upholds-transgender-bathrooms-students-do-not-have-a-fundamental-priv

as sleeping facilities on overnight trips.[31]

Given no option to challenge this new school policy, a significant number of parents took their children out of the school (94 fewer students were enrolled the following year), objecting to the transgender "ideological indoctrination" being imposed on impressionable youth. The option for parents who hold to the Biblical/Natural Law perspective that there are two sexes increasingly is to enroll their children in a private, religious school or to home-school.

MENSTRUATION FOR ALL

In one school district in the United Kingdom, children are to be taught that "all genders" can have menstrual periods. The Brighton & Hove City Council approved this guidance in a nod to transgender rights advocates.[32]

Transgenderism has even affected academic research. Research at Brown University established the following finding: "Rapid-onset gender dysphoria' (ROGD, a newly discovered feeling that one's psychological identity is opposite to one's biological sex) among teens and young adults may be a social contagion linked with having friends who identify as LGBT, an identity politics peer culture, and an increase in internet use." This claim was yanked from the Ivy League university's news releases accompanied by a statement apologizing for publicizing their own professor's research.[33]

RAPID ONSET GENDER DYSPHORIA

The American College of Pediatricians found that the vast majority of pre-pubertal children experiencing gender dysphoria usually revert

---

31   Katherine Kersten, "Transgender Conformity," *First Things,* December 2016.

32   Helena Horton, "Boys Can Have Periods Too, Children to be Taught in Latest Victory for Transgender Campaigners," *The Telegraph,* December 16, 2018.

33   "Brown Statement on Gender Dysphoria Study," *News from Brown,* March 19, 2019, https://www.brown.edu/news/2019-03-19/gender

to the gender identity of their biological sex by late adolescence. They critiqued the new treatment standard for gender dysphoria in children for assuming that it is innate and because the treatments involve suppression of puberty using powerful drugs followed by the use of cross-sex hormones—a combination that results in *lifetime sterility*.[34] Furthermore, those who had transition surgery were *19 times more likely than average to die by suicide*.[35]

Like other social contagions, including cutting, anorexia, and bulimia, rapid onset gender dysphoria is often associated with pre-existing psychological problems such as anxiety and depression.[36] But unlike those other body image neuroses, this one gets immediate and full support, "affirmative care," for the patient's stated identity, including "top surgery," which refers to double mastectomies, with student health plans or Obamacare health insurance paying the bill. Such gender transition treatments involve significant risks. The puberty blockers stunt growth and decrease bone density. Individuals taking these hormones require lifelong monitoring for a number of dangerous side effects, including cancer and deep vein thrombosis. Given such lifelong impacts, the use of sex-reassignment treatments in children amounts to a massive uncontrolled experiment. [37]

Many health clinics furnish testosterone hormones to young women without requiring any psychological evaluation. Most therapists and psychiatrists, especially in the District of Columbia and 14 states which have laws prohibiting "efforts to change a patient's gender identity," offer immediate affirmation of teens' self-diagnosis, oblivious to parental concerns. Not all medical professionals give in to patients' demands, but most, fearing ostracism and legal penalties, do.[38]

---

34 "Gender Dysphoria in Children," *American College of Pediatricians*, November, 2018.

35 Cecilia Dhejne et al., "Long-term follow-up of transsexual persons undergoing sex reassignment surgery: cohort study in Sweden," PLOS ONE 6 (February 2011): e16885.

36 Katherine Kersten, "Transgender Conformity."

37 Ibid., 4.

38 Abigail Shrier, "When Your Daughter Defies Biology, *Wall Street Journal,* January 6, 2019.

POST-CHRISTIAN MAN

In December 2018, the Church of England released guidance for church leaders on how to hold a special ceremony to "recognize liturgically a person's gender transition." Such ceremonies should have a "celebratory character" in which the individual could share their testimony so that the congregation can "affirm them in their identity" and could include a service renewing baptismal commitment as the most appropriate setting.[39]

The Church of England is not alone. The Episcopal Church in the U.S., the Union for Reform Judaism, the United Church of Christ, Unitarian Universalist Association, the Evangelical Lutheran Church of America, the Presbyterian Church (U.S.A.), and United Methodist Church have all embraced transgender inclusion policies.[40]

As discussed by Katherine Kersten in *First Things,* the new post-Christian worldview rejects not only God, but also the idea that we are created with a purpose in an ordered universe. The "post-Christian man" views his body as a canvas on which to express his identity and exert his will. The preoccupation of many to cover their bodies with tattoos and piercings is an example. The more contrary to nature this new self is, the more "authentic" it can claim to be.[41]

As discussed in chapter one, the Gnostic impulse rejects physical reality as evil. It seeks a higher, hidden knowledge, creating a magical reality unwilling to recognize physical limitations. Today's transgender crusade can be seen as the latest chapter of this denial. It is inherently authoritarian because it has to be. Both nature and common sense oppose it. Critics who draw attention to reality must be discredited, silenced, or denounced as bigots. Otherwise, the Gnostic fantasy world would quickly disintegrate.[42]

---

39 "Church of England backs gender transition services," The Christian Institute, December 18, 2018, www.christian.org.uk.

40 Aleksandra Sandstrom, "Religious groups' policies on transgender members vary widely," Pew Research Center, December 2, 2015.

41 Katherine Kersten, "Transgender Conformity." p. 6.

42 Ibid.

12

THE END OF CATHOLICISM

For a village [Vatican City] where the overwhelming majority have sworn a vow of celibacy there is an unusual preoccupation with sexual matters. Homosexuality, if not rife within the Vatican, is constantly evident, and is a frequent factor in career advancement. Young attractive priests, invariably referred to as Madonni, *use their charm to accelerate their promotion. Certain bishops have found the need to work late in a locked room with only a* Madonno *to assist them. Satanic masses have happened regularly with hooded semi-naked participants and porn videos have been shown to a carefully selected audience.*

DAVID YALLOP, THE POWER AND THE GLORY

Even the most loyal of Catholics and their faithful priests must concede there is something rotten in the Church. Not only did Cardinal Bernard Law protect Father John Geoghan, who abused 100 Catholic boys over a career of seduction, molestation and rape, the cardinal moved him from parish to parish like a Mafia don providing safe houses for one of his button men. Rather than act as the good shepherd who lays down his life for his sheep, Law covered up the predator tracks of the wolf preying on his lambs.

PATRICK J. BUCHANAN, MARCH 20, 2002

IN 1972, in the midst of the sexual revolution, the Catholic Theological Society of America established a committee to conduct a study on human sexuality with the hope of "providing some helpful and illuminating guidelines in the present confusion."[1] The committee's pronouncements represented a sharp repudiation of every traditional teaching regarding sexual morality. The proper meaning of sexuality, the committee concluded, was not the satisfaction of an animal urge but the means by which people can break out of their isolation and "attain communion with one another." Sexual congress, whether premarital or extra-marital, was thus elevated to the status of a sacrament.[2] Regarding sexual morality, the committee decided that sex was moral if it contributed toward "integration" (i.e., communion with the partner). "Destructive sexuality," in the committee's opinion, "resulted in personal frustration and interpersonal alienation."[3]

The door was now open for Catholics to join the sexual revolution. Married couples were not bound to employ the missionary position; masturbation was not mortal sin; and homosexual acts were not unnatural. A 1981 Knights of Columbus study of eighteen to thirty-year-old Catholics in the United States showed that 90% disagreed with the pronouncements of *Humanae Vitae* and 88% disagreed with the Catholic norms on divorce and premarital sex.[4] From 1973 to 1983, the rate of divorce among Catholics grew from one in seven to one in four. A 1985 Gallup poll showed that the general Catholic population had become more tolerant of premarital sex than Protestants—only

---

1   Anthony Kosnik, William Carroll, and Agnes Cunningham, Ronald Modras, and James Schulte, *Human Sexuality: New Directions in American Catholic Thought* (New York: Paulist Press, 1977), p. xi.

2   Ibid., pp. 82-86.

3   Ibid., p. 86.

4   1981 Knights of Columbus-sponsored study in George A. Kelly, "Schooling and the Values of People," *Columbia*, Volume 29, June 1986.

33% disapproving, compared to the Protestants' 46%.[5] According to the same poll, 77% of U.S. Catholics said they relied on their own conscience rather than the proclamations of the Church in making sexual decisions.[6]

A LOST IDENTITY

The moral teachings of the Church had granted Catholics a distinct identity, a means by which Catholics identified themselves to others. But by 1970, the Catholic substructure with its own blend of rituals and rules, mystery, and manners vanished from the American scene. The editors of *Newsweek* on October 4, 1971 concluded: "Largely because of Vatican Council II and the turmoil that has followed, there is now as much diversity in theology and lifestyle among Catholics as there is among U.S. Protestants. A Catholic, in effect, is anyone who he says he is, and his attitude toward the Church is likely to be shaped essentially by his income, education, and where he floats in America's still bubbling melting pot."[7]

In 1999, shortly before he died of bone and liver cancer, Monsignor Luigi Marinelli, who had worked at the Vatican for 45 years, testified that a gay lobby had emerged as a dominant force within the Roman Curia under the pontificate of Paul VI and began to use sex as a carrot for advancement to ambitious up-and-coming clerics. In his memoir *Via col vento in Vaticano* [*Gone with the Wind in the Vatican*], Marinelli wrote that being a practicing gay prelate "can help a hopeful candidate advance more quickly and cause a rival to lose the desire to present himself for promotion. The one who gives himself from the waist down has a better chance than the one who gives his heart and soul to the service of God and his brothers. For many in the Curia, the beautiful

---

5   Ibid.

6   Gallup poll in Thomas C. Reeves, "Not So Christian America," *First Things*, October 1996, http://www.firstthings.com/article/1996/10/001-not-so-christian-america

7   Editorial Staff, "Has the Church Lost Its Soul?" *Newsweek*, October 4, 1971, p. 81.

boy attracts more goodwill and favor than the intelligent one."[8]

The list of alleged gay Catholic clerics included the names of Cardinal Tarcisio Bertone, who became the Vatican Secretary of State, Bishop Mauro Parmegiani, reigning cleric of Tivoli, Archbishop Josef Wesolowski, Apostolic Nuncio to the Dominican Republic, and Monsignor Francisco Camaldo, Official of the Vicariate of Rome at the Vatican.[9] Under Bertone's direction, the Vatican purchased properties in Rome that served to house gay saunas and massage parlors where priests paid for sex. The most notorious of these places was Europa Multiclub, the largest gay bathhouse in Italy. Tales of Vatican dignitaries frequenting Multiclub captured headlines in Rome's tabloids, and the website for Multiclub promoted special "bear nights" where hairy young men stripped and changed into clerical outfits.[10]

THE PINK POPE

The most prominent name on the list of gay clerics was that of Giovanni Montini, who reigned over the Church as Paul VI. Testimony about the pope's sexual proclivity was from several reliable sources, including Franco Bellegrandi. A member of the honor guard of the Sovereign Pontiff (*camarieri di spada i cappa*), Bellegrandi served as a professor of Modern History at Innsbruck University (Austria) and as a correspondent for *L'Osservatore Romano*, the Vatican newspaper. In his book *Nikita Roncalli: Controvita di un Papa*, Bellegrandi writes: "When he was Archbishop of Milan, he was caught by the police one night wearing civilian clothes and in not so laudable company. Actually, for many years

---

8   Luigi Marinelli, quoted in Gary Posner, *God's Bankers: A History of Money and Power at the Vatican* (New York: Simon and Schuster, 2015), p. 463.

9   Leo Zagami and Brad Olsen, *Pope Francis: The Last Pope? Money, Masons, and Occultism in the Decline of the Catholic Church* (San Francisco, CA: CCC Publishing, 2015), pp. 16-18.

10   Michael Day, "Vatileaks Scandal: Vatican Properties 'Used as Brothels and Message Parlors Where Priests Pay for Sex,'" *Independent* (UK), November 10, 2015, http://www.independent.co.uk/news/world/europe/vatileaks-scandal-vatican-properties-used-as-brothels-and-massage-parlours-where-priests-pay-for-sex-a6729251.html

he has been said to have a special friendship with a red-haired actor. This man did not make any secret of his relationship with the future Pope. The relationship continued and became closer in the years ahead."[11]

The red-haired actor and lifetime lover of Paul VI, whom Bellegrandi describes, reportedly was Paolo Carlini, who appeared in *Roman Holiday* (1953) with Audrey Hepburn and Gregory Peck and *It Started in Naples* (1960) with Clark Gable and Sophia Loren.[12] As long as Paul VI occupied the papal throne, Carlini was allowed to come and go as he wished within Vatican City. He often was seen taking the elevator to the papal bedchamber in the dead of night.[13]

Under Paul VI, according to Bellegrandi, offices within the Vatican were suddenly staffed by effete young men in tight-fitting uniforms with make-up on their faces. These newcomers replaced venerable old employees who were suddenly fired or removed to a different post. Bellegrandi writes: "The *Gendarmeria Pontificia* [the Vatican police] had to steer carefully along those floating mines and keep one eye closed— and sometimes both eyes—hushing up reports, and discouraging a diligent editor or two. I underwent such an experience myself."[14]

The relationship of the pope to the movie actor might have remained concealed from the public, save for Paul VI's denunciation of homosexuality and other "perversions" on December 29, 1975. In his "Declaration on Certain Questions concerning Sexual Ethics," the pope condemned homosexuality as "a serious depravity" that represented "a sad consequence of rejecting God."[15] This statement struck several members of

11   Franco Bellegrandi, *Nikita Roncalli: Controvita di un Papa* (Rome: Eiles, 2009), pp. 85-86.

12   Paul Hoffman, *Oh Vatican! A Slightly Wicked View of the Holy See* (New York: Congdon and Weed, 1984), p. 151.

13   Bellegrandi, *Nikita Roncalli*, p. 86.

14   Ibid., pp. 91-92.

15   Paul VI, "Declaration on Certain Questions concerning Sexual Ethics," an encyclical letter, December 29, 1975, http://www.vatican.va/roman_curia/congregations/cfaith/documents/rc_con_cfaith_doc_19751229_persona-humana_en.html

the European gay community as "galling hypocrisy." Roger Peyrefitte, a former French diplomat, published an article in *Tempo*, an Italian news journal, which exposed the Holy Father's long-standing affair with Carlini.[16] The article created a furor, causing Paul VI to appear on the balcony of St. Peter's to denounce the "horrible and slanderous accusations." But Peyrefitte remained steadfast and repeated his accusations on a host of television news programs that were broadcast throughout Italy.[17]

QUEER CARDINALS

Cardinal Joseph Bernardin was one of the most influential religious figures in the history of the American church. He was the creator of the National Conference of Catholic Bishops and the United States Catholic Conference.[18] According to his biographer, Eugene Kennedy, Bernardin "was the senior active American prelate among the country's more than 350. But his influence far exceeded his seniority. His writing and speaking on national and even global issues caused him to eclipse megabishops of the past."[19] On November 13, 1993, the cardinal was accused of numerous coercive sexual acts against Steven Cook, a seminarian from the Archdiocese of Cincinnati, and of engaging in "sexual satanic rites" with seminarians in Winona, Minnesota.[20] The $10 million lawsuit against Bernardin was settled and sealed out of court. Cook, however, never retracted his charges nor did he say they were inaccurate.[21] In accordance with Bernardin's last request, the Windy

---

16   Marian T. Horvat, "Paul VI's Homosexuality: Rumor or Reality?" *Tradition in Action*, February 1, 2006, http://www.traditioninaction.org/HotTopics/a02tPaulV_Accusations.html

17   Ibid.

18   Likoudis, *Amchurch Comes Out,* p. 137.

19   Eugene Kennedy, quoted in Ibid., p. 138.

20   Matt C. Abbott, "Ex-Priest Ellis Hatsham 'Returns,'" *Renew America*, April 19, 2011, http://www.renewamerica.com/columns/abbott/110419

21   Likoudis, *Amchurch Comes Out,* p. 139.

City Gay Chorus performed at his funeral Mass at the Holy Name Cathedral in Chicago in 1996.[22]

Cardinal Theodore McCarrick, Archbishop of Washington, DC, was charged with making sexual advances on two priests and one ex-priest during his well-known "sleepovers" at his shore home in New Jersey.[23] Cardinal John Wright, who presided over the Archdiocese of Pittsburgh, had been known to have a predilection for boys going back to his days as a priest in Boston. Fr. Raymond Page would take boys out to a holiday home in Massachusetts for Wright to sodomize. In the spirit of charity, the cardinal gave the boys $20 for their cooperation.[24] At Vatican II, Wright was a strong advocate for reform, especially in the areas of ecumenism and religious freedom.

Notable among the practicing homosexual American cardinals was Cardinal Francis Spellman, one of the most influential Catholic clerics of the 20th Century. After his death, members of the media discovered that Spellman was well-known in New York's gay community as "Nelly." One of Spellman's lovers was a Broadway dancer who appeared in the show "One Touch of Venus." Several nights a week, the cardinal would send his limousine to pick up the dancer for bouts of rough and tumble sex. When the dancer asked Spellman how he could get away with living such a debauched life, the cardinal answered, "Who would believe it?"[25]

---

22   David Gibson, "Pope Francis Breathes New Life into Cardinal Bernardin's Contested Legacy," *Religious News Service*, October 14, 2013, http://religionnews.com/2013/10/24/pope-francis-breathes-new-life-cardinal-bernardins-contested-legacy/

23   Margaret Galitzin, "When Cardinals Are Outed for Their Homosexuality," *Tradition in Action*, March 8, 2013, http://www.traditioninaction.org/HotTopics/N002-Cardinals.htm

24   Randy Engel, "The Homosexual Colonization of the Catholic Church," *New Oxford Review* November 2006, http://www.newengelpublishing.com/pages/New-Oxford-Review.html

25   Michelangelo Signorile, "Cardinal Spellman's Dark Legacy," *Strausmedia*, May 7, 2002, http://www.nypress.com/cardinal-spellmans-dark-legacy/

SEMINARY SEXCAPADES

By the end of Paul VI's reign, 40% to 60% of the young men in Catholic seminaries studying for the priesthood were practicing homosexuals.[26] The gay environment was so pronounced at St. John's Provincial Seminary in Plymouth, Michigan that the school came to resemble the set of *Fellini's Satyricon* rather than a place for spiritual formation. Homosexual acts between the seminarians took place in open settings. During the night, aggressive gays would cruise the dormitory from room to room in search of new partners. By 1985, the seminary had become so notorious as a homosexual hothouse that it was shut down by the Vatican.[27]

At St. Mary's Seminary in Baltimore, which became known as "the Pink Palace," the students regularly dressed in leather or lavender silk for a night of frolicking on the "block," Baltimore's answer to Greenwich Village. School vans provided the transportation. The rector of the seminary said, "We don't ask our candidates about their sexual orientation. It would be a violation of a man's civil rights to deny him ordination on those grounds."[28]

"OUT, PROUD, AND OPEN"

At St. Mary's of the Lake in Mundelein, Illinois (commonly known as "Mundelein"), new students were often coerced into having sex with upperclassmen and the priests who served on the faculty. Instructors managed to convince the aspirants to the priesthood that homosexual acts were not a violation of the virtue of chastity. Coming out parties for the closet seminarians became gala events that were celebrated by dining, drinking, and dancing. Few were able to retain their orthodox beliefs in such a bacchanalian setting. One student sent this complaint to Father John Canary, the rector at Mundelein:

---

26   Michael S. Rose, *Goodbye, Good Men: How Liberals Brought Corruption into the Catholic Church* (Washington, DC: Regnery Publishing, 2002), pp. 55-87.

27   Ibid., p. 58.

28   Ibid., p. 56-57.

Upon my arrival at Mundelein, I assumed there would be some "gay" students. I also assumed that I could handle that. I am a straight man, not a homophobic monster, Still nothing prepared me for the "underculture" of homosexuality that has been supported by the formation staff. . .

It's pretty offensive to a straight guy, because if I ever brought a woman in, played dance music rather than show tunes, and told jokes about which classmates were coupling with whom, I'd be booted out in a minute. . . . . It's common knowledge there are "gay couples" [at Mundelein] and I mean "couples" not friends.

The other problem at Mundelein is that if a straight student complains about this, he gets blackballed as a "conservative." There are several of us who are trying to be chaste. It's difficult, but to have to live among this gay culture is too much. To be at events where guys seem to have their CAM [campus] priest's blessing to be "out, proud, and open" about their love life really bothers me. And I am not alone.[29]

Students, such as Michael Shane who penned the above complaint, were classified as morally rigid and sent to psychologists for vocational counseling. At the counseling sessions, they were encouraged to be tolerant of all manners of sexual expression. If they failed to take this counseling to heart, they were driven out of the seminary as spiritually unfit for ordination.[30]

OUR SEXUALITY

In order to mold the students into "open and affirming" clerics, *Our Sexuality* became a standard text at the Oblate School of Theology in San Antonio, Texas. This work by Robert Crooks and Karla Baur, two "good Catholic authors," taught that those studying for the priesthood must relinquish many of their "biases," including the belief that sex is only for reproduction. The authors said:

---

29   Fr., Michael Shane, quoted in Ibid., pp. 60-61.

30   Ibid., pp. 61-65.

Many people have learned to view activities and other practices—such as masturbation, sexual fantasy, and anal intercourse—with suspicion. The same is true of sexual activity between members of the same sex, which certainly does not fit into the model of intercourse for reproduction. All these noncoital sexual behaviors have been defined at some time as immoral, sinful, perverted, or illegal. We will present them in this text as viable sexual options for those who choose them.[31]

They insisted that students must abandon the traditional teachings of the Church concerning sexual morality as expressed by St. Thomas Aquinas. Aquinas, according to *Our Sexuality*, ". . . maintained that human sexual organs were designed for procreation and that any other use—as in homosexual acts, oral-genital sex, anal sex, or sex with animals—was against God's will and therefore heretical. Aquinas's teachings were so influential that from then on homosexuals were to find neither refuge nor tolerance anywhere in the Western World."[32]

Once ordained, many of the priests who graduated from these "hotbeds of homosexuality" came under the jurisdiction of gay bishops. They had been trained to be open and accepting of homosexual coupling. They had been exposed to teachers who insisted that seminarians adopt a non-judgmental stance toward sexual deviancy. They had been encouraged by clerical formation teams to emerge from their closets and to acknowledge their sexual orientation. Those who fancied that these methods of preparing men for Holy Orders were all well and good remained blithely unaware that 10% of the new prelates were pedophiles.[33]

---

31 Robert Crooks and Karla Baur, *Our Sexuality* (Belmont, California: Wadsworth, 2008), p. 9. See also Ibid., p. 100.

32 Ibid., p. 11.

33 "Catholic Church Pays $655 Million in Abuse Cases," *Agence France-Presse*, March 8, 2008.

THE JOHN JAY STUDY

On February 27, 2004, the John Jay College of Criminal Justice revealed in a study that had been commissioned by the U.S. Conference of Catholic Bishops, that between 1950 and 2002, 4,392 U.S. priests had been charged with sex abuse and that the allegations had been made by more than 10,667 alleged victims. The study contained the following findings:

- 81% of the victims were male.

- Females tended to be younger than the males. Data analyzed by the researchers showed that the number and proportion of sexual misconduct directed at girls under 8 years old was higher than that directed at boys the same age

- 22.6% were age 10 or younger; 51% were between the ages of 11 and 14; and 27% were between the ages to 15 to 17 years.

- A substantial number (almost 2,000) of very young children were victimized by priests during this time period.

- In 6,696 (72%) cases, an investigation of the allegation was carried out. Of these, 4,570 (80%) were substantiated; 1,028 (18%) were unsubstantiated; 83 (1.5%) were found to be false. In 56 cases, priests denied the allegations.

- More than 10% of these allegations were characterized as not substantiated because diocese could not determine whether the alleged abuse actually took place.

- In 20% of the cases, the priest was deceased or inactive at the time of the receipt of the allegation and typically no investigation was conducted.

- In 38.4% of allegations, the abuse was alleged to have occurred within a single year, in 21.8% the alleged abuse lasted more than a year but less than 2 years, in 28% between 2 and 4 years, in 10.2% between 5 and 9 years, and, in under 1%, 10 or more years.

Concerning the 4,392 priests, the study displayed the following results:

- 56% had one reported allegation against them; 27% had two or three allegations against them; 14% had four to nine allegations against them; and 3% (149 priests) had 10 or more allegations against them. These 149 priests were responsible for almost 3,000 victims, or 27% of the allegations.

- The allegations were substantiated for 1,872 priests and unsubstantiated for 824 priests. The researchers thought the charges to be credible for 1,671 priests and not credible for 345 priests. The 298 priests and deacons who had been completely exonerated were not included in the study.

- 50% were 35 years of age or younger at the time of the first instance of alleged abuse

- Almost 70% had been ordained before 1970.

- Fewer than 7% were reported to have themselves been victims of physical, sexual, or emotional abuse as children. Although 19% had alcohol or substance abuse problems, 9% were reported to have been using drugs or alcohol during the instances of abuse.[34]

PROSECUTION UNDER RICO

By the close of the first decade of the 21st Century, U. S. bishops received complaints of child sexual abuse by approximately 6,000 priests—5.6% of the country's Catholic clerics. Five hundred twenty-five were behind

---

34   "The Nature and Scope of Sexual Abuse of Minors by Catholic Priests and Deacons" (*The John Jay Report*), John Jay College of Criminal Justice, The City University of New York, February 2004, http://www.usccb.org/issues-and-action/child-and-youth-protection/upload/The-Nature-and-Scope-of-Sexual-Abuse-of-Minors-by-Catholic-Priests-and-Deacons-in-the-United-States-1950-2002.pdf

bars, and over 3,000 civil and criminal lawsuits were pending.[35] The cost of this scandal exceeded $3 billion, forcing eight dioceses to seek bankruptcy protection.[36] Ten percent of the Roman Catholic priests in America had been accused of pedophilia—a number so alarming that legal activists have called upon federal and state attorneys to prosecute such clerics under the guidelines of the Racketeering Influenced and Corrupt Organization Act (RICO), thereby, once again, treating the Roman Catholic Church as a criminal and corrupt organization.[37]

A GLOBAL PROBLEM

This problem of pedophilia, of course, was not confined to America. It extended to Ireland, Canada, the United Kingdom, Latin America, Belgium, France, Germany, and Australia, increasing the cost to $10 billion and creating financial havoc in dioceses and parishes throughout the world. This mounting problem had been addressed by the continuous rotation of problematic and perverse priests between dioceses and a conspiracy of silence among the Curia. Not only had John Paul II condoned this practice but he also went on to insist that the abusers were, in fact, the victims. Cardinal Ratzinger said: "It has to do with the reflection of our highly sexualized society. Priests are also affected by the general situation. They may be especially vulnerable, or susceptible, although the percentage of abuse cases is no higher than in other occupations."[38]

John Paul II's refusal to demand the dismissal of priests from holy office who had been found guilty of child molestation has been likened

---

35 Michael D. Shaffer, "Sex Abuse Crisis Is a Watershed in the Roman Catholic Church's History in America," *Philadelphia Inquirer*, June 25, 2012.

36 Annysa Johnson and Paul Gross, "Archdiocese of Milwaukee Files for Bankruptcy Protection," *Milwaukee Journal Sentinel*, January 4, 2011, http://www.jsonline.com/features/religion/112878494.html, accessed May 24, 2014.

37 "Catholic Church Pays $655 Million in Abuse Cases," *Agence France-Presse*, March 8, 2008.

38 Benedict XVI (Joseph Ratzinger), quoted in David Yallop's *The Power and the Glory: Inside the Dark Heart of John Paul II's Vatican* (New York: Carroll and Graf, 2007), p. 352.

to the silence of Pope Pius XII during the Nazi Holocaust.[39] One of the pope's greatest shames was giving sanctuary to Cardinal Law, who resigned in disgrace from the Archdiocese of Boston in 2002. Another unforgivable act was the pope's stubborn and self-righteous defense of Marcial Maciel Degollado, a Mexican priest who serially abused adolescent seminarians, some as young as 12, and several of his own illegitimate children.[40]

U.N. CONDEMNATION

On January 16, 2014, the Roman Catholic Church became the first and only religious institution to be condemned by the United Nations. The global organization took the Vatican to task for transferring abusive priests from parish to parish rather than turning them over to the police. Monsignor Charles Scicluna, the Vatican's former sex crime prosecutor, admitted to a U.N. committee on Human Rights that the Holy See had been "slow" to face the crisis and that "certain things need to be done differently."[41]

But neither Monsignor Scicluna nor the other members of the Vatican committee could provide an answer to a question raised by Sara Oviedo, the U.N. human rights investigator. Ms. Oviedo asked how the Vatican, given its zero-tolerance policy toward clerical sex abuse, could continue, as a religious institution, "to cover up and obscure these kinds of cases?"[42] Nor could the Vatican committee offer a response to Maria Rita, another U.N. investigator, who questioned: "If these events continue to be hidden and covered up, to what extent will children be affected?"[43]

---

39   Jason Berry, *Lead Us Not into Temptation: Catholic Priests and Sexual Abuse of Children* (Chicago: University of Illinois Press, 2000), pp. vii-xii.

40   Maureen Dowd, "Pope Saint, Victims Asterisks," Commentary, *Scranton Times-Tribune*, April 24, 2014.

41   Monsignor Charles Scicluna, quoted in "U.N. Committee Criticizes Vatican for Allegedly Enabling Child Sex Abuse," *Daily News*, January 16, 2014, http://www.nydailynews.com/news/world/u-n-committee-criticizes-vatican-allegedly-enabling-child-sex-abuse-article-1.1581758

42   Sara Oviedo, quoted in Ibid.

43   Maria Rita, quoted in Ibid.

A CARDIAC INCIDENT

Archbishop Josef Wesolowski, the papal nuncio to the Dominican Republic, was accused in June 27, 2014 with picking up boys on the waterfront, paying them to perform sexual acts, and taking pornographic pictures of them. As soon as the charges were filed by Dominican officials, Wesolowski was whisked away to the Vatican and placed in protective custody. The requests for his extradition were denied on the grounds that the Polish prelate possessed diplomatic immunity.[44] He was the highest-ranking Catholic cleric to be labeled a pedophile.

The uproar over the incident caused Pope Francis to set a trial date for Wesolowski, who would become the first person ever to be tried at a criminal court within the Vatican. The trial never occurred. On August 27, 2017, the archbishop was found dead within his Vatican residence at 5 AM. His death was attributed to a "cardiac incident."[45]

A FORTRESS IMPREGNABLE

Largely because of the pedophilia scandal, the Holy See by 2005 began to display deficits in excess of $12 million. However, the Roman Curia remained blithely unconcerned about these mounting shortfalls. They knew that real worldly riches of the Church remained safe and secure within the Apostolic Palace, which houses the Vatican Bank. Dioceses may be sued and fall into bankruptcy. Parochial schools, universities, and hospitals may be strapped with multi-million-dollar settlements. But the accounts within the Institute for Works of Religion (IOR), commonly referred to as the Vatican Bank, remain out of the reach of altar boys who were sexually molested by their parish priests. As a sovereign state, the Holy See cannot be subjected to any ruling by any

---

44   Elisabetta Poroledo, "Josef Wesolowski, Ex-Archbishop Accused of Sexual Abuse, Dies at 67," *New York Times*, August 28, 2015, http://www.nytimes.com/2015/08/29/world/europe/jozef-wesolowski-polish-ex-archbishop-accused-of-child-sexual-abuse-is-found-dead.html

45   Cindy Wooden, "Former Nuncio Dies in Vatican Residence while Awaiting Sex Abuse Trial," *Catholic News Service*, September 1, 2015, http://www.catholicnews.com/services/englishnews/2015/former-nuncio-dies-in-vatican-residence-while-awaiting-sex-abuse-trial.cfm

foreign court. It remains an institution with over $50 billion in securities; gold reserves that exceed those of some industrialized nations; real estate holdings that equal the total area of many countries; and opulent palaces containing the world's greatest art treasures.[46] Such wealth will remain and grow even though the contributions of the Catholic faithful have been cut back to a trickle.

---

46 Richard Behar, "Washing Money in the Holy See."

PART THREE

SCIENCE AND SKEPTICISM

13

THE GOSPEL OF DARWIN

It was Darwin's greatest accomplishment to show that the directive organization of living beings can be explained as the result of a natural process, natural selection, without any need to resort to a Creator or other external agent.

FRANCISCO J. AYALA, DARWIN'S GREATEST DISCOVERY, 2007

It is no coincidence that, historically, both the Nazis and the communists exhibited a religious adherence to the Gnostic myth of Darwinism. Smith writes: "In place of an Eschaton which ontologically transcends the confines of this world, the modern Gnostic envisions an End within history, an Eschaton, therefore, which is to be realized within the ontological plane of this visible universe." According to Vatican insider Malachi Martin, the Italian humanists who eventually created speculative Masonry, reconstructed the concept of gnosis, and transferred it to a thoroughly this-worldly plane. Both Nazism and communism were birthed by organizational derivations of Masonry.

PHILLIP D. COLLINS, "DARWINISM AND THE RISE OF GNOSTICISM," 2005

THE ABANDONMENT OF THE GOD of the Old Testament has been accelerated by the claims of contemporary science.

The creation account in the opening chapter of Genesis has been debunked and discredited by findings that the earth is not stationary in space, let alone the center of the universe, but rather a planet that revolves around the sun; that the earth is not a flat plane covered by a dome-like solid firmament but rather a sphere in space that is perpetually spinning on an axis; that dinosaurs roamed the face of the earth 260 million years before the first creature resembling a human being appeared; and, finally, that human beings were not created in the image and likeness of God but rather evolved from sea creatures in the primordial slime.

This last finding, for fundamentalists, has been the most devastating, since it relates human beings not to a Divine Being but rather a Gibbon ape.

Darwinism.

Darwinism has captured the scientific world by storm with dire consequences for those who uphold a literal interpretation of the Book of Genesis. Those preachers and teachers who have tried to disprove the theory of evolution have been silenced by Clarence Darrow in the famous "monkey trial" of 1925.

Evolution, as embraced by the academic world, served to support the tenets of Gnosticism, including the teaching that the vast majority of mankind were of no greater importance or significance in the vast scheme of things than ants or amphibians, and that true "gnosis" or "knowledge" resided in man's awareness of his true origin.

The Clergy Letter Project of 2004 was designed to show that "religion and science can be compatible" and to endorse evolution.[1] It now claims to have the signatures of 16,000 Christian Clergy. Similar statements have been signed by 737 Rabbis, 592 Unitarians, and 56

---

1   Michael Zimmerman, Founder, *The Clergy Letter Project*, 2004, http://www. theclergyletterproject.org/

Buddhists according to their website. These signatories are not laymen in the pews. These are pastors, religious professors, and theologians. They are the leaders and opinion makers for the people in the pews.

THE DARWINIAN CREDO

According to their website, The Clergy Letter Project has been officially endorsed by the Southwestern Washington Synod of the Evangelical Lutheran Church in America, the Southeast Florida Diocese of the Episcopal Church, the Presbytery of the Cascades (101 Presbyterian churches), the United Methodist Church worldwide in 2008, and the Presbyterian Church (USA) in 2016.[2] The following is their statement of Darwinian faith:

> We the undersigned, Christian clergy from many different traditions, believe that the timeless truths of the Bible and the discoveries of modern science may comfortably coexist. We believe that the theory of evolution is a foundational scientific truth, one that has stood up to rigorous scrutiny and upon which much of human knowledge and achievement rests. To reject this truth or to treat it as "one theory among others" is to deliberately embrace scientific ignorance and transmit such ignorance to our children. We believe that among God's good gifts are human minds capable of critical thought and that the failure to fully employ this gift is a rejection of the will of our Creator. To argue that God's loving plan of salvation for humanity precludes the full employment of the God-given faculty of reason is to attempt to limit God, an act of hubris. We urge school board members to preserve the integrity of the science curriculum by affirming the teaching of the theory of evolution as a core component of human knowledge. We ask that science remain science and that religion remain religion, two very different, but complementary, forms of truth.[3]

---

2   Ibid.

3   Ibid.

Support for a "theistic" Darwinian perspective also comes from Francis Collins and Karl Giberson in a book, *Language of Science and Faith,* published by InterVarsity Press, an extension of InterVarsity Christian Fellowship/USA, an evangelical organization: "The model for divinely guided evolution that we are proposing here thus requires no 'intrusions from outside' for its account of God's creative process, except for the origins of natural laws guiding the process."[4]

In their view, God is the origin of matter and the natural laws that guide it. The properties of matter were enough to bring about all living things without any further direct action by God. This eliminates the problem of any conflict with science, because modern evolutionary theory also holds that matter by itself evolved over a long period of time into all living things.[5]

A PASSIVE GOD

A significant plurality of Jews and Christians (62%) accept materialist evolution for the origin of plant and animal species as a proven fact.[6] Genesis 1-3 is now viewed as a fascinating myth. The "God" of Theistic Evolution may have once been active in the creation of matter and the natural laws guiding it, but had no input in the formation of different life forms and the human race, which arose from unguided natural processes, As theologian Wayne Grudem explains: "According to theistic evolution, God did not act directly, discreetly, or discernably in time to create plants, animals, or man. Indeed, theistic evolution insists that after the creation of the universe at the Big Bang, God did not actively make anything, but merely upheld (or observed) the ongoing natural

---

4   Karl Giberson and Francis Collins, *Language of Science and Faith* (Downers Grove, IL: InterVarsity, 2011), p. 115.

5   Denis Alexander, *Creation or Evolution: Do We Have to Choose? 2nd ed.* (Oxford and Grand Rapids: MI: Monarch, 2014), p. 436.

6   "New Poll Asks Christians, Do You Believe in Evolution," *Black Christian News,* February 7, 2019, blackchristiannews.com/2019/02/new-poll-asks-christians-do-you-believe-in-evolution/

processes that were themselves directly responsible for the origin of all life forms."[7]

But is Darwin's theory of evolution really a "proven fact" that the modern church must accept, with revisions to Biblical faith that lead to envisioning a disinterested, passive God of "theistic evolution?"

A HASTILY ARRANGED MARRIAGE

Stephen Meyer, a geophysicist and professor of science at Whitworth University, writes:

Theistic evolutionists say that God used the evolutionary process to create the diversity of life on Earth. This statement represents the central claim of theistic evolution—namely, that God as Creator employed the processes of random variation and natural selection to cause plants, animals, and indeed every living thing, to come to be...But a skeptic might wonder if this marriage of Christian theism and evolutionary theory has not been rather hastily arranged. Although the bride and groom are smiling in the reception line, when they happen to glance sidelong at each other, their smiles vanish. A skeptic might further observe that the bona fides of the groom, neo-Darwinian theory, have been in doubt for some time—not, however, from the bride's overeager, churchgoing family, anxious to secure what they hope will be a conflict-diminishing marriage, but from the groom's secular and visibly morose side of the aisle. The stony expressions of his materialistic kin suggest a deeply significant, but largely neglected, story.[8]

7   Wayne Grudem, "Biblical and Theological Introduction: The Incompatibility of Theistic Evolution with the Biblical Account of Creation and with Important Christian Doctrines" in *Theistic Evolution: A Scientific, Philosophical, and Theological Critique*, J. P. Moreland, Stephen C. Meyer, Christopher Shaw, Ann K. Gauger, Wayne Grudem, & 20 more, eds., (Wheaton, IL: Crossway,, 2017), p. 74.

8   Stephen C. Meyer, "Neo-Darwinism and the Origin of Biologic Form and Information," in *Theistic Evolution: A Scientific, Philosophical, and Theological Critique*, J. P. Moreland, Stephen C. Meyer, et al., eds., (Wheaton, IL: Crossway, 2017), p. 106.

As described by Meyer, the proposed "marriage" between Christian theism and neo-Darwinian evolutionary theory remains threatened by the largely neglected story of the growing disillusionment with Darwin among secular scientists who are well aware of the current scientific research that undermines the key pillars of his theory.

Darwin assumed a "Tree of Life" starting with some original life form. From there all other species evolved, making a branching structure where all species in existence can be traced back to that original unknown species. He assumed some primordial soup, a "warm little pond,"[9] could accomplish the deed of spontaneous generation when a bolt of lightning is added.

BASICS OF DARWIN'S THEORY

What exactly does his Theory of Evolution state? Francisco Ayala in the *Encyclopedia Britannica* provides this summary:

> Evolution theory in biology postulat(es) that the various types of plants, animals, and other living things on Earth have their origin in other preexisting types and that the distinguishable differences are due to modifications in successive generations. The theory of evolution is one of the fundamental keystones of modern biological theory. The virtually infinite variations on life are the fruit of the evolutionary process. All living creatures are related by descent from common ancestors. Humans and other mammals descend from shrewlike creatures that lived more than 150 million years ago; mammals, birds, reptiles, amphibians, and fishes share as ancestors aquatic worms that lived 600 million years ago; and all plants and animals derive from bacteria-like microorganisms that originated more than 3 billion years ago. Biological evolution is a process of descent with modification. Lineages of organisms change through generations; diversity arises because the lineages that descend

---

9   Peretó, Juli; Bada, Jeffrey L.; Lazcano, Antonio (2009). "Charles Darwin and the Origin of Life." *Origins of Life and Evolution of Biospheres.* 39 (5): 395–406. Charles Darwin's letter to Joseph Dalton Hooker, March 29, 1863.

from common ancestors diverge through time....Natural selection occurs because individuals having more-useful traits, such as more-acute vision or swifter legs, survive better and produce more progeny than individuals with less-favorable traits.[10]

FOSSIL RECORD FAILURE

Darwin himself admitted in *On the Origin of Species* that if the fossil record did not turn up the "missing links" that he needed and future discoveries did not show a slow and gradual progression of more and more complex species, then his theory was wrong.[11] Since 1859 the totality of the fossil record has expanded 1,000 times until it can be assumed to be very nearly complete. At least it can be accurately analyzed for conclusions because there is sufficient data for the required scientific accuracy.

If Darwinian evolution were true, then by simple logic the number of transitional forms between species should far outnumber the resultant species. Therefore, the fossil record should show evidence of a vast number of transitional fossils. Logic would dictate that transitional forms are equally likely to fossilize. Darwin said, "the number of intermediate and transitional links, between all living and extinct species, must have been inconceivably great."[12] In fact, however, gradual changes of one species into another do not appear in the fossil record. Species appear already fully formed. As explained by Jonathan Wells, author of *Icons of Evolution:* "This vastly improved knowledge of Cambrian and Precambrian fossils has aggravated Darwin's problem

10   Francisco Jose Ayala, "Evolution," Evolution: Scientific Theory," Encyclopedia Britannica online, Updated: Jan. 11, 2019, https://www.britannica.com/science/evolution-scientific-theory

11   Charles Darwin, *On The Origin of Species by Natural Selection or the Preservation of Favored Races in the Struggle for Life*, (New York, D. Appleton and Company, 1861). Full scanned text online at http://darwin-online.org.uk/converted/pdf/1861_OriginNY_F382.pdf

12   Charles Darwin., *On the Origin of Species by Means of Natural Selection* (Ontario, Broadview Press Ltd., 2003) p. 270.

rather than alleviated it. Many paleontologists are now convinced that the major groups of animals really did appear abruptly in the early Cambrian. The fossil evidence is so strong, and the event so dramatic, that it has become known as 'the Cambrian explosion,' or 'biology's big bang.'"[13]

Stephen J. Gould, was a paleontologist, evolutionary biologist, and historian of science, as well as a strong believer in materialistic evolution. However, he refuted Darwinian gradualism based on the fossil record by writing:

> The extreme rarity of transitional forms in the fossil record persist as the trade secret of paleontology. The evolutionary trees that adorn our textbooks have data only at the tips and nodes of their branches; the rest is inference, however reasonable, not the evidence of fossils. . . . We fancy ourselves as the only true students of life's history, yet to preserve our favored account of evolution by natural selection we view our data as so bad that we never see the very process we profess to study.[14]

THE CAMBRIAN EXPLOSION

The fossil record shows that most species when they first appear are fully formed. The body plan is complete. It changes very little from then on.

The fossil record also shows that the vast majority of species appear around the same time. In a relatively narrow window of historical time of about 20 to 25 million years, now called the Cambrian Explosion, almost all animal phyla, or groups, and most living species, appear. After that fossils change very little over time until they either go extinct or are still alive today. Stephen Meyer, author of *Darwin's Doubt*, explains:

> Despite the scope of his synthesis, there was one set of facts that trou-
> bled Darwin—something he conceded his theory couldn't adequately

---

13   Jonathan Wells, *Icons of Evolution: Science or Myth? Why Much of What We Teach about Evolution Is Wrong* (Washington, DC: Regnery Publishing, 2000), p. 37.

14   Stephen J. Gould, "Evolution's Erratic Pace," *Natural History*, vol. 86 (May 1987), p. 14.

explain, at least at present. Darwin was puzzled by a pattern in the fossil record that seemed to document the geologically sudden appearance of animal life in a remote period of geologic history, a period that at first was commonly called the Silurian, but later came to be known as the Cambrian. During this geological period, many new and anatomically sophisticated creatures appeared suddenly in the sedimentary layers of the geologic column without any evidence of simpler ancestral forms in the earlier layers below, in an event paleontologists today call the Cambrian Explosion.[15]

The few million years of the Cambrian Explosion represent about 2% of a timeline stretching from the beginning of time until today. So, what the fossil record is saying is that nothing much was happening for a really long time, then suddenly life exploded on the scene. Since that time, things have remained very much constant and stable. This is a total denial of Darwin's slow and gradual process, as Jonathan Wells in *Icons of Evolution* maintains:

> Is the fossil record sufficiently fragmented to explain the absence of Precambrian ancestors for Cambrian animals? Most paleontologists don't think so. Enough good sedimentary rocks from the late Precambrian and Cambrian have now been found to convince paleontologists that if there had been ancestors, and they had fossilized, they would have been discovered by now.[16]

THE MISSING TREE OF LIFE

The fossil record does not show anything close to Darwin's so-called Tree of Life. A particular species will pop up suddenly out of nowhere without any ancestors. Some adaptations or changes may take place, bigger or smaller or such, but then the species either goes extinct or still

---

15   Stephen C. Meyer, *Darwin's Doubt: The Explosive Origin of Animal Life and the Case for Intelligent Design* (San Francisco, HarperOne, Jun 3, 2014), pp. 6-7.

16   Jonathan Wells, *Icons of Evolution*, p. 42.

exists. Meyer explains: "Echoing these views, a January 2009 cover story and review article in *New Scientist* observed that today the tree-of-life project 'lies in tatters, torn to pieces by an onslaught of negative evidence.' As the article explains, 'Many biologists now argue that the tree concept is obsolete and needs to be discarded,' because the evidence suggests that 'the evolution of animals and plants isn't exactly tree-like.'"[17]

Most evolutionists will admit that the classical statements of Darwin have been refuted, or at least been unsubstantiated by the fossil record or by experimental data. As summarized by Michael Denton, an Australian molecular biologist:

> Since Darwin's time the search for missing links in the fossil record has continued on an ever-increasing scale. So vast has been the expansion of paleontological activity over the past one hundred years that probably 99.9% of all paleontological work has been carried out since 1860. Only a small fraction of the hundred thousand or so fossil species known today were known to Darwin.[18]
>
> Despite the tremendous increase in geological activity in every corner of the globe and despite the discovery of many strange and hitherto unknown forms, the infinitude of connecting links has still not been discovered and the fossil record is about as discontinuous as it was when Darwin was writing the Origin. The intermediates have remained as elusive as ever and their absence remains, a century later, one of the most striking characteristics of the fossil record.[19]

A MATTER OF BAD MATH

In April 1966 a group of distinguished mathematicians, including some Nobel Prize winners, gathered at the Wistar Institute Symposium:

---

17   Stephen C. Meyer, *Darwin's Doubt,* p 119.

18   Michael Denton, *Evolution: A Theory in Crisis* (Chevy Chase, MD, Adler & Adler; 2002), pp. 160-1.

19   Ibid., p. 146.

Mathematical Challenges to the Neo-Darwinian Theory of Evolution.[20] It was chaired by the Nobel Prize winner, Sir Peter Medawar, and only the most distinguished authorities in their fields were invited. In one example of mathematical presentations, *Inadequacies of Neo-Darwinian Evolution as a Scientific Theory,* Murray Eden showed that it would be impossible for even a single ordered pair of genes to be produced by DNA mutations in the bacteria, E. coli, with 5 billion years in which to produce it. His estimate was based on 5 trillion tons of the bacteria covering the planet to a depth of nearly an inch during that 5 billion years. The genes of E. coli contain over a trillion (10^{12}) bits of data. Eden also showed the mathematical impossibility of protein forming by chance.[21]

Follow-up conferences became more and more contentious between evolutionists and mathematicians. But the mathematicians had established that even allowing for sudden change and multiple steps at once (not Darwinism), one still cannot make enough changes to account for all the cellular developments necessary to produce one simple bacteria. Darwinism was officially refuted mathematically in 1966.

DNA REPAIR

In a more recent example, the Nobel Prize in Chemistry in 2015 was given to three men who discovered that DNA can repair itself when it is incorrectly copied during cell division.[22] They discovered three different abilities of DNA to repair itself. The conclusion was that for

---

20   Paul S. Moorhead and Martin M. Kaplan, Eds, *Mathematical Challenges to the Neo-Darwinian Interpretation of Evolution,* (Philadelphia, Wistar Institute Press, 1967). Book Review by John L. Harper, *Science Magazine,* April 26, 1968, Vol. 160, Issue 3826, pp. 408, http://science. sciencemag.org/content/160/3826/408.

21   Murray Eden, "Inadequacies of Neo-Darwinian Evolution as a Scientific Theory," *Mathematical Challenges to the Neo-Darwinian Interpretation of Evolution,* (Philadelphia, Wistar Institute Press, 1967), p. 18.

22   The Royal Swedish Academy of Sciences, The Nobel Prize in Chemistry 2015. (Stockholm, Sweden, NobelPrize.org, October 7, 2015) https://www.nobelprize.org/prizes/chemistry/2015/ press-release/

every 1,000 incorrect copies or mutations, at least 999 would be successfully repaired.

These discoveries make mutation as a source for change even less mathematically possible. Any significant random mutation that could possibly survive will be overwhelmed very quickly before it is fixed in the population.

CODES FOR NEW SPECIES

Since DNA was discovered in 1953, better instruments and research have revealed undreamed-of realities. There is enough DNA in a human body to be stretched end to end and reach to the sun and back 300 times.[23] A pinhead of DNA has the information content of paperback books stacked from the earth to the moon 500 times.[24]

All that information within living cells is not random. It is coded. Scientists are gradually understanding different parts of that coding. Coded information can mean only one thing, namely that it originates from an intelligent source. There is no evidence that a random process can produce useful coded information. Furthermore, the design had to exist in an intelligent mind before the code in order for the code to specify a precise outcome.

IRREDUCIBLE COMPLEXITY

Additional challenges to the Theory of Evolution have emerged. In Darwin's day, scientists conducted their studies with very rudimentary microscopes and could not reveal the workings inside of the tiny cell. Thanks to modern microscopes, biologists now compare the complexity in a cell to that of an entire city.

---

23   Anthony T. Annunziato, "DNA Packaging: Nucleosomes and Chromatin," *Nature Education*, 1(1):26, 2008. https://www.nature.com/scitable/nated/article?action=showContentInPopup&contentPK=310

24   Werner Gitt, "Dazzling Design in Miniature: DNA Information Storage," *Creation*, Issue 20, December 6, 199, https://wernergitt.com/articles/english/item/20205-dazzling-design-in-miniature-dna-information-storage

The concept of "irreducible complexity" has been put forth by Michael Behe, a biochemist, in his book, *Darwin's Black Box: The Biochemical Challenge to Evolution.*[25] If a system is "irreducibly complex," this simply means that you cannot take away any single piece at all because if you do, it won't work. Behe uses the example of the mousetrap to try to illustrate his point. It has only five parts, but if you took away any one of them, it would not work. It cannot be accidentally assembled by a slow and gradual process of one piece at a time. Nothing functions until the total assembly is completed.

Behe studied the biochemistry of bacteria for over 20 years and particularly the bacteria's flagellum, its propulsion system. He discovered that over 40 proteins are involved, the system is assembled in an orderly, sequential fashion, and it finally functions similar to an outboard motor on a boat. At no point in the assembly process does the flagellum function until the end. This violates Darwin's idea of incremental and accidental progression of functioning stages. Behe writes: "Manufacturing machines build other molecular machines, as well as themselves. Cells swim using machines, copy themselves with machinery, ingest food with machinery. In short, highly sophisticated molecular machines control every cellular process. Thus, the details of life are finely calibrated, and the machinery of life enormously complex."[26]

The concept of "irreducible complexity" is a paradigm changer. It can now be identified everywhere one looks. Each time one recognizes it one might also note there is a little sign flashing, "No Darwinism here."

THE BRICK, NOT THE BLUEPRINT

A whole new field of science is now opening up called "epigenetics," which is changing scientific thinking about DNA. It is discovering that DNA is only a part of the process of life. DNA is merely analogous to

---

25   Michael J. Behe, *Darwin's Black Box: The Biochemical Challenge to Evolution* (New York: Free Press, March 13, 2006), p. 5.

26   Ibid.

the bricks used to build a house. It is not the blueprint. The blueprint must lie someplace else other than within the DNA. The same bricks could be used to build a mansion or a shack. The design or blueprint is not in the DNA itself. Therefore random mutations of DNA cannot even be considered any longer as the major source for evolution. It's only changing the bricks and not the house. Jonathan Wells writes: "And the three-dimensional arrangement of proteins in a cell requires spatial information that precedes their synthesis and is specified independently of DNA. Therefore, DNA does not contain a program for embryo development, and mutations in DNA cannot provide the raw materials for anatomical evolution."[27]

THE EVIDENCE IGNORED

Such findings remain ignored by contemporary Christians. Darwinism has become such an integral aspect of modern thought that it became integrated into Christian theology by such thinkers as Teilhard de Chardin. In the spirit of Gnosticism, de Chardin saw an evolution of humanity from the primitivism of the Old Testament to a union with the all-embracing God of love, personified by Jesus. This movement, De Chardin wrote, would culminate in ". . . a new religion (let's call it an improved Christianity, if you like) whose personal God is no longer the great 'neolithic' landowner of times gone by, but the Soul of the world as demanded by the cultural and religious stage we have now reached. . . ."[28] The end of evolution, according to de Chardin, would be man joining with other men to make a kind of simple organism with a single Personal God. When that goal was reached, he said, "Everything that is hard, crusty, or rebellious. . . all that is false and reprehensible. . .

---

27   Jonathan Wells, "Why DNA Mutations Cannot Accomplish What Neo-Darwinism Requires" in *Theistic Evolution: A Scientific, Philosophical, and Theological Critique*, eds. J. P. Moreland, Stephen C. Meyer, et.al. (Wheaton, IL, Crossway, November 30, 2017), p. 237.

28   Pierre Teilhard de Chardin, *Letters to Leontine Zanta* (New York: Harper and Row, 1969), p. 114.

all that is physically or morally evil will disappear . . . Matter will be absorbed into Spirit. . . ."[29] In political terms, this union would result in totalitarianism. He wrote: "The synthesis of the (Christian!) God of the Above and the (Marxist!) God of the Ahead: this is the only God whom we shall in the future be able to adore in spirit and in truth."

Teilhard also asserted in *The Future of Man* that "the modern totalitarian regimes, whatever their initial defects, are neither heresies nor biological regressions: they are in line with the essential trend of 'cosmic' movement." In *Science and Christ,* he wrote: "Fascism represents possibly a blueprint, rather successfully done, of the world of tomorrow."[30] Such statements did not result in de Chardin's excommunication from the Church, but rather his veneration by Pope Benedict XVI and other leading spokesmen of contemporary Christianity.[31]

---

29   Pierre Teilhard de Chardin, quoted in Mary Lukas and Ellen Lukas, *Teilhard* (Garden City, New York: Doubleday, 1977), p. 50.

30   Pierre Teilhard de Chardin, quoted in Ellen Myers, "Pantheism Mysticism vs. Created Reality," *Creation Social Science and Humanities Society*, Vol. IV, 1981, creationism.org/csshs/v04n3p04. htm

31   "Benedict XVI Praises the Cosmic Liturgy of Teilhard de Chardin," *Tradition in Action*, July 24, 2009, https://www.traditioninaction.org/ProgressivistDoc/A_120_RatzTeilhardl.html

14

DARWIN'S DESCENDANTS

Throughout the first six decades of the twentieth century, hundreds of thousands of Americans and untold numbers of others were not permitted to continue their families by reproducing. Selected because of their ancestry, national origin, race or religion, they were forcibly sterilized, wrongly committed to mental institutions where they died in great numbers, prohibited from marrying, and sometimes even unmarried by state bureaucrats. In America, this battle to wipe out whole ethnic groups was fought not by armies with guns nor by hate sects at the margins. Rather, this pernicious white-gloved war was prosecuted by esteemed professors, elite universities, wealthy industrialists and government officials colluding in a racist, pseudoscientific movement called eugenics. The purpose: create a superior Nordic race.

EDWIN BLACK, *WAR AGAINST THE WEAK*, 2012

NOTHING HAS PROPELLED the abandonment of the Old Testament more than the theory of evolution which undermines the Biblical premise that man is made in the image and likeness of God, a teaching set forth in the very first chapter of Genesis.

If the Bible begins on such a false note, then the entire Pentateuch lacks credibility. The story of Adam and Eve becomes, at best, a moral allegory, and, at worst, a simple fable that arose from the desert tribes of ancient Mesopotamia.

Moreover, if the God of the Old Testament is not really the author and father of mankind, then man's spiritual nature—the fact that he can transcend matter by his very speech—testifies to the existence of a spiritual realm far removed from the workings of the Demiurge depicted in Genesis, who gave rise to the sad spectacle of human history.

THE BIRTH OF EUGENICS

In 1798 the English economist Thomas Malthus published "An Essay on the Principle of Population," in which he theorized that a finite or arithmetically growing food supply would limit the exponentially expanding human population, leading to catastrophic famines and wars. He advocated population control and even argued that, in many instances, charitable assistance continued generational poverty and consequently made little sense in the natural scheme of human progress.[1]

In the 1850s, agnostic English philosopher Herbert Spencer published *Social Statics,* in which he declared that human society was determined by the uncaring laws of science, not the will of a compassionate, powerful God. He popularized a new term, "survival of the fittest." Since the human race was evolving according to its inherited nature, the "fittest" would naturally thrive and advance society, while the "unfit" would become more impoverished. The suffering of the lower classes was the necessary result of the laws of nature. Spencer wrote: "The whole effort of nature is to get rid of such, and to make room for the better . . . If they are not sufficiently complete to live, they die, and it is best they should die."[2]

---

1 Thomas R. Malthus, *An Essay on the Principle of Population,* as selected by Donald Winch, Cambridge: Cambridge University Press, 1992, pp. 100-101.

2 Herbert Spencer, *Social Statics,* New York: Robert Schalkenback Foundation, reprint, 1970, pp. 58-60, 289-290, 339-340.

SOCIAL DARWINISM

In 1859, Charles Darwin published *On the Origin of Species*. His theory of natural selection described the survival competition of all living things in environments of limited resources and hostile predators. He made it clear that his theory "is the doctrine of Malthus applied with manifold force to the whole animal and vegetable kingdoms; for in this case, there can be no artificial increase of food, and no prudential restraint from marriage."[3]

Darwin was theorizing about the "natural world," but it wasn't long before leading thinkers were distilling the ideas of Malthus, Spencer, and Darwin into a new concept that they called "social Darwinism." Social planners rallied around the idea that in the struggle to survive in a harsh world, many individuals were less worthy and even destined to wither away as a natural part of progress.[4]

Such views rejected the Biblical view expressed in Genesis 1:26-27 ("Let us make man in our image, after our likeness. . . . So God created man in his own image, in the image of God he created him; male and female he created them") and the teaching that all human beings were created in God's image, thereby possessing inherent worth and value. But they attracted two admirers, who possessed an animus towards Judeo-Christian teachings: Karl Marx and Friedrich Engels.

EVOLUTION MELTS INTO MARXISM

With the publication of Darwin's theory, materialists like Marx and Engels could confidently claim they had an overarching explanation of the origins of all life on earth. It was not God, but random variation and natural selection which produced all species from single cells to the most complex self-conscious beings. The immutable forces of nature were the driving power of history and life.

---

3   Charles Darwin, *The Origin of the Species*, New York: D. Appleton & Co., 1881, chapter 3, p. 114.

4   Robert C. Bannister, *Social Darwinism: Science and Myth in Anglo-American Social Thought*, Philadelphia: Temple University Press, 1979, p. xii.

Only 1,250 copies of the first edition of *On the Origin of Species* were printed, and they all sold in one day. One of those who obtained a copy was Friedrich Engels, then living in Manchester.[5] Three weeks later, he wrote to Karl Marx: "Darwin, by the way, whom I'm reading just now, is absolutely splendid. There was one aspect of teleology that had yet to be demolished, and that has now been done. Never before has so grandiose an attempt been made to demonstrate historical evolution in Nature, and certainly never to such good effect."[6]

One year later Marx wrote that Darwin's writings effectively ended the need to consider design or purpose in the material world, as discussed in "metaphysics" or "teleology," since they could be attributed to purely material forces: "Darwin's work is most important and suits my purpose in that it provides a basis in natural science for the historical class struggle. . . . Despite all shortcomings, it is here that, for the first time, 'teleology' in natural science is not only dealt a mortal blow but its rational meaning is empirically explained."[7]

THE BASIS OF DIALECTICAL MATERIALISM

Although Darwin's own political views were far from radical, his insights were used as weapons in the battle to establish materialist "science" as the basis for Marx's dialectic understanding of the violent evolution of societies.[8] When Karl Marx published the second edition of his first volume of *Capital* in 1873, he sent a copy to Darwin inscribed "Mr.

---

5   Ian Angus, "Marx and Engels...and Darwin? The Essential Connection between Historical Materialism and Natural Selection," *International Socialist Review*, Issue #65, May 2009. https://isreview.org/issue/65/marx-and-engelsand-darwin

6   Karl Marx and Friedrich Engels, *Marx-Engels Collected Works, vol. 40* (Moscow: Progress Publishers, 1975), p. 441.

7   Karl Marx and Friedrich Engels, *Marx-Engels Collected Works, vol. 41,* (Moscow: Progress Publishers, 1975), pages 246-7. From Marx's letter to the German socialist Ferdinand Lasalle. https://isreview.org/issue/65/marx-and-engelsand-darwin

8   Angus, *"Marx and Engels...and Darwin?"*

Charles Darwin, On the part of his sincere admirer, Karl Marx."[9] In 1883, at Marx's funeral, Engels said, "Just as Darwin discovered the law of development of organic nature, so Marx discovered the law of development of human history."[10]

Marx, who was looking for a scientific, materialistic justification for revolution by the masses, found his answer in the notion of evolution. The idea of survival of the fittest could be appropriated for his purpose of justifying class struggle as the driving force of history. Even as the development of more advanced life forms was driven by naturalistic forces, Marx maintained that progress in the human realm was inexplicably always upward, driven by materialist forces and violent revolution.

In *Socialism: Utopian and Scientific,* Engels praised Darwin's victory in dealing "the metaphysical conception of Nature the heaviest blow," and replacing a conception that could include a non-material cause with one that sees dialectic and materialist forces as the source of evolutionary progress. He wrote:

> Nature works dialectically and not metaphysically . . . she does not move in the eternal oneness of a perpetually recurring circle, but goes through a real historical evolution. In this connection, Darwin must be named before all others. He dealt the metaphysical conception of Nature the heaviest blow by his proof that all organic beings, plants, animals, and man himself, are the products of a process of evolution going on through millions of years.[11]

THE RISE OF EUGENICS

Another influential movement enamored with the vision of "Social

---

9   Ben Waggoner, "Did Karl Marx send a copy of Das Kapital to Charles Darwin? If so, why?" *Quora,* Updated November 30, 2018, https://www.quora.com/Did-Karl-Marx-send-a-copy-of-Das-Kapital-to-Charles-Darwin-If-so-why

10 Karl Marx and Friedrich Engels, *Marx-Engels Collected Works*, vol. 40 (Moscow: Progress Publishers, 1975), p. 467.

11 Ibid., p. 301.

Darwinism" was the Eugenicists. The term "eugenics" was actually invented in 1883 by Francis Galton, Charles Darwin's cousin. He wanted to better the human race through propagating the British elite in large numbers and decreasing other "feeble-minded" peoples. The 1st International Eugenics Congress was held in London in 1912 and presided over by Charles Darwin's son, Major Leonard Darwin.[12]

Eugenics advocacy groups started in England, spread throughout Europe, but found their greatest reception in the United States in the early 1900s. A dedicated group of American sociologists, economists, physicians, scientists, and activists provided the intellectual momentum to institutionalize and organize the American eugenics movement. American believers such as Charles Davenport courted and convinced the rich to support the study and control of increasing human degeneracy.[13]

They founded the American Breeders Society in 1903 and also the Cold Springs Harbor Laboratory, Long Island, NY, which tracked millions of families for their genetic histories. The U.S. Supreme Court ruled in 1927 that forced sterilization of the handicapped does not violate the U.S. Constitution. Justice Oliver Wendall Holmes said, ". . . three generations of imbeciles are enough."[14]

HUMAN ZOOS

Very few people alive today know the sordid history of scientific racism in America. A new video documentary called *"Human Zoos"* describes this reality at the beginning of the 20th century:

---

12 Curators of The University of Missouri, *"Charles Davenport and the Eugenics Record Office,"* Controlling Heredity: The American Eugenics Crusade: 1870-1940, Revised March 16, 2012, https://library.missouri.edu/exhibits/eugenics/davenport.htm.

13 Ibid.

14 History.com Editors, *"Eugenics,"* History.com, A&E Television Networks, November 15, 2017, https://www.history.com/topics/germany/eugenics

In September 1906, nearly a quarter of a million people flocked to the Bronx Zoo in New York City. Many came for a startling new exhibit in the Zoo's Monkey House. But it wasn't a monkey they came to see. It was a man. His name was Ota Benga. A pygmy from the African Congo, Ota Benga was exhibited in a cage along with monkeys.

Benga was not alone. He was one of literally thousands of indigenous peoples who were put on public display throughout America in the early twentieth century. Often touted as "missing links" between man and apes and as examples of the "lower" stages of human evolution, these native peoples were harassed, demeaned, and jeered at. Their public display was arranged with the enthusiastic support of the most elite members of the scientific community, and it was promoted uncritically by America's leading newspapers. [15]

EUGENICAL STERILIZATION

By 1920, two years before the publication of Laughlin's influential "Eugenical Sterilization in the United States (1922)," 3,200 individuals across the country were reported to have been involuntarily sterilized. That number tripled by 1929, and by 1938 more than 30,000 people were claimed to have met this fate. More than half of the states adopted Laughlin's law, with California, Virginia, and Michigan leading the sterilization campaign. [16]

The U.S. Federal Government, state governments, and wealthy institutions contributed to this racism until well after World War II, as documented by Edwin Black:

---

15   John G. West, *Human Zoos: America's Forgotten History of Scientific Racism,* (Written and directed by John G. West and edited by Rachel Adams. Released Aug. 28, 2018. 55 min.) HumanZoos.Org, https://humanzoos.org/synopsis/. Above text from the film summary. (Accessed January 29, 2019)

16   Philip K. Wilson, *Eugenics,* (Chicago, *Encyclopedia Britannica,* Genetics, 2019) https://www. britannica.com/science/eugenics-genetics

Elements of the philosophy were enshrined as national policy by forced sterilization and segregation laws, as well as marriage restrictions, enacted in twenty-seven states. In 1909, California became the third state to adopt such laws. Ultimately, eugenics practitioners coercively sterilized some 60,000 Americans, barred the marriage of thousands, forcibly segregated thousands in "colonies," and persecuted untold numbers in ways we are just learning. Before World War II, nearly half of coercive sterilizations were done in California, and even after the war, the state accounted for a third of all such surgeries.[17]

Black goes on to incriminate the Carnegie Institution, the Rockefeller Foundation, and the Harriman railroad fortune as funding scientific racism. In 1904, the Carnegie Institution established a laboratory complex at Cold Spring Harbor on Long Island that stockpiled millions of index cards on ordinary Americans, as researchers carefully plotted the removal of families, bloodlines, and whole peoples.[18]

THE "UNFIT" AND THE "FIT"

Probably the most infamous eugenicist is Margaret Sanger, founder of Planned Parenthood. One can see in her own words that "the unbalance between the birth rate of the 'unfit' and the 'fit'" was "the greatest present menace to civilization."[19] Sanger went on to list the groups that needed to be eliminated:

Feeble-minded persons, epileptics, idiots, imbeciles, insane people, tubercular, those with any loathsome or contagious disease, paupers,

---

17   Edwin Black, "Eugenics and the Nazis—the California Connection," *San Francisco Chronicle*, November 9, 2003, Page D–1. http://www.hartford-hwp.com/archives/45/299.html.

18   Edwin Black, *War Against the Weak: Eugenics and America's Campaign to Create a Master Race*, Washington, DC, Dialog Press; Expanded edition, April 30, 2012, xviii.

19   Margaret Sanger, "The Eugenic Value of Birth Control Propaganda," New York University, *The Public Writings and Speeches of Margaret Sanger*, October, 1921, https://www.nyu.edu/projects/sanger/webedition/app/documents/show.php?sangerDoc=238946.xml

professional beggars, those likely to become a public charge, criminals, prostitutes, or for purposes of prostitution in any form; illiterates, those over 16 years unable to read English or any other language—all are refused admission and procedure for the enforcement of these measures is mandatory. I think it is good legislation. Unfortunately, it is merely negative and not selective legislation…

If it is necessary to keep such types out of the country why is it not just as important to stop their breeding?[20]

Birth Control does not mean contraception indiscriminately practiced. It means the release and cultivation of the better elements in our society, and the gradual suppression, elimination and eventual extinction, of defective stocks—those human weeds which threaten the blooming of the finest flowers of American civilization.[21]

While I personally believe in the sterilization of the feeble-minded, the insane and syphilitic, I have not been able to discover that these measures are more than superficial deterrents when applied to the constantly growing stream of the unfit.[22]

This distinction between the fit, the somewhat fit, and the completely unfit bore a strong resemblance to the writings of Marcion and Valentinus, who placed all of humanity in three water-tight categories, the elect or the Illuminated, who possessed true knowledge (*gnosis*) and a strong spark of divinity within them; the psychics, who were capable of

---

20 Margaret Sanger, "The Necessity for Birth Control," New York University, *The Public Writings and Speeches of Margaret Sanger*, December 19, 1928, https://www.nyu.edu/projects/sanger/webedition/app/documents/show.php?sangerDoc=129046.xml.

21 Margaret Sanger, "High Lights in the History of Birth Control," New York University, *The Public Writings and Speeches of Margaret Sanger*, October 1923, https://www.nyu.edu/projects/sanger/webedition/app/documents/show.php?sangerDoc=306641.xml

22 Margaret Sanger, "Birth Control and Racial Betterment," New York University, *The Public Writings and Speeches of Margaret Sanger*, February 1919, https://www.nyu.edu/projects/sanger/webedition/app/documents/show.php?sangerDoc=143449.xml

obtaining salvation; and the vast majority of humanity who ate, drank, married, and died eternally.[23]

THE GERM PLASM

"Feeblemindedness" was a very broad category of deplorables including members of races (like blacks) who were considered by Darwinian biologists of the time to be "lower" on the evolutionary scale. "Feebleminded" persons could appear perfectly normal to everyone else. That's why they were so dangerous, according to eugenicists. The feeble-minded could appear so ordinary that non-feebleminded persons might marry them and then spread their defective "germ plasm to the next generation."[24]

Sanger and other eugenicists argued that the feeble-minded must be prevented from reproducing through compulsory sterilization. Black writes about ". . . simple mountain people (who) were systematically sterilized under a Virginia law compelling such operations for those ruled unfit. . . ." He continues as follows:

> Often, the teenage boys and girls placed under the surgeon's knife did not really comprehend the ramifications. Sometimes they were told that they were undergoing an appendectomy or some other unspecified procedure. Generally, they were released after the operation. Many of the victims did not discover why they could not bear children until decades later when the truth was finally revealed to them by local Virginia investigative reporters and government reformers. . . ."[25]

---

23 W. H. C. Frend, *The Early Church* (Philadelphia: J. P. Lippincott, 1966), p. 65.

24 John G. West, *Darwin Day In America: How Our Politics and Culture Have Been Dehumanized in the Name of Science* (Wilmington, DE: Intercollegiate Studies Institute; November, 2007), p. 134.

25 *The Lynchburg Story,* dir. Stephen Trombley, prod. Bruce Eadie, Worldview Pictures, 1993, videocassette, as discussed in Edwin Black, *War Against the Weak: Eugenics and America's Campaign to Create a Master Race,* p. 4.

Black goes on to describe a woman who was sterilized at age eleven:

Mary Donald was equally pained when she recalled her years of anguish following her sterilization at Lynchburg when she was only eleven. Several years later, she was "released" to her husband-to-be, and then enjoyed a good marriage for eighteen years. But "he loved kids," she remembered, "I lay in bed and cried because I couldn't give him a son," she recounted in her heavily accented but articulate mountain drawl. "You know, men want a son to carry on their name. He said it didn't matter, But as years went by, he changed. We got divorced and he married someone else." With these words, Mary broke down and wept. [26]

HITLER'S INSPIRATION

The American eugenics campaign of mass sterilization and involuntary incarceration of "defectives" came to the attention of Adolf Hitler in Germany decades after it was initiated in America. Prior to World War II, the Nazis practiced eugenics with the open approval of eugenics advocates in the U.S.[27] As Joseph DeJarnette, superintendent of Virginia's Western State Hospital, stated in 1934, "Hitler is beating us at our own game."[28]

Hitler proudly told his comrades how closely he followed American eugenic legislation. "Now that we know the laws of heredity," he told a fellow Nazi, "it is possible to a large extent to prevent unhealthy and severely handicapped beings from coming into the world. I have studied with interest the laws of several American states concerning prevention of reproduction by people whose progeny would, in all probability, be of no value or be injurious to the racial stock."[29]

---

26   Ibid.

27   Edwin Black, *War Against the Weak: Eugenics and America's Campaign to Create a Master Race*, p. 7.

28   "Delegates Urge Wider Practice of Sterilization," *Richmond Times-Dispatch*, January 16, 1934.

29   Ibid.

EVOLUTIONARY ZEALOTS

Government resources and huge institutions have financed the Darwinian cause. The results are predictable. The "science is settled" argument has been invoked as a way to end many discussions of scientific importance.[30] It also carries with it the psychological hammer of coercion by bullying any dissent from the established orthodoxy. It should be noted that this is not faithfulness to the Scientific Method.

Ultimately, Darwinism became a well-entrenched and even unchallengeable dogma. Schools refused to allow for any ideas that were not materialistic. The following is the policy statement on evolution from the website of the National Association of Biology Teachers:

> Evolutionary biology rests on the same scientific methodologies the rest of science uses, appealing only to natural events and processes to describe and explain phenomena in the natural world. Science teachers must reject calls to account for the diversity of life or describe the mechanisms of evolution by invoking non-naturalistic or supernatural notions, whether called "creation science," "scientific creationism," "intelligent design theory," or similar designations. Ideas such as these are outside the scope of science and should not be presented as part of the science curriculum. These notions do not adhere to the shared scientific standards of evidence gathering and interpretation.[31]

In other words, instead of evaluating contrarian ideas based on the quality of their evidence, students must ignore ideas and evidence that conflict with their preconceived dogmas.

If natural law is "survival of the fittest" and the end goal of history

---

30 Martin Cothran, "Science's Useful Fallacy," Memoria Press, https://www.memoriapress.com/articles/sciences-useful-fallacy/

31 National Association of Biology Teachers, *"NABT Position Statement on Teaching Evolution,"* Accessed: Jan. 29, 2019, https://nabt.org/Position-Statements-NABT-Position-Statement-on-Teaching-Evolution

is going to be a more advanced race, then it becomes the right and even the responsibility of the evolved elite to help the process along. Given ongoing widespread fears about overpopulation, akin to Malthusian beliefs in the 19th century, the Global Community organization advocates sharp reductions in global population:

> The Global Community proposes a tight global policy, benignly implemented, or it will be very nasty indeed. In practice, a human population of 10 to 12 billion would be too uncomfortably high and would add a high strain on world resources. What kind of world population would be reasonable? What goal should we aim at? A population should be small enough to be sustainable indefinitely and still allow plenty of leeway for ourselves and other lifeforms. It should also be large enough to allow the formation of healthy civilizations. We propose a world population of 500 million.[32]

Given that such elitists openly assert that 500 million is their preferred world population and the current world population approaches 7.7 billion people,[33] fifteen of every sixteen humans would have to be somehow eliminated, clear enough evidence that Social Darwinism and Eugenics beliefs are alive and well in the second decade of the 21st century.

EUGENIC GNOSTICS

These beliefs have gained renewed impetus by the resurgence of Gnosticism, since the followers of Marcion and Valentinus believed that procreation would only serve the evil Demiurge who fashioned this vale of tears. They encouraged their followers to desist from acts of sexual congress and advocated a policy of zero population growth.[34]

---

32   The Global Community, "Our Overpopulated Planet," GlobalCommunityWebNet.com, Global Dialog, 2007, http://globalcommunitywebnet.com/globalcommunity/overpopulatedplanet.htm

33   http://www.worldometers.info/world-population/ , accessed March 4, 2019.

34   Frend, *The Early Church*, p. 65.

This attitude was reflected as follows by Roy Scranton in his op-ed piece of July 26, 2018 for *The New York Times*:

> I cried two times when my daughter was born. First for joy, when after 27 hours of labor the little feral being we'd made came yowling into the world, and the second for sorrow, holding the earth's newest human and looking out the window with her at the rows of cars in the hospital parking lot, the strip mall across the street, the box stores and drive-throughs and drainage ditches and asphalt and waste fields that had once been oak groves. A world of extinction and catastrophe, a world in which harmony with nature had long been foreclosed.
>
> My partner and I had, in our selfishness, doomed our daughter to life on a dystopian planet, and I could see no way to shield her from the future.[35]

Marcion would have been hard-pressed to state the Gnostic view of the world in a more compelling manner.

---

35 Roy Scranton, https://www.nytimes.com/2018/07/16/opinion/climate-change-parenting.html

15

THE SANCTITY OF LIFE

Before I formed you in the womb I knew you, and before you were born I consecrated you; I appointed you a prophet to the nations.

JEREMIAH 1:5

But even though one of them should accidentally implant the seed of his natural emission prematurely and the woman becomes pregnant, listen to a more dreadful thing that such people venture to do. They extract the fetus at the stage which is appropriate for their enterprise, take this aborted infant, and cut it up in a trough with a pestle. And they mix honey, pepper, and certain other perfumes and spices with it to keep from getting sick, and then all the revelers in this [herd] of swine and dogs assemble, and each eats a piece of the child with his fingers. And now, after this cannibalism, they pray to God and say, "We were not mocked by the archon of lust, but have gathered the brother's blunder up!" And this, if you please, is their idea of the "Perfect Passover."

EPIPHANIUS, "GNOSTICS," PANARION 26.5,4-6, AD 375

EARLY CHRISTIANS INHERITED the Judaic belief in the innate dignity of life in the womb. In this way, they separated themselves from surrounding pagan cultures by rejecting abortion and infanticide.[1] Both ancient Romans and Greeks were tolerant of abortion, and accepted the argument that a fetus did not become formed and begin to live until at least forty days after conception for a male, and around eighty days for a female. Aristotle had written: ". . . when couples have children in excess, let abortion be procured before sense and life have begun; what may or may not be lawfully done in these cases depends on the question of life and sensation. . . ."[2]

In the ancient world, undesirable children were frequently abandoned in a practice called "exposure."[3] The choice to discard one's children was the legal right of the head of the household in the Roman Empire, and was usually made within the first eight days of the baby's life. Greek philosopher Plutarch had taught that until that time, the child was more akin to vegetation than an actual human.[4] In some parts of the Roman Empire, abortion and killing infants was so common that populations decreased as a result.[5]

A.R. Colon explains that exposure was practiced by both the rich and poor for a myriad of reasons: "An infant could be abandoned without penalty or social stigma for many reasons, including an anomalous appearance, being an illegitimate child or grandchild or a child of

---

1   Fr. William Saunders, "The Sanctity of Human Life," *Catholic Education Resource Center*, 2003, https://www.catholiceducation.org/en/culture/catholic-contributions/the-sanctity-of-human-life.html

2   Aristotle, *Politics, Book VII, Classic Wisdom Weekly*, https://classicalwisdom.com/greek_books/politics-by-aristotle-book-vii/7/

3   N.S. Gill, "Roman Exposure of Infants," *ThoughtCo.*, February 2, 2019, https://www.thoughtco.com/roman-exposure-of-infants-118370

4   John Ortberg, *Who Is This Man?* (Grand Rapids, Michigan: Zondervan, 2012), p. 28.

5   William P. Saunders, "Church Has Always Condemned Abortion," *The Arlington Catholic Herald*, September 19, 2016, https://www.catholicherald.com/News/Church_Has_Always_Condemned_Abortion/

infidelity, family poverty, parental conflict, or being one of too many children. Sometimes they were given to friends, but more often than not they were abandoned to the elements, and death resulted from hypoglycemia and hypothermia. Sometimes the infant was devoured by the dogs that scavenged public places. . . ."[6]

Early Christians worked against infanticide by prohibiting its members from practicing it and by providing relief for the poor through taking in babies who had been left to die by their pagan parents. Political protection of the newborn began with edicts passed by Trajan in AD 103, and continued with Constantine, due to his conversion to Christianity, in the early part of the fourth century. The killing of infants was made illegal in AD 374, thanks to a proclamation by Emperor Valentinian.[7]

The *Didache,* considered one of the earliest authoritative documents of Christianity, describes the way of life and the way of death. The way of life demands that Christians "shall not murder a child by abortion nor commit infanticide."[8] Christians were forbidden to murder any child, born or unborn. The second-century Christian apologist Tertullian, one of the formative figures in the development of Christianity, was adamantly against abortion. He wrote: "It is not permissible for us to destroy the seed by means of illicit manslaughter once it has been conceived in the womb, so long as blood remains in the person."[9] Tertullian cited Jeremiah to make the claim that we must preserve the life that God has already sanctified in the womb:

6   Ibid.

7   "Roman vs. Christian Treatment of Children," https://ntbc.wordpress.com/roman-vs-christian-treatment-of-children/

8   Tim Sauder (translator), *Didache,* 2, https://davidmathiraj.files.wordpress.com/2012/12/didache-01.pdf

9   Tertullian, *Apologia,* cap 25, line 4, http://www.priestsforlife.org/magisterium/earlychurchfathers/tertullian.html

Thus, you read the word of God, spoken to Jeremias: "Before I formed thee in the womb, I knew thee." If God forms us in the womb, He also breathes on us as He did in the beginning: "And God formed man and breathed into him the breath of life." Nor could God have known man in the womb unless he were a whole man. "And before thou camest forth from the womb, I sanctified thee." Was it, then, a dead body at that stage? Surely it was not, for "God is the God of the living and not the dead."[10]

Athenagoras, Hippolytus, Basil the Great, Ambrose, Jerome, and John Chrysostom were among many other church fathers who were also adamantly anti-abortion.[11]

THE QUESTION OF ENSOULMENT

Augustine accepted Aristotle's belief regarding the progression of life in the womb: human beings began in a vegetative or plant-like existence, progressed to an animal soul, and finally gained a human soul. Nevertheless, Augustine denounced the procedure of abortion: "No woman should take drugs for purposes of abortion, nor should she kill her children that have been conceived or are already born. If anyone does this, she should know that before Christ's tribunal she will have to plead her case in the presence of those she has killed."[12]

The mistaken biological theories of Aristotle never changed the early Church's sentiment that abortion was deeply sinful at every stage. Abortion in the beginning stages of pregnancy was viewed as attacking a being who was being prepared by God to receive an eternal soul (e.g. Psalm 139:13-1).

---

10   Tertullian, *De Anima*, 26.5, http://www.priestsforlife.org/magisterium/earlychurchfathers/
        tertullian.html

11   Albert Mohler, "The Real Story of Christianity and Abortion," *Table Talk, September 2017.*

12   Rollin Grams, "The Christian Church's Stance on Abortion," *Bible and Mission*, May 4, 2017,
        https://bibleandmission.blogspot.com/2017/05/the-christian-churchs-stance-on-abortion.html

Thirteenth-century theologian Thomas Aquinas drew heavily on Aristotle's thought in his writings, including the ancient Greek philosopher's theory that the rational human soul is absent in the first few weeks of pregnancy. Nonetheless, Aquinas considered abortion to be a serious transgression at every stage, stating that it is a sin "against nature" to reject God's gift of a new life. Although some church penalties were more punitive for an abortion performed after "ensoulment," abortion at all stages continued to be seen as a grave moral evil.[13]

While the debate on when the soul enters the body continued during the ensuing centuries, the Protestant Reformers maintained a strong stance against all abortion. In his *Commentary on Genesis*, Martin Luther noted: "How great, therefore, the wickedness of human nature is! How many girls there are who prevent conception and kill and expel tender fetuses, although procreation is the work of God! Indeed, some spouses who marry and live together in a respectable manner have various ends in mind, but rarely children." The God who declares that we are to be fruitful and multiply regards it as a great evil when human beings destroy their offspring.[14]

Echoing Luther, John Calvin in his commentary on Exodus 21:22, wrote:

". . .the unborn, though enclosed in the womb of his mother, is already a human being, and it is an almost monstrous crime to rob it of life which it has not yet begun to enjoy. If it seems more horrible to kill a man in his own house than in a field, because a man's house is his most secure place of refuge, it ought surely to be deemed more atrocious to destroy the unborn in the womb before it has come to light."[15]

---

13 "History of Church Teaching on Abortion," *US Bishops Issue Fact Sheet,* September 4, 2008, http://catholic-church.org/ejtyler/catholic_life/Abortion.html

14 Luther, Martin, *Commentary on Genesis, Vol. I: Luther on the Creation* (Project Gutenberg Ebook #48193, 2015).

15 Calvin, John, *Commentaries on the Four Last Books of Moses* (Ulan Press, San Bernardino, California, 2012), p. 18.

ROE V. WADE

While abortion has been regularly performed throughout the history of the United States, and was legal in several states until the Supreme Court's decision in 1973, it was traditionally considered shameful and not something to flaunt. The 1973 *Roe v. Wade* Supreme Court ruling established abortion as a constitutional right and therefore mandated that it be made available in all states. *Roe* received significant criticism in the legal community,[16] with the decision being widely seen as an extreme form of judicial activism.[17]

In the 1973 issue of the *Yale Law Journal*,[18] the American legal scholar John Hart Ely criticized *Roe* as a decision that "is not constitutional law and gives almost no sense of an obligation to try to be." Ely added: "What is frightening about *Roe* is that this super-protected right is not inferable from the language of the Constitution, the framers' thinking respecting the specific problem in issue, any general value derivable from the provisions they included, or the nation's governmental structure." Harvard Law Professor Laurence Tribe had similar thoughts: "One of the most curious things about *Roe* is that, behind its own verbal smokescreen, the substantive judgment on which it rests is nowhere to be found."[19]

THE CHURCH WEAKENS

Historically, the Roman Catholic church has maintained one of the

---

16 Roger Dworkin, *Limits: The Role of the Law in Biomedical Decision Making* (Indianapolis: Indiana University Press, 1996), pp. 28-36.

17 Linda Greenhouse, *Becoming Justice Blackmun: Harry Blackmun's Supreme Court Journey.* (New York: Times Books, 2005), pp. 135-6.

18 Ely, John Hart. "The Wages of Crying Wolf, 82 *Yale Law Journal* 920 (1973), https:// digitalcommons.law.yale.edu/cgi/viewcontent.cgi?referer=&httpsredir=1&article=5116&context =fss_papers

19 Tribe, Laurence (1973). "The Supreme Court, 1972 Term – Foreword: Toward a Model of Roles in the Due Process of Life and Law." *Harvard Law Review.* 87, p. 7.

strongest anti-abortion stances, opposing the procedure under nearly all circumstances. Abortion is considered a sin meriting excommunication, and pro-choice stances are rejected in many traditional Catholic communities. A large percentage of ordinary churchgoers and church officials, however, are willing to accept a more permissive attitude towards abortion. In the United States, many priests have been granted authority to give absolution for abortion, an act once reserved solely for bishops. Nearly half of U.S. Catholics believe abortion should be legal in all or nearly all cases, according to data from a 2014 Pew Research Center study.[20]

PROTESTANTS AND ABORTION

Since *Roe v. Wade,* a number of Protestant churches have weakened their stance against abortion. Following the 1973 ruling, the United Methodist Church began to support a woman's choice to abort under safe medical procedures. Over the next 40 years, the UMC continued to debate and reconsider their position on abortion. In 2018, the church proposed to amend their mission statement to "recognize tragic conflicts of life that might justify abortion." Rather than using the word "abortion," the church has substituted the term "reproductive health." Additionally, the statement no longer discusses the sanctity of preborn life, nor the alarming recent increase in abortions.[21]

Similarly, the United Church of Christ has adopted the expression "reproductive justice" to describe its support of a woman's right to have an abortion. In 2016, UCC activists applauded the U.S. Supreme Court ruling to deny Texas limitations to abortion that would have shut down nearly 80 percent of abortion clinics in the state. The Court ruled

---

20   Weston Williams, "Has Pope Francis Softened the Catholic Stance on Abortion?," *Christian Science Monitor,* November 21, 2016, https://www.csmonitor.com/World/Europe/2016/1121/Has-Pope-Francis-softened-the-Catholic-stance-on-abortion

21   Katie Anderson, "United Methodist New Belief: We Support Legal Access to Abortion," *Human Defense,* August 30, 2018, https://humandefense.com/united-methodist-church-proposes-new-belief-we-support-legal-access-to-abortion/

unconstitutional the 2013 Texas law banning abortions after 20 weeks of pregnancy, requiring abortion clinics to meet the same standards as hospital-style surgical centers, and mandating that a doctor have admitting privileges at a hospital within 30 miles of the facility where he or she performs abortions.[22]

UCC pastor Rev. John Dorhauer commended the Supreme Court ruling which struck down the Texan law by writing: "As a longtime advocate for women's reproductive health, and now as the general minister and president of a denomination whose longstanding support for the same is deep and rich, I celebrate this decision. I recognize it as a crucial victory in the ongoing battle to protect a woman's constitutional right to maintain control of her body and her reproductive health."[23]

Three years prior to *Roe v. Wade,* the Presbyterian Church USA published a study which described abortion as being a helpful aid for unwanted pregnancies; phrases such as "personal choice" and "responsible decision" regarding abortion began to appear in ecclesiastical reports. In the early 1980s, Presbyterians approved a policy which asserted that abortion was a "stewardship responsibility"; many Presbyterians today earnestly support the Religious Coalition for Reproductive Choice.[24]

JEWS AND ABORTION

While Jews have divergent views on a wide range of topics, on abortion they are essentially united. According to a 2012 survey released by the Public Religion Research Institute (PRRI), 93% of American Jews support some manner of legalized abortion. In addition, Jews are the sole group

---

22 Manny Fernandez, "Abortion Restrictions Become Law in Texas, but Opponents Will Press Fight," *New York Times,* July 18, 2013.

23 Ernest L. Ohlhoff, "Abortion: Where Do the Churches Stand?'" http://www.pregnantpause.org/people/wherchur.htm

24 "Abortion/Reproductive Choice Issues," *Presbyterian Church USA/Presbyterian Mission,* February 23, 2016, https://www.presbyterianmission.org/blog/2016/02/23/abortion-issues-2/

surveyed by PRRI in which a plurality support abortion in *every* case.[25]

Nevertheless, two large Orthodox Jewish religious organizations, the Rabbinical Council of America (RCA) and Agudath Israel of America, released a statement condemning the January 2019 New York state law legalizing late-term abortions: "Jewish law opposes abortion, except in cases of danger to the mother. Most authorities consider feticide an act of murder; others deem it an act akin to the murder of potential life. The RCA maintains that 'abortion on demand,' even before twenty-four weeks from the commencement of pregnancy, is forbidden There is no sanction to permit the abortion of a healthy fetus when the mother's life is not endangered."[26]

Although some Orthodox women protest this conservative stance, Jewish tradition teaches that a human fetus has status and dignity, and that abortion is prohibited in the vast majority of pregnancies.[27]

WHEN DOES LIFE BEGIN?

In the early 1970s, most supporters of abortion believed that the embryo or developing fetus consisted of nothing more than a clump of cells. But now doctors have extensive information regarding the development of human life in the womb. By the first month, the baby's heart is beating approximately 113 beats per minute. By the eighth week, the kidneys, liver, brain, and lungs are all beginning to function. The fingers and toes are separate and the *external* genitalia are formed.[28] A baby can suck its thumb as early as twelve weeks.[29]

---

25   Roger Price, "The Curious Consensus of Jews on Abortion," *Judaism and Science*, January 10, 2013, https://www.judaism and science.com/the-curious-consensus-of-jews-on-abortion/

26   Sales, Ben, "Orthodox Rabbis Compare Abortion to Murder—and Orthodox Women Are Angry about It," *Jewish Telegraph Agency*, January 31, 2019, https://www.jta.org/2019/01/31/culture/orthodox-groups-come-out-swinging-against-new-yorks-abortion-law

27   Ibid.

28   Stephanie Watson, "How Pregnancy Works," *How Stuff Works*, https://health.howstuffworks.com/pregnancy-and-parenting/pregnancy/conception/pregnancy2.htm

29   MNS, "15 Mind-Blowing Things Babies Can Do In The Womb" *WOW,* September 2, 2016, https://www.babygaga.com/15-mind-blowing-things-babies-can-do-in-the-womb/

In 1981, a U.S. Senate judiciary subcommittee requested medical professionals to testify to a special committee regarding the beginning of human life. During the hearings, Dr. Alfred M. Bongiovanni, professor of pediatrics and obstetrics at the University of Pennsylvania, stated:

> I have learned from my earliest medical education that human life begins at the time of conception. . . I submit that human life is present throughout this entire sequence from conception to adulthood and that any interruption at any point throughout this time constitutes a termination of human life. . .I am no more prepared to say that these early stages [of development in the womb] represent an incomplete human being than I would be to say that the child prior to the dramatic effects of puberty...is not a human being. This is human life at every stage. . . .[30]

In March 2017, the American College of Pediatricians released the following statement:

> The predominance of human biological research confirms that human life begins at conception—fertilization. At fertilization, the human being emerges as a whole, genetically distinct, individuated zygotic living human organism, a member of the species Homo sapiens, needing only the proper environment in order to grow and develop. The difference between the individual in its adult stage and in its zygotic stage is one of form, not nature. This statement focuses on the scientific evidence of when an individual human life begins.[31]

---

30 Randy Alcorn, "Scientists Attest to Life Beginning at Conception," *eternal perspective ministries*, March 8, 2010, https://www.epm.org/resources/2010/Mar/8/scientists-attest-life-beginning-conception/

31 "When Human Life Begins," *American College of Pediatricians*, March 2017, https://www.acpeds.org/the-college-speaks/position-statements/life-issues/when-human-life-begins

In the 21st century, a majority of U.S. doctors and medical experts have come to the conclusion that human life begins at conception.[32] Irish professor William Reville, from the University College Cork explains:

> An individual human life begins at conception when a sperm cell from the father fuses with an egg cell from the mother, to form a new cell, the zygote, the first embryonic stage. . . The zygote is the start of a biological continuum that automatically grows and develops, passing gradually and sequentially through the stages we call fetus, baby, child, adult, old person and ending eventually in death. The full genetic instructions to guide the development of the continuum, in interaction with its environment, are present in the zygote. Every stage along the continuum is biologically human and each point along the continuum has the full human properties appropriate to that point. . . .[33]

Ashley Montague, a geneticist and professor at Harvard and Rutgers, is not a supporter of the anti-abortion movement. Nevertheless, he maintains: "The basic fact is simple: life begins not at birth, but conception."[34] This scientific conclusion, however, appears to have done little to prevent increasingly liberal pro-choice legislation.

LEGALIZED INFANTICIDE

The Reproductive Health Act (RHA), a New York state statute, which was passed on January 22, 2019, pushes the "abortion envelope" even further than Roe v. Wade. The RHA allows for:

---

32   Katherine Weber, Majority of US Doctors Believe Pregnancy Begins at Conception, According to Survey, November 18, 2011, https://www.christianpost.com/news/majority-of-us-doctors-believe-pregnancy-begins-at-conception-according-to-survey.html

33   William Reville, "Opinion Letters," *Independent,* January 20, 2013, https://www.independent.ie/opinion/letters/embryo-starts-the-continuum-of-life-28960991.html

34   Ashley Montague, *Life Before Birth* (New York: Signet Books, 1977), p. vi.

- Late-term abortions for the "life and health of the mother." The word "health" is now a subjective term open to a wide variety of interpretations.

- The removal of the requirement that abortionists be licensed doctors. Now, nurse practitioners, physician assistants, and others are able to carry out abortions.[35]

- Taking away safeguards for accidental live births. An infant who has remained alive during an abortion can now be murdered outside the womb.

- Removing punishment for illegal and involuntary abortions, such as when a criminal attempts to cause a miscarriage by drugs or physical violence against a mother.[36]

The new law states: "The New York Constitution and United States Constitution protect a woman's fundamental right to access safe, legal abortion…" The term "fundamental right" bears special significance in the philosophy of law. Naming abortion as "a fundamental right" could nullify an individual's right of conscience or religious freedom. This new protocol could be used as a tool to stifle pro-life and religious groups, and coerce physicians and health professionals to execute abortions despite their personal beliefs.[37]

Shortly after the RHA bill was passed, abortion supporters in Virginia, Vermont, and Rhode Island began promoting comparable legislation. At this writing, there are eight states that have no gestational limits on

---

35 Nurses and midwives have been in training to perform abortions by organizations such as the Clinton Health Access Initiave, Partners in Health, Planned Parenthood, and Ivy League schools for over two decades.

36 "Cuomo, Hillary Clinton push to expand late-term abortion in New York with state Legislature," *The Guardian,* January 17, 2019, https://www.texasrighttolife.com/cuomo-hillary-clinton-push-to-expand-late-term-abortion-in-new-york-with-state-legislature/

37 Ibid.

abortion: Alaska, Colorado, New Hampshire, New Jersey, New Mexico, Oregon, Vermont, and New York, along with Washington, D.C.[38]

Ending the lives of unborn babies in the third trimester indicates that the aim of the abortion lobby is not the protection of maternal health in circumstances of hazardous pregnancy, but is rather the right to destroy an unwanted child whose existence poses no risk to maternal health. The only motivation to terminate a late-term pregnancy is that the woman (or someone who is pressuring her to abort) wants the child to be dead rather than alive. Dr. Omar Hamada, former chief medical officer at Advon Healthcare, has delivered more than 2,500 babies. He shared on social media one day after the Reproductive Health Act was passed: "I want to clear something up so that there is absolutely no doubt. There's not a single fetal or maternal condition that requires third trimester abortion. Not one. Delivery, yes. Abortion, no. There is absolutely no medical reason to kill a near term or term infant. For any reason."[39]

Having an abortion reverses the fundamental maternal principle of mother as protector and provider. Rather than sacrificing herself for the sake of her child's well-being, women sacrifice the life of their child for a variety of reasons; having a baby would interfere with their education, their work, or their ability to care for dependents. Women also cite economic difficulties, relationship problems, and simple lack of readiness.[40]

---

38   Melissa Barnhart, "7 states already allow abortion up to birth—not just New York," *The Christian Post*, January 30, 2019, https://www.christianpost.com/news/7-states-already-allow-abortion-up-to-birth-not-just-new-york.html

39   Heather Clark, "OB/GYNs, Nurses Speak Out Against NY Abortion Law: It Is Never Necessary to Kill Baby for Health, Life of Mother," *Christian News*, January 28, 2019, https://christiannews.net/2019/01/28/ob-gyns-nurses-speak-out-against-ny-abortion-law-it-is-never-necessary-to-kill-baby-for-health-life-of-mother/

40   Lawrence B. Finer, Lori F. Frohwirth, Lindsay A. Dauphinee, Susheela Singhand, Ann M. Moore, "Reasons U.S. Women Have Abortions: Quantitative and Qualitative Perspectives," *Perspectives on Sexual and Reproductive Health*, 2005, 37(3):110.

BUCKETS OF BABY PARTS

Though not widely publicized, pathologists have been traumatized as a result of being required to deal with the remains of dead babies sent to them from abortion clinics. In a YouTube testimony, one young female pathologist who identified herself only as "Dr. B" recounted the horror she felt being presented with "buckets and buckets of dead baby parts" that she was forced to examine while working in a hospital.[41] One pathologist identifying himself as "Andy Milonakis," wrote on social media:

> . . . We get a fair number of fragmented fetuses from abortion pro-
> cedures and they come in a container with formalin. The fact that
> they're all hacked up is disturbing to begin with. . . . One incident
> really freaked me, it was a boy fetus, at least 3+ pounds, around 24+
> weeks. It sat decomposing because the rest of the staff was AFRAID
> of it, I'm not joking. Then the chief of staff told me to deal with it
> because I was the FNG (f-kcin new guy) so I went to work. Pulled
> out 2 well-formed arms and then the torso, headless. The head was at
> the bottom of the container, when I pulled it, he had this expression
> of such utter horror it flipped me wayyyy out, my PA saw it and ran
> literally left work and went on disability (I'm serious here). It was like
> a headless screaming baby, like it had been born at least for a split
> second to realize it was screwed and let out one agonal yelp…I'm
> not joking. . . . [42]

PROFITING FROM FETAL TISSUE

Selling fetal tissue has proven lucrative for the abortion industry. Through its National Institutes of Health division, the U.S. Department

---

41   "Powerful testimony of Dr. B ex-atheist pathologist," https://www.youtube.com/watch?v=eJ8_
     m5R8eR0, accessed May 20, 2019.

42   Van Maren, Jonathon, "What Happens to Unborn Babies After Abortion? Pathologists
     Share the Horrors," *Lifenews.com*, October 23, 2013, https://www.lifenews.com/2013/10/23/
     what-happens-to-unborn-babies-after-abortion-pathologists-share-the-horrors/

of Health and Human Services (HHS) spends $100 million in taxpayer money annually on projects using fetal organs and tissues from abortions. In 2017, $20 million of federal funds was spent on fetal experimentation being conducted in government facilities owned and operated by HHS.[43]

Advanced Bioscience Resources, Inc. (ABR) has served as one of the main suppliers of fetal tissue to Health and Human Services. ABR has worked closely with abortion clinics across the country, and is one of the oldest wholesalers of aborted fetal body parts in the United States. Founded in 1989, ABR has made tens of millions of dollars in transactions over freshly aborted baby body parts. ABR profits by harvesting and purchasing tiny livers, lungs, and brains from healthy fetuses terminated at 4, 5, and 6 months in abortion clinics, and re-sells the body parts to taxpayer-funded research laboratories at huge mark-up prices. Organs, tissues, and cells are stitched into rodents to create so-called "humanized mice." Supporters of these chimeric procedures argue that researchers have been able to find new therapies and drugs for human immune systems and blood disorders. They contend that by implanting freshly aborted baby hearts, lungs, livers, and brains into laboratory rodents, the fields of hematology and immunology have benefited greatly.[44]

The Center for Medical Progress (CMP), founded by David Daleiden, interacted extensively with the leadership of ABR on several occasions from 2013 to 2015 during CMP's major investigative journalism study on fetal trafficking. In 2013, ABR's Procurement Manager Perrin Larton confirmed ABR's extensive supply of aborted fetal parts to government researchers at NIH. In the secretly filmed video by CMP, Larton explained how ABR is careful to make sure that the 21- and 22-week fetuses scheduled for organ harvesting were not exterminated

---

43   Daleiden, David, "Why are taxpayers buying parts of aborted babies?," *Washington Examiner*, October 23, 2018, https://www.washingtonexaminer.com/opinion/op-eds/why-are-taxpayers-buying-parts-of-aborted-babies

44   Ibid.

with feticides like digoxin before the abortion. She stated that she has watched multiple fetuses targeted for harvesting be delivered whole in the abortion clinics.[45]

THE MARCION CONNECTION

The grisly experimentation with late-term aborted babies demonstrates a gross disregard for human life. Although the scientific community now concurs that life begins at conception, the killing of both the unborn and born continues. As shown earlier, much of the Judeo-Christian community also supports these ancient practices. How can the traditionally religious view of the sanctity of human life be reconciled with these unholy procedures?

In order to justify killing human life, a judgment must be made that some lives are more valuable than others. The Marcion infiltration of the modern-day church may provide an explanation. According to Marcion, all of humanity fit into one of three categories: ". . . the elect or the Illuminated, who possessed true knowledge (*gnosis*) and a strong spark of divinity within them; the psychics, who were capable of obtaining salvation; and the vast majority of lost humanity who ate, drank, married, and died eternally. . . ."[46]

---

45   Daleiden, David, "Special Report: Advanced Bioscience Resources," *The Center for Medical Progress*, September 10, 2018, https://www.centerformedicalprogress.org/human-capital/special-report-advanced-bioscience-resources/

46   W. H. C. Frend, *The Early Church* (Philadelphia, Lippincott, 1968) p. 65.

PART FOUR

JESUS AND THE NEW TESTAMENT

16

THE QUEST FOR JESUS

Christianity is basically an historical religion. That is to say, it is not founded primarily in universal principles, but in concrete events, actual historical happenings. The most important of these is the life of a little-known Jewish carpenter who was born in a stable, died at the age of thirty-three as a criminal rather than a hero, never travelled more than ninety miles from his birthplace, owned nothing, attended no college, marshaled no army, and instead of producing books did his own writing in the sand. Nevertheless, his birthday is kept across the world and his death day sets a gallows against every skyline. Who, then, was he?

HUSTON SMITH, *THE RELIGIONS OF MAN*

He comes to us as One unknown, without a name, as of old, by the lakeside, He came to those men who knew Him not. He speaks to us the same word, "Follow thou me!" and sets us to the tasks which He has to fulfill for our time. He commands. And to those who obey Him, whether they be wise or simple, He will reveal Himself in the toils, the conflicts, the suffering which they shall pass through in His fellowship, and, as an ineffable mystery, they shall learn in their own experience Who He is.

ALBERT SCHWEITZER, *THE QUEST OF THE HISTORICAL JESUS*

HE HAS BEEN CALLED THE "PRINCE OF PEACE," and yet He said: "Do not suppose that I have come to bring peace to the earth. I did not come to bring peace, but a sword" (Matt. 10:34).

He has been celebrated as a prophet of non-violence and yet He drove the money changers from the temple court with a whip of cords, saying: "Get these out of here! How dare you turn my Father's house into a market?" (John 2:16).

He has been hailed as a teacher who taught men to turn the other cheek and not to resist an evil person, but he confronted and cursed the scribes and Pharisees as "a brood of vipers," asking: "How will you escape being condemned to hell?" (Matt. 23:33).

He has been worshipped as "the Son of God," who brought a new understanding of the Supreme Being to mankind, and yet He said: "Do not think that I have come to abolish the Law or the Prophets; I have not come to abolish them but to fulfill them. For truly I tell you, until heaven and earth disappear, not the smallest letter, not the least stroke of a pen, will by any means disappear from the Law until everything is accomplished. Therefore, anyone who sets aside one of the least of these commands and teaches others accordingly will be called least in the kingdom of heaven, but whoever practices and teaches these commands will be called great in the kingdom of heaven. For I tell you that unless your righteousness surpasses that of the Pharisees and the teachers of the law, you will certainly not enter the kingdom of heaven" (Matt. 5:17-20).

Who was Jesus?

This question has confronted mankind for two thousand years and few have provided a satisfactory answer. Indeed, His very disciples seemed uncertain of His identity. When Jesus asked His disciples, "Who do people say the Son of Man is?" They answered: "Some say John the Baptist; others say Elijah; and still others Jeremiah or one of the prophets" (Matt: 6:14).

THE QUEST FOR THE HISTORICAL JESUS

In the midst of the Age of Reason and Enlightenment, several scholars set out to establish once and for all the identity of the Jesus of history as opposed to the Jesus of religious veneration. The first major attempt to bring the methods of critical analysis was a work called *The Aims of Jesus and His Disciples* by Hermann Samuel Reimarus, a professor of Oriental languages at Hamburg. Reimarus postulated an intense difference between who Jesus actually was and what His disciples proclaimed him to be. Jesus, he believed, was a Jewish reformer who became increasingly fanatical and politicized; but he failed to re-establish the Kingdom of David. His cry of dereliction on the cross signaled the end of His expectation that God would act to support Him. His disciples fell back on a different model of Messiahship, proclaiming that Jesus had been "raised" from the dead, and would bring the end of the world. They, too, were disappointed. But instead of crying out in despair, they founded the primitive Christian church.[1]

A second landmark in the quest for the historical Jesus was *The Life of Jesus* by David Friedrich Strauss, another German professor. In this work he patently rejected the supernatural aspects of the gospels and described the church's handling of the historical information about Christ as myth. He accepted a bare-bones framework of Jesus' life, including events such as his baptism by John the Baptist, his teaching and making of disciples, as well as His death due to the hostility of the Pharisees. The early disciples, Strauss believed, turned the historical Jesus into something He was not by a twofold process. In the first place, they interpreted the events of Jesus' life as fulfillment of prophecy and Old Testament belief and expectation to establish Him as Messiah. Secondly, they created myths and legends about him through the vehicle of community belief. "The historical Jesus was thus turned into the divine Messiah by the pious, but erroneous devotion of the church."[2]

---

1   *Fragments from Reimarus* (London: William and Norgate, 1879), pp. 24-31.

2   David Strauss, quoted in Michael Burer, "A Survey of Historical Jesus Studies: From Reimarus to Wright," *Bible.org,* May 27, 2004, https://bible.org/article/survey-historical-jesus-studies-reimarus-wright

ALBERT SCHWEITZER'S CONCLUSION

At the turn of the 20th Century, the quest for the historical Jesus was led by Albert Schweitzer, the noted physician, theologian, philosopher, and musicologist. After years of analyzing the evidence, Schweitzer wrote: "There is nothing more negative than the result of the critical study of the Life of Jesus. The Jesus of Nazareth, who came forward publicly as the Messiah, who preached the ethic of the Kingdom of God, who founded the Kingdom of God upon earth, and died to give His work its final consecration, never had any existence."[3]

Schweitzer's conclusion was based largely upon the almost complete lack of any mention of Jesus by sources other than the New Testament. Within the Roman world in which He lived, Jesus appeared to be a figure of little consequence. The few references to him are brief and tendentious.

THE ROMAN REFERENCES

The historian Tacitus, writing in the midst of the Second Century after a great fire had engulfed Rome which many people believed had been set by Emperor Nero so that he could rebuild the city in accordance with his personal taste, wrote:

> But all human efforts, all the lavish gifts of the emperor, and the propitiations of the gods, did not banish the sinister belief that the conflagration was the result of an order. Consequently, to get rid of the report, Nero fastened the guilt and inflicted the most exquisite tortures on a class hated for their abominations, called Christians by the populace. Christus, from whom the name had its origin, suffered the extreme penalty during the reign of Tiberius at the hands of one of our procurators, Pontius Pilatus, and a most mischievous super-stition, thus checked for the moment, again broke out not only in Judaea, the first source of the evil, but even in Rome, where all things

3   Albert Schweitzer, *The Quest of the Historical Jesus* (New York: Macmillan, 1968), p. 398.

hideous and shameful from every part of the world find their center and become popular. Accordingly, an arrest was first made of all who pleaded guilty; then, upon their information, an immense multitude was convicted, not so much of the crime of firing the city, as of hatred against mankind. Mockery of every sort was added to their deaths. Covered with the skins of beasts, they were torn by dogs and perished, or were nailed to crosses, or were doomed to the flames and burnt, to serve as a nightly illumination, when daylight had expired. Nero offered his gardens for the spectacle, and was exhibiting a show in the circus, while he mingled with the people in the dress of a charioteer or stood aloft on a car. Hence, even for criminals who deserved extreme and exemplary punishment, there arose a feeling of compassion; for it was not, as it seemed, for the public good, but to glut one man's cruelty, that they were being destroyed.[4]

Another Roman reference to Jesus resides in a letter of Pliny the younger, the governor of Bithynia-Pontus (now in modern Turkey), to the Emperor Trajan, circa AD 112. In the letter, Pliny reported of the emergence of a mad sect in his province whose members "recite a hymn to Christus as to a god," and "oblige themselves by a sacrament [or oath], not to do anything that was ill." Pliny informed the emperor that he has had questioned several members of the sect and, if they admitted more than three times that they worshipped "Christus," he put them to death. Since the matter of Christians was new to him, Pliny asked the emperor if he had adopted the proper measures. Trajan responded as follows:

You have taken the method which you ought in examining the causes of those that had been accused as Christians, for indeed no certain and general form of judging can be ordained in this case. These people are not to be sought for; but if they be accused and convicted, they are to be punished; but with this caution, that he who denies himself to

---

4   Tacitus, (AD 109) *The Annals*, translated by Alfred John Church and William Jackson Brodribb, *The Internet Classics Archive*, http://classics.mit.edu/Tacitus/annals.11.xv.html

be a Christian, and makes it plain that he is not so by supplicating to our gods, although he had been so formerly, may be allowed pardon, upon his repentance. As for libels sent without an author, they ought to have no place in any accusation whatsoever, for that would be a thing of very ill example, and not agreeable to my reign.[5]

The third and final Roman reference comes from the biographer Suetonius, who in his *Life of Claudius* (25:4), wrote: "As the Jews were making constant disturbances at the instigation of Chrestus [sic], he expelled them from Rome."[6]

THE JEWISH REFERENCES

The only other outside sources for the historical Jesus are Jewish. The Talmud—the religious laws of Judaism and the collection of comments and interpretations concerning them—includes this passage:

On the eve of Passover Yeshu was hanged. For forty days before the execution took place, a herald went forth and cried, "He is going forth to be stoned because he has practiced sorcery and enticed Israel to apostasy. Any one who can say anything in his favor, let him come forward and plead on his behalf." But since nothing was brought forward in his favor he was hanged on the eve of the Passover!—Ulla retorted: Do you suppose that he was one for whom a defense could be made? Was he not a Mesith [enticer] concerning him Scripture says, Neither shalt thou spare, neither shalt thou conceal him? With Yeshu however it was different, for he was connected with the government. Our Rabbis taught: Yeshu had five disciples, Matthai, Nakai, Nezer, Buni, and Todah.[7]

---

5   "Letters of Pliny the Younger and the Emperor Trajan" (AD 112), translated by William Whiston, *Frontline*, Public Broadcasting System (PBS), April 1998, https://www.pbs.org/wgbh/pages/frontline/shows/religion/maps/primary/pliny.html

6   Suetonius, "The Life of Claudius" (AD 115), *Early Christian Writings,* http://www.earlychristianwritings.com/suetonius.html

7   "The Execution of Yeshu ha Notzri on the Eve of Passover—Talmud, Sanhedrin 431" (188 A.D.), *Yeshu ha-Nootzri,* May 11, 2017, http://yeshuhanotzri.blogspot.com/2016/02/execution-of-yeshu-ha-notzri-on-eve-of.html

Another reference to Jesus comes from Josephus, who in his *Antiquities of Judaism* mentioned the execution of "the brother of Jesus, who was called Christ, whose name was James, and some others."[8]

THE LACK OF EVIDENCE

Such a paucity of references to Jesus by His contemporaries has caused New Testament scholar Gunther Bornkamm to conclude: "These pagan and Jewish sources are of importance only in so far as they confirm the fact which was also otherwise well known, that in the early days it never occurred even to the fiercest adversary of Christianity to doubt the historical existence of Jesus at all. However, the non-Christian allusions to him contribute practically nothing. We learn from them that contemporary historiography, as far as they knew of Jesus' appearance at all, considered it anything but an epoch-making event."[9]

THE NAGGING QUESTIONS

Historians know a great deal about figures from the past: the medical problems of Julius Caesar, Cleopatra's dress size, the shape of Mark Antony's mouth, and the sex life of Marcus Tullius Cicero.[10] Why, then, is so little known about Jesus, about His appearance, about the first thirty years of His life, about His trial in a Roman court of law and His public execution? Why is there no historical verification from non-Christian sources of a Jewish rabbi who raised a ruckus in Jerusalem, was nailed to a cross, and rose from the dead? Surely the ancient Jews kept records of the proceedings of the Sanhedrin? And the Roman overlords

---

8   Josephus, *The Antiquities of the Jews* (AD 93), Book XX, Chapter 9, translated by William Whiston, *Wikisource*, https://en.wikisource.org/wiki/The_Antiquities_of_the_Jews/Book_XX#Chapter_9

9   Gunther Bornkamm, *Jesus of Nazareth* (New York: Harper and Row, 1975), p. 28.

10   "A. J. Sillett, "The Unhealthy Sex Life of Marcus Tullius Cicero?" *What Would Cicero Do?* 1987, https://whatwouldcicerodo.wordpress.com/2013/12/18/the-unhealthy-sex-life-of-marcus-tullius-cicero/

who governed Palestine would have kept their own records.

What happened to them?

THE LOST DOCUMENTS

Such records as may have existed in Rome were probably destroyed by the great fire of AD 64 which gutted the buildings containing the Empire's archives. Among the archives would have been the records of Herod Antipas, the tetrarch of Galilee and Peraea, and of Pontius Pilate, who served as the governor of Palestine.[11] The Jewish records were devoured by the dogs of war.

In AD 66, the Jews mounted a full-scale rebellion against Roman rule. The suicidal nature of the revolt was measured by the fact that it took the Romans four years to recapture Jerusalem and the last outlying fortress at Masada. In the process, the entire countryside was laid to waste. The population of Palestine was decimated. The Romans put thousands to the sword, sold thousands more into slavery, and sent the remaining Jews into exile. The city of Jerusalem was destroyed, including the Temple which Herod the Great had begun in 20 BC and to which the finishing touches had been added just eight years earlier.[12]

Believing that the Jewish religion was the cause of the rebellion, the Romans systematically destroyed every synagogue in the country, leaving not a stone unturned. Religious landmarks were crushed, and the sacred writings and commentaries, the scrolls from the Sanhedrin, the records of the scribes, were confiscated and put to the torch. If the materials upon which records were written were of good quality, the texts were scraped down and soaked off so that the parchment could be reused.[13]

---

11   Kelly Shannon, "Memory, Religion and History in Nero's Great Fire: Tacitus, 'Annals' 15: 41-7," *The Classical Quarterly*, Vol. 62, No. 2, December 2012, https://www.jstor.org/stable/23470136?seq=1#page_scan_tab_contents

12   David Green, "This Day in Jewish History: The Roman Siege of Jerusalem," *Haaretz*, July 9, 2012, https://www.haaretz.com/jewish/70-c-e-the-roman-siege-of-jerusalem-ends-1.5155728

13   Robert Coughlan, "Who Was the Man Jesus?" *Life*, December 24, 1964.

SLANTED TESTIMONY

Apart from the scant references in the writings of Tacitus, Pliny the Young, Suetonius, the Babylonian Talmud, and Josephus, the only other information about the life of Jesus comes from the New Testament. Of its twenty-seven books, twenty-three are concerned with matters that came after the earthly ministry of Jesus came to an end. The first four books—the Gospels of Matthew, Mark, Luke, and John—present the story of His life through the perspective of faith. The Gospels were written decades after the death of Jesus, and the evangelists, according to New Testament scholars, never laid eyes on Jesus. The information they received about Him came from the verbal testimony of His followers that had been passed on to the primitive church.[14]

And the testimonies of the four evangelists remain problematic for most scholars since they seem to disagree on matters pertaining to His birth, His death, and His resurrection. What's more, they leave out a great deal of information, including the appearance of Jesus and His personal qualities, and they reveal almost nothing about His life before His ministry, which is to say, nearly His whole life.[15]

THE SYNOPTIC PROBLEM

In the language of theology, the Gospels of Matthew, Mark, and Luke are called "synoptic," since they share a common view of the life and times of Jesus.[16] These Gospels tell much the same story in much the same way, although their testimonies appear conflicting. Mark, for example, fails to mention the Nativity. Matthew and Luke agree that Mary, the mother of Jesus, was betrothed to a man called Joseph and that she was a virgin when she gave birth. However, both Gospel writers

---

14   Hugh Anderson, *Jesus: Great Lives Observed* (Englewood Cliffs, New Jersey: Prentice Hall, 1967), p. 6.

15   Coughlan, "Who Was the Man Jesus?"

16   Bart Ehrman, "The Synoptic Gospels: A Historian's Perspective," *The Great Courses Daily*, n. d., https://www.thegreatcoursesdaily.com/synoptic-gospels-historians-approach/

provide genealogies to show that Jesus was a descendant of King David through the male line—that is, the line of Joseph. This incongruity is intensified by the fact that the genealogies differ. Scholars also point out discrepancies between the three Gospels in the accounts of the Passion of Jesus and His Resurrection. These discrepancies have caused those who have embarked on the quest for the historical Jesus to conclude that much of the material in the synoptic gospels came from the oral tradition, a tradition that involved the process of myth-making. New Testament historian Hugh Anderson writes:

> The first three Gospels (commonly called the Synoptic Gospels because of their close literary interrelationships) were produced in the period from about AD 65 to 95. That is to say that a time of over thirty years elapsed from the death of Jesus around AD 30 to the writing of Mark, first of the Synoptic Gospels, about AD 65. The materials on which Mark and the Synoptic writers who followed him drew for their compilation of their Gospels were the traditions of Jesus' words and deeds, which had first of all circulated by word of mouth among various Christian communities during the generation after his crucifixion. If we are to have any acquaintance at all with the problems of reconstructing Jesus' history, we have to form some impression of this interim era of oral tradition. In the course of oral transmission, the Christian communities kept alive those traditions of Jesus' sayings and acts which could be turned to practical use in meeting the varied situations of their daily lives, in preaching, in mission, in cult and liturgy. We should not be surprised to find in this whole fluid process traditions about Jesus were steadily reshaped, adapted, and heightened in color, especially since those responsible for passing them on were every day witnessing new converts won and new conquests made in the name of Jesus Christ, their Lord.[17]

---

17 Anderson, *Jesus*, p. 6.

THE QUEST FOR JESUS

A JACKDAW'S NEST

The Gospel of John is a jackdaw's nest of mixed problems for historians. His Gospel, according to Bornkamm, is so different in character in relation to the other three, and such a product of a "developed theological reflection," that it must be treated as a "secondary source."[18] Indeed, almost everything about John's Gospel *is* different. A few examples are as follows:

- The Synoptics suggest that the ministry of Jesus lasted only one year, and they mention only one visit to Jerusalem. In John's Gospel, His ministry lasted about three years, during which Jesus made several trips to the city of David.

- The Synoptics make the same selection of major scenes from the life of Jesus, describe them in much the same way, and place them in the same chronological order. John, however, makes his own selection of the stories and places them in a different order and under different circumstances. The cleansing of the Temple is a case in point. In the Synoptics, this event occurs at the end of Jesus's career, while John places it at the beginning.

- In the Synoptics, Jesus seldom speaks of Himself directly, makes no claims of His Messiahship, and remains so reticent about His status and identity that He urges people who have decided that He is the Son of God to keep this revelation a secret. John, however, provides Jesus with a new, streamlined personality, removes any doubts about His Messiahship, and presents Him as constantly asserting His divinity by a series of metaphors: "I am the light of the world," "I am the bread of life," "I am the good shepherd," "I am the true vine," "I am the Way, the Truth, and the Life." Within this Gospel, Jesus utters a total of 120 "I am" statements," and another 234 "I" statements, such as "I glorify," "I speak," and "I know."

---

18   Bornnkamm, *Jesus of Nazareth*, p. 14.

- In addition, John employs mysticism, symbolism, and Neo-Platonic language that is completely lacking in the Synoptics. This is evidenced by the very opening of his Gospel: "In the beginning was the Word, and the Word was with God, and the Word was God. He was with God in the beginning. Through him all things were made; without him nothing was made that has been made. In him was life, and that life was the light of all mankind. The light shines in the darkness, and the darkness has not overcome it." (John 1:1-5).[19]

THE BRICK WALL

The results of the quest of the historical Jesus caused Rudolf Bultmann, professor of New Testament at the University of Marburg, to conclude: "I do indeed think that we can now know almost nothing concerning the life and personality of Jesus."[20] Since little could be known of the historical Jesus, Bultmann and his disciples focused their complete attention on the *kerygma* or proclamation of the early church about Jesus. Such a focus came with the acknowledgment that the Gospels consist only of tradition and, therefore, by definition, of adulteration.[21]

Christians, Bultmann argued, must be content with the fact that the *kerygma* existed—that the early Christians viewed Jesus as a person worthy of faith and devotion. The tradition that they passed on about Jesus, Bultmann maintained, provides the only reason for modern man to have faith in Him as well. It is for Bultmann unnecessary, even sacrilegious for anyone to try to look behind the tradition in search for a historical figure.[22] With this admission of resignation and futility, the quest for the historical Jesus came to an abrupt and inglorious end.

---

19   Coughlan, "Who Was the Man Jesus?"

20   Rudolf Bultmann, *Jesus and the Word* (New York: Scribner's, 1934), p. 8.

21   Rudolf Bultmann and Five Critics, *Kerygma and Myth* (New York: Harper Torchbooks, 1961), http://media.sabda.org/alkitab-2/Religion-Online.org%20Books/Bultmann,%20Rudolf,%20et.%20al.%20-%20Kerygma%20and%20Myth.pdf

22   Ibid.

THE RESULTS OF THE QUEST

Thanks to the quest, Jesus became a nebulous figure that lacked historical credibility. The Gospels became reflecting pools into which every minister and priest could look to uncover the verification of their own ideology. For exponents of liberation theology, He became a militant figure who sought to overthrow Roman rule. For New Age believers, He became a meek and mild figure who spread a message of tolerance and universal benevolence. For left-wing scholars, He became a fierce advocate for human rights and social justice.

Within mainline denominations, including the United Church of Christ, Jesus transformed into a cosmic and transcendent figure who embraced all lifestyles and all expressions of religious belief and established a religion that freed all of mankind from the demanding laws of the Old Testament, including the Ten Commandments. This Jesus condoned the worship of false gods (including Allah), the marriage of practicing homosexuals, the practice of late-term abortion, and the establishment of gun control.[23] These developments occurred because the denominations not only rejected the teachings of the Gospels but also the *kerygma* of primitive Christianity—the very proclamations about Jesus that Bultmann insisted all Christians must accept and affirm. In this way, the Jesus of Marcion was brought back to life.

The case for the claims of traditional believers in Jesus seemed hopeless until a Bedouin boy cast a stone at one of the goats who had strayed from his flock on the western coast of the Dead Sea and heard something shatter.

---

23   John Dart, "UCC Has Been Progressive Pacesetter," *Christian Century*, July 18, 2013, https://www.christiancentury.org/article/2013-07/ucc-has-been-progressive-pacesetter

17

JESUS: THE EVIDENCE

If the Essenes preserved their Scrolls, would the early Christians who resembled them in so many ways, have neglected their documents—and may they now be locked away in clay jars in some unknown cave in the Jordan wilderness, waiting for another Bedouin boy to throw some lucky stone? These speculations could go to include many "missing" documents, not only Christian but Jewish and Roman key chapters of both Josephus and Tacitus for instance and the true reports of Pontius Pilate, not the forged ones. What seems highly probable is that the discoveries will go on and that they will include some important and surprising ones.

ROBERT COUGHLAN, "WHO WAS THIS MAN JESUS," *LIFE*, 1964

I am here trying to prevent anyone saying the really foolish thing that people often say about Him: "I'm ready to accept Jesus as a great moral teacher, but I don't accept His claim to be God." That is the one thing we must not say. A man who was merely a man and said the sort of things Jesus said would not be a great moral teacher. He would either be a lunatic—on the level with a man who says he is a poached egg—or else he would be a Demon of Hell. You must make your choice. Either this man was, and is, the Son of God, or else a madman or something worse. You can shut Him up for a fool, you can spit at Him and kill Him as a demon; or else you can fall at His feet and call Him Lord and God. But let us not come with any patronizing nonsense about His being a great moral teacher. He has not left that open to us. He did not intend to.

C. S. LEWIS, *MERE CHRISTIANITY*

WHAT SHATTERED, the Bedouin boy discovered that day in 1947, was a clay jar within a concealed cave. Next to the jar, he saw an ancient black scroll. Exploring the cave, he found six more jars—all of which contained ancient manuscripts that were made of papyrus and copper. The boy took the scrolls to an antiques dealer in Bethlehem who bought them for $28.[1]

The discovery of the shepherd eventually caught the attention of Dr. John C. Trevor of the American Schools of Oriental Research. An expedition was mounted to comb the Qumran caves for more ancient manuscripts. Eventually, a collection of 981 different scrolls were found in eleven caves.[2]

The scrolls were subjected to radiocarbon and paleographic dating which showed that they had been written between 200 BC and AD 68. These findings were upheld by X-ray and Particle Induced X-ray Emission tests by the National Institute of Nuclear Physics in Sicily.[3]

THE DEAD SEA SCROLLS

The scrolls represented the sacred literature of the Essenes, one of the major Jewish sects in existence at the time of Jesus. The Essenes were an ascetic community who sought seclusion from worldly evils within the caves of Qumran near the Dead Sea. Here, in the darkness, they awaited the impending arrival of the judgment of God and the end of the world.[4] They saw themselves as the "true Israel," the "children of light" who were engaged in a struggle against the "children the darkness."[5]

---

1   Leon Levy, "Dead Sea Scrolls," Digital Library, Israel Antiquities Authority, 2012, https://www.deadseascrolls.org.il/learn-about-the-scrolls/introduction

2   Ibid.

3   Ibid.

4   Robert Coughlan, "Who Was the Man Jesus?" *Life,* December 24, 1964.

5   Hugh Anderson, *Jesus: Great Lives Observed* (Englewood Cliffs, New Jersey: Prentice Hall, 1967), p. 31.

The Essenes bore striking similarity to the early Christians. Both were eschatological communities—expecting the imminent transformation of the world. Drawing from the Book of Daniel, both believed in the coming of the "Son of Man," who would bring about the Day of Judgment. Both used baptismal rites, not animal sacrifice, as a means of repentance. Both shared sacred meals of bread and wine as Messianic banquets. Both groups shared all their goods in common and relinquished all their worldly possessions. Both were rigidly disciplined and lived in strict obedience to the law of Moses.[6]

NEW LIGHT ON JOHN'S GOSPEL

What remained most startling about the Dead Sea Scrolls was the fact that they contained the same language and imagery that had been dismissed as late Hellenistic in the Gospel of John. Like the Essenes, John makes persistent use of such phrases as "the spirit of truth," "the light of the world," "walking in darkness," and "the children of light." The similarities between the scrolls and the fourth gospel can be witnessed by a comparison of John's prologue with the opening of an Essene manuscript called the "Manual of Discipline."

> He was with God in the beginning
> Through Him all things came to be,
> Not one thing had its being but through Him (John 1:2-3).

> All things came to pass by His knowledge,
> He establishes all things by His design
> And without Him nothing is done (Manual 11:11).[7]

---

6   Moshe Dann, "The Essenes and the Origins of Christianity," *The Jerusalem Post*, July 13, 2018, https://www.jpost.com/Jerusalem-Report/The-Essenes-and-the-origins-of-Christianity-562442

7   Ian Wilson, *Jesus: The Evidence* (San Francisco: Harper Collins, 1996), pp. 33-34.

The parallelisms are reinforced by numerous other passages, including this juxtaposition between John 8 and the Essenes' *Rule of the Community*:

> I am the light of the world; he who follows me will not walk in darkness (John 8:12).

> All the children of righteousness are ruled by the Prince of Light and walk in the ways of light, but all the children of falsehood are ruled by the Angel of Darkness and walk in the ways of darkness. (Rule of the Community, 3).[8]

These findings caused Reinhold Niebuhr to conclude: "It was assumed that much of the critical work on the New Testament had been done, and, in a sense, finished. The discovery of the Scrolls not only aroused tremendous public interest but also demonstrated that frontiers are never closed in historical studies."[9]

AN EYEWITNESS ACCOUNT

In the wake of the discovery of such similarities, prominent British scholars began to reassess the historicity of John's Gospel. Aileen Guilding in *The Fourth Gospel and Jewish Worship*, showed that the Gospel's construction is based on the Jewish cycle of feasts and the practice of completing the reading of the Torah in a three-year cycle. Guilding concluded that John was, most likely, an eyewitness to the accounts he recorded in his Gospel since he provides detailed and accurate references to the geographical features of Jerusalem before it was destroyed by the Romans.[10] For example, John mentions a Pool of Siloam (John 9:7), the remains of which have been unearthed in Jerusalem, and a "Gabbatha" or pavement where Pilate sat in judgment

---

8   Dann, "The Essenes and the Origins of Christianity."

9   Reinhold Niebuhr, quoted in Coughlin, "Who Was This Man Jesus?"

10   Wilson, *Jesus, the Evidence*, p. 34.

over Jesus, an area of Roman paving that now resides within the crypt of the Convent of the Sisters of Our Lady of Zion in the midst of the City of David.[11] In addition, Oxford scholars C. F. Burney and A. T. Olmstead have argued forcibly that John's Gospel was composed in Aramaic, not much later than AD 40.[12]

In his Gospel, John observes: "There *is* in Jerusalem at the Sheep-Pool, a place with five colonnades, called in Hebrew Bethesda (5:2)." This site, according to British historian John A. T. Robinson, was obliterated in the destruction of the city, only to be discovered in the 1960s by a team of archaeologists. But the fourth evangelist emphatically says at the time of his writing "is" not "was." For Robinson, this provides proof that the fourth Gospel may represent an eyewitness account."[13]

"THE RYLANDS FRAGMENT"
The theory that the Fourth Gospel may have been written at a date much earlier than the late 2nd Century as supposed by Bultmann and company is supported by one of the earliest surviving fragments of any Gospel—canonical or non-canonical—is a scrap of papyrus on display at the John Rylands Library on the campus of Manchester University in England. On the front of this fragment is the Greek text of John 18:31-34: "So Pilate said to them, 'Take Him yourselves, and judge Him according to your law.' The Jews said to him, 'We are not permitted to put anyone to death,' to fulfill the word of Jesus which He spoke, signifying by what kind of death He was about to die. Therefore, Pilate entered again into the Praetorium, and summoned Jesus and said to Him, 'Are You the King of the Jews?' Jesus answered, 'Are you saying this on your own initiative, or did others tell you about Me?'" On the back of the fragment is John 18:37-38: "'You are a king, then!' said

---

11   Ibid., pp. 34-35.

12   Ibid., p. 34.

13   John A. T. Robinson, *Can We Trust the New Testament* (Grand Rapids, Michigan: William B. Eerdmans Publishing Company, 1977), pp. 85-86.

Pilate. Jesus answered, 'You say that I am a king. In fact, the reason I was born and came into the world is to testify to the truth. Everyone on the side of truth listens to me.' 'What is truth?' retorted Pilate. With this he went out again to the Jews gathered there and said, 'I find no basis for a charge against him.'"[14]

This scrap from an ancient codex or "small book" was found in Egypt, hundreds of miles from Ephesus in Turkey, where John purportedly wrote his Gospel. Such small books were carried by early Christians as they spread the "good news" throughout the Greco-Roman world. Analysis of the papyrus and the handwriting indicate that it was written circa AD 100, seventy years after the death of Jesus.[15]

THE MAGDALEN MANUSCRIPT

Equally shattering to the claims of Biblical scholars from Hermann Samuel Reimarus to Rudolf Bultmann was the recent re-evaluation of three papyrus fragments that had been purchased in 1901 by the Reverend Charles Bousfield Huleatt, a British missionary, from an antiques dealer in Luxor, Egypt.[16] When pieced together, the fragments, written in Greek, contained the following 26 lines from the 24th chapter of Matthew's Gospel:

As they were eating, Jesus took some bread and blessed it. Then he broke it in pieces and gave it to the disciples, saying, "Take this and eat it, for this is my body." And he took a cup of wine and gave thanks to God for it. He gave it to them and said, "Each of you drink from it, for this is my blood, which confirms the covenant between God and his people. It is poured out as a sacrifice to forgive the sins of many. Mark my words—I will not drink wine again until the day I

---

14   Wilson, *Jesus: The Evidence*, p. 21.

15   "What Is the Significance of This Fragment?" University of Manchester Library, n. d., https://www.library.manchester.ac.uk/search-resources/special-collections/guide-to-special-collections/st-john-fragment/what-is-the-significance/

16   Chuck Missler, "The Magdalen Papyrus: Astonishing Rediscovery," *Koinonia House*, April. 2001, http://www.khouse.org/articles/2001/333/

drink it new with you in my Father's Kingdom." Then they sang a hymn and went out to the Mount of Olives. On the way, Jesus told them, "Tonight all of you will desert me. For the Scriptures say, 'God will strike the Shepherd, and the sheep of the flock will be scattered.'"

In 1994, Carsten Peter Thiede, Director of the Institute of Basic Epistemological Research in Paderborn, Germany, used a scanning laser microscope to more carefully examine these fragments. Such a microscope can differentiate between the twenty micrometer (millionth of a meter) layers of papyrus, measuring the height and depth of the ink, and provide accurate dating, and determine the angle of the stylus used by the scribe. Thiede astounded the scholastic world by concluding that the Magdalen fragments were either an original from Matthew's Gospel, or an immediate copy, written while Matthew and the other disciples were still alive. Matthew's skills in shorthand, Thiede maintained, were evident in his inclusion of the extensive discourses, which he apparently was able to record verbatim. The Magdalen papyrus discovery remains distinctive since it was dated strictly on the basis of physical evidence rather than a literary theory or historical suppositions.[17]

And so, it came to pass that the theories of the form, textual, philological, and literary analysis of the four Gospels by many of the world's leading scholars have come to naught. Mark may not have been the first to compile his Gospel. In all likelihood, that distinction belongs to Matthew, as traditionalists throughout the centuries have maintained. And the Gospel of John, in which Jesus seems to speak like a Neo-Platonist, is the most Hebraic of all the New Testament accounts and appears, like the Gospel of Matthew, to have been written by an eye witness.

But can the four Gospels be trusted?

This question, above all others, begs an answer, since the four evangelists contradict one another in so many ways, even in their accounts of the Resurrection.

---

17   Ibid.

18

JESUS: THE RESURRECTION

Fellow Israelites, listen to this: Jesus of Nazareth was a man accredited by God to you by miracles,
wonders and signs, which God did among you through him, as you yourselves know. This man
was handed over to you by God's deliberate plan and foreknowledge; and you, with the help of
wicked men, put him to death by nailing him to the cross. But God raised him from the dead,
freeing him from the agony of death, because it was impossible for death to keep its hold on him. . . .

ACTS 2:22-24

THE EARLY CHRISTIANS consisted of the twelve disciples, Matthias having been elected to replace Judas Iscariot; Galileans, who had accompanied Jesus on his fateful trip to Jerusalem; women, including Mary Magdalene, whom Jesus had cured of an unknown illness, and Mary, the mother of Jesus; and His brothers, including James, who would become the leader of the early church (Acts 1:14).[1] They spent a great

---

1   Robert Coughlan, "Who Was the Man Jesus?" *Life*, December 25, 1964.

deal of time at the Temple and its encircling courtyards. For the most part, they gathered at the eastern wall, known as Solomon's Portico. They came together to pray, to exchange stories of Jesus, and to spread the "good news" to anyone who would listen.[2]

APOSTOLIC PROCLAMATIONS

The "good news," which became crystallized into the Apostle's Creed, represented the following proclamations of the first community (*ecclesia*) of believers: Jesus was the long-awaited Messiah, who would restore the earthly kingdom of the Jews. He was a descendant of David, who came to His fellow Jews under the guise of the "suffering servant" foretold by the prophet Isaiah. Jesus was raised in Galilee as a devout Jew. He underwent circumcision and a bar mitzvah, worshipped at the Temple, and became a rabbi. Like John the Baptist, He upheld the need for repentance and spiritual rebirth through the waters of Baptism. He affirmed the necessity of upholding every letter of the law and had rebuked those who sought to Hellenize the religion of Abraham, Moses, David, and the prophets. He taught in parables and His message centered on the coming Kingdom. He displayed an affinity for those on the fringes of society: the poor, the widows, the diseased, and the dispossessed. He condemned the rulers in vituperative language for their failure to heed the spirit of the law. He performed miracles and drove out demons. As a Pharisee, Jesus believed in angels and spirits, the resurrection of the dead, and a Final Judgment. He amassed a sizeable following and journeyed to Jerusalem, where He, in an act of violence, drove the money-changers from the Temple. He was arrested, condemned as a common criminal, and crucified at Calvary. Three days after His death, Jesus rose from the dead and appeared to His followers. He ascended into heaven, where He remains seated at the right hand of God. He will come again in glory to judge the wicked and to establish the New

---

2   Ibid.

Israel.[3] This Second Coming would happen soon. It could take place tomorrow, today, or the very next hour. That's why the early Christians spent their days at the Temple, where He was destined to appear on "that great and dreadful day."[4]

But He didn't come.

THE MOVEMENT BEGINS

And, after the weeks and months passed by, the disciples deemed it necessary to proclaim the *gospel* or "good news" not only to their fellow Jews but to all the inhabitants of the Greco-Roman world. This mission required direction and coordination which was provided by the Church Council at Jerusalem under James. James, as the younger brother of Jesus, was the proper leader because the early Christians remained determined to establish a caliphate under the bloodline of Jesus within the boundaries of Judaism.[5] Since the *eschaton* ("the end of the age") was at hand, there was no time to record the words and deeds of Jesus on parchment. The only necessity was proclaiming the word as far and near as possible within the remaining time.[6]

A GAGGLE OF GOSPELS

Eventually, the words and deeds were recorded not only by Matthew, Mark, Luke, and John, but a host of others who produced *The Gospel of Thomas, The Gospel of Philip, the Gospel of Truth, The Secret Gospel of James,* and *The Gospel to the Egyptians.*[7] These works contain accounts of the boy Jesus and His mother. In the *Gospel of Thomas*, the young

---

3   "The Kerygma," *Bible Lessons International*, 2014, http://www.freebiblecommentary.org/special_topics/kerygma.html

4   Coughlin, "Who Was the Man Jesus?"

5   W. H. C. Frend, *The Early Church* (Philadelphia: J. P. Lippincott, 1966), p. 38.

6   Coughlin, "Who was the Man Jesus?"

7   Elaine Pagels, *The Gnostic Gospels* (New York: Vintage Books, 1989), pp. xv-xvi.

Jesus, while playing along the banks of a stream on the Sabbath, forms twelve sparrows out of clay, clapped His hands, brings the clay figures to life, and causes them to fly. When the son of a scribe takes Jesus to task for performing such a trick on the Sabbath, Jesus curses the boy and causes him to wither like a fig tree. The parents of the boy beg Jesus to restore their son to life. Jesus reluctantly complies, "leaving only some small member to continue withered that they might take warning."[8]

In *The Secret Gospel of James*, Salome, after hearing of the miraculous birth of Jesus from a midwife who had attended the delivery, sets out to verify Mary's alleged "intactness" for herself. As Mary lay sleeping, Salome sneaks into the cave and "puts forward her finger to test Mary's condition" only to have her finger singed for her sinful curiosity.[9]

ORDER FROM CHAOS

By the second century, so many gospels were in circulation throughout the Greco-Roman world that it was hard to tell who had the "good news" straight. The problem was settled by Irenaeus who said that all Christians must look to the Church of Rome for authentic doctrine, since this church had been established by Peter and Paul, who had passed on true teachings to their episcopal successors. He wrote:

> It is possible, then, for everyone in every church, who may wish to know the truth, to contemplate the tradition of the apostles which has been made known to us throughout the whole world. And we are in a position to enumerate those who were instituted bishops by the apostles and their successors down to our own times, men who neither knew nor taught anything like what these heretics rave about. . . .
>
> But since it would be too long to enumerate in such a volume

---

8   *The Gospel of Thomas*, The Lost Books of the Bible, SacredTexts.Com, http://www.sacred-texts. com/bib/lbob/lbob08.htm

9   *The Secret Gospel of James,* quoted in *Women and Religion: A Feminist Sourcebook for Christian Thought*, edited by Elizabeth Clark and Herbert Richardson (New York: Harper and Row, 1977), p. 35.

as this the successions of all the churches, we shall confound all those who, in whatever manner, whether through self-satisfaction or vainglory, or through blindness and wicked opinion, assemble other than where it is proper, by pointing out here the successions of the bishops of the greatest and most ancient church known to all, founded and organized at Rome by the two most glorious apostles, Peter and Paul—that church which has the tradition and the faith with which comes down to us after having been announced to men by the apostles. For with this Church, because of its superior origin, all churches must agree, that is, all the faithful in the whole world. And it is in her that the faithful everywhere have maintained the apostolic tradition.[10]

All well and good, save for the fact that the four gospels that became the official canon of the Church contain discrepancies and inconsistencies on the central proclamation of the early church, i.e., that Jesus of Nazareth rose from the dead.

CONTRADICTIONS IN "EVERY MAJOR DETAIL"
What accounts for such contradictions?

This question cannot be ignored in a world that is becoming increasingly secular. Moreover, the claim that the four evangelists were eyewitnesses to the events that they record only serves to exacerbate the problem. Regarding the contradictions, Paul Ehrman writes: "The Gospels are so problematic for historians who want to know what really happened. This is especially true for the Gospel accounts of Jesus' resurrection. They are filled with discrepancies, some of which cannot be reconciled. In fact, the Gospels disagree on nearly every detail in their resurrection narratives."[11] Similarly, Paul Tobin says: "Contradictions

---

10 Irenaeus, "Against the Heresies," III in *The Apostolic fathers: Justin Martyr and Irenaeus*, translated by A. Cleveland Coxe, Volume I, *The Ante Nicene Fathers* (Grand Rapids: William B. Eerdmans Publishing Company, 19801), pp. 415-416.

11 Bart D. Ehrman, *How Jesus Became God: The Exaltation of a Jewish Prophet from Galilee* (New York: HarperOne, 2014), p. 133.

exist in almost every detail between the four gospels accounts of the events surrounding the discovery of the empty tomb. . . . All the other details contradict each other so blatantly that we have no reason whatsoever to believe any of them to be historically true. . . The very variant nature of the reports of Jesus' [post-resurrection] appearances in the gospels speaks against their historicity. . . the gospels and other New Testament sources can't even present us with a harmonious witness to the events surrounding the appearances of the risen Jesus. It goes without saying that no weight can be given to accounts which contradict each other in every major detail."[12]

NOT GETTING THE FACTS STRAIGHT

Matthew says that two women—Mary Magdalene and "the other Mary" (28:1) went to the tomb on Easter morning (28:1) Mark maintains that three made the visit (Mary Magdalene, Mary, the mother of James, and Salome (16:1). Luke mentions a group of women, including a mysterious Joanna (24:1, 10), while John writes that only one woman (Mary Magdalene) made an appearance (20:1).

Matthew records that a violent earthquake took place (28:2), while the other evangelists remain silent about this extraordinary detail. Matthew and Mark insist that the women saw one angel at the tomb (Matthew 28:2-3). Luke writes of two men "in clothes that gleamed like lightning" (24:4). John speaks of "two angels in white, seated where Jesus' body had been, one at the head and the other at the foot." (20:12).

Matthew says that the tomb was closed when Mary Magdalene arrived and that an angel came down from heaven, rolled back the stone, and sat on it (28:2). The other evangelists testify that the tomb was already opened when Mary Magdalene (and, according to Mark and Luke, other women) arrived.

Matthew, Luke, and John say that the disciples were immediately

---

12   Paul Tobin, *The Rejection of Pascal's wager: A Skeptic's Guide to the Bible and the Historical Jesus* (Bedfordshire, England: Authors OnLine, 2009), pp. 542, 554.

informed by Mary Magdalene (and, in Luke's case, a gaggle of women) of the open tomb (Matthew 28:8; Luke 24:9-11; John 20:2). Mark writes: "Trembling and bewildered, the women went out and fled from the tomb. They said nothing to anyone, because they were afraid" (16:8).

In John's Gospel, Mary Magdalene weeps at the tomb because the body of Jesus is missing. Turning around, she sees someone standing before her but doesn't realize that it was Jesus. The passage continues as follows:

> He [Jesus] asked her, "Woman, why are you crying? Who is it you are looking for?"
>
> Thinking he was the gardener, she said, "Sir, if you have carried him away, tell me where you have put him, and I will get him."
>
> Jesus said to her, "Mary."
>
> She turned toward him and cried out in Aramaic, "Rabboni! (which means Teacher).
>
> Jesus said, "Do not hold on to me, for I have not yet ascended to the Father. Go instead to my brothers and tell them, 'I am ascending to my Father and your Father, to my God and your God'" (20:15-17).

Matthew, however, insists that Mary Magdalene and the other Mary, far from weeping at the empty tomb, were rather "filled with joy." What's more, in Matthew (as well as Mark), Jesus allows the women to touch Him. Matthew writes: "So the women hurried away from the tomb, afraid yet filled with joy, and ran to tell his disciples. Suddenly Jesus met them. 'Greetings,' he said. They came to him, clasped his feet and worshiped him. Then Jesus said to them, 'Do not be afraid. Go and tell my brothers to go to Galilee; there they will see me'" (Matthew 28: 8-10).

A PIOUS INVENTION?

Even a cursory comparison of the four Gospels has caused scholars such as Earl Doherty to conclude: "There is not a single example of a common resurrection appearance between any two, let alone three, of Matthew, Luke, or John's accounts. There is a common factor in the women... but even here the details are different and incompatible. There is also a certain commonality in that the appearances are to followers of Jesus... but beyond that, all the details of the appearances are widely divergent and, in many respects, thoroughly irreconcilable. . . It doesn't take an abundance of logical thought to conclude that the overwhelmingly compelling deduction to be made, taken with the fact that Mark contains no resurrection appearances whatsoever, is that all the descriptions of such appearances in the canonical Gospels are the invention of the later evangelists."[13]

But surely something happened on that Easter morning that caused a group of men and women to leave home and family in order to spread the word that a prophet from Galilee had risen from the dead at a certain time and place in linear history.

What?

THE HALLUCINATION HYPOTHESIS

Some conclude that the accounts of the resurrection sprang from an apostolic hallucination. Rudolph Bultmann argues: "The historian can perhaps to some extent account for that faith [in the resurrection] from the personal intimacy which the disciples had enjoyed with Jesus during his earthly life and so reduce the resurrection appearances to a series of subjective visions."[14] Similarly, Johannes Weiss contends that "the appearances were not external phenomenon but were merely the goals of an inner struggle in which faith won the victory over doubt. . . . The appearances were not the basis of their faith, though so it seemed to them, so much as its product and result."[15]

But this hypothesis remains highly problematic. By definition, a

---

13   Earl Doherty, *Challenging the Verdict: A Cross-Examination of Lee Strobel's "The Case for Christ"* (Ottawa: Age of reason Publications, 2001), p. 186.

14   Rudolph Bultmann, *The Theology of the New Testament*, Volume I (New York: Scribner's, 1951), p. 45.

15   Johannes Weiss, *Earliest Christianity*, Volume I (New York: Harper and Row, 1959), p. 30.

hallucination is a private event, a purely subjective experience void of any external reference or object. Psychologist Gary Collins writes: "Hallucinations are individual occurrences. By their very nature only one person can see a given hallucination at a time. They certainly aren't something which can be seen by a group of people. Neither is it possible that one person could somehow induce a hallucination in somebody else. Since a hallucination exists only in this subjective, personal sense, it is obvious that others cannot witness it."[16] But the evangelists insist that the risen Jesus appeared to many different people at different times and places. He appeared to Mary Magdalene, to Peter, to two disciples on the road to Emmaus, to the apostles, to the apostles as a group with a skeptic named Thomas who wouldn't believe unless he had touched the risen Jesus. Moreover, the Apostle Paul maintains that the risen Jesus appeared, not only to him, but also to five hundred people at one time.[17]

Even if the disciples fell prey to some post-hypnotic suggestion or strange form of group psychosis that made the dead and buried Jesus appear alive and well before them, the hypothesis fails to take into account the reportedly very real emptiness of the tomb.[18]

THE RESUSCITATION HYPOTHESIS

Another hypothesis is that Jesus did not die on the cross. This notion was set forth by D. H. Lawrence in *The Man Who Died*. In this story, Jesus was taken down from the cross too early, revived in the tomb, and petrified His disciples when He appeared before them in the flesh. The resuscitated Jesus then headed off to Egypt to enjoy conjugal bliss with

---

16   Gary Collins, quoted in Gary R. Gromacki, "The Historicity of the Resurrection of Jesus Christ, Part Two," *Associates for Biblical Research*, April 20, 2014, http://www.biblearchaeology. org/post/2014/04/20/The-Historicity-of-the-Resurrection-of-Jesus-Christ-Part-2.aspx

17   Ibid.

18   Ian Wilson, *Jesus: The Evidence* (San Francisco: HarperCollins, 1996, p. 150.

a priestess of Isis, who mistook Him as the pagan god Osiris.[19] A similar theory is set forth in the supposedly factual *Holy Blood, Holy Grail* by Michael Baigent, Richard Leigh, and Henry Lincoln. According to this account, Jesus was revived by Mary Magdalene, his paramour, in a cave outside of Jerusalem. He made an appearance before His disciples to say, Adieu, before heading off with the former prostitute to rear a family in the south of France.[20] In *The Passover Plot*, yet another rendition of this same theory, author Hugh Schonfield argued that the sponge offered to Jesus on the cross (John 19:29-30) was soaked not in vinegar but some drug to induce an appearance of death. Unfortunately, a soldier thrust his lance into the side of Jesus, thereby actually killing Him and causing the Passover plot, which was mounted to convince the Jews that the prophet from Galilee was the Messiah to misfire. Schonfield concluded his work of "nonfiction" by stating that the man seen by Mary Magdalene at the tomb was someone who had been sent by to try to revive the dead Jesus. The Resurrection, therefore, was simply an unfortunate case of mistaken identity.[21]

The notion of the resuscitation of Jesus was debunked over one hundred and fifty years ago not by a fundamentalist zealot but rather by the Tubingen lecturer David Strauss, who believed that the accounts of the Resurrection were pious myths. In his *New Life of Jesus* (1865), Strauss wrote: "It is impossible that a being who had stolen half dead out of the sepulcher, who crept about weak and ill and wanting medical treatment. . . could have given the disciples the impression that he was a conqueror over death and the grave, the Prince of life: an impression that lay at the bottom of their future ministry. Such a resuscitation could by no

---

19   D. H. Lawrence, "The Man Who Died," Project Gutenberg, May, 2007, gutenberg.net.au/ebooks07/0700631h.html

20   Michael Baigent, Richard Leigh, and Henry Lincoln, *Holy Blood, Holy Grail* (New York: Delta, 2004), pp. 352-360.

21   Hugh J. Schonfield, *The Passover Plot* (New York: Disinformation Company, 2005), pp. 127-183.

possibility have changed their sorrow into enthusiasm, have elevated their reverence into worship."[22]

THE TRUTH OF THE RESURRECTION
What happened on Easter morning?

The evidence of the Resurrection is internal—lodged within the Epistles of Paul, which predate the four gospels and remain the earliest Christian documents. In his first letter to the Corinthians, Paul states that the Resurrection remains the indispensable part of the Gospel:

> Now, brothers and sisters, I want to remind you of the Gospel I preached to you, which you received and on which you have taken your stand. By this gospel you are saved, if you hold firmly to the Word I preached to you. Otherwise, you have believed in vain.
>
> For what I received I passed on to you as of first importance: that Christ died for our sins according to the Scriptures, that he was buried, that he was raised on the third day according to the Scriptures, and that he appeared to Cephas, and then to the Twelve. After that, he appeared to more than five hundred of the brothers and sisters at the same time, most of whom are still living, though some have fallen asleep. Then he appeared to James, then to all the apostles, and last of all he appeared to me also, as to one abnormally born.
>
> For I am the least of the apostles and do not even deserve to be called an apostle, because I persecuted the church of God. (1 Corinthians 15:1-9).

This passage is remarkable since Paul states clearly and unequivocally that the risen Jesus had been seen not only by him, by Simon Peter, by the other disciples, but also more than five hundred other people who were still alive in AD 55 when he was putting these words to papyrus.[23]

---

22   David Strauss, *The Life of Jesus for the People,* Second Edition (London: Williams and Norgate, 1879), p. 412.

23   Wilson, *Jesus: The Evidence,* p. 151. See also "The First and Second Letter to the Corinthians," *Dating the New Testament,* n. d., www.datingthenewtestament.com/Corinthians.htm

Paul went on to write:

But if it is preached that Christ has been raised from the dead, how can some of you say that there is no resurrection of the dead? If there is no resurrection of the dead, then not even Christ has been raised. And if Christ has not been raised, our preaching is useless and so is your faith. More than that, we are then found to be false witnesses about God, for we have testified about God that he raised Christ from the dead. But he did not raise him if in fact the dead are not raised. For if the dead are not raised, then Christ has not been raised either. And if Christ has not been raised, your faith is futile; you are still in your sins. Then those also who have fallen asleep in Christ are lost. If only for this life we have hope in Christ, we are of all people most to be pitied (1 Corinthians 15:12-19).

The Resurrection, therefore, was the central proclamation of the early church. Without belief in this event, faith was meaningless.

Regarding the significance of this testimony, Edwin M. Yamauchi, Associate Professor of History at Oxford, Ohio, writes: "What gives a special authority to [Paul's] list as historical evidence is the reference to most of the five hundred brethren being still alive. St. Paul says in effect: 'If you don't believe me, you can ask them.' Such a statement in an admitted genuine letter written within thirty years of the event is almost as strong evidence as one could hope to get for something that happened nearly two thousand years ago."[24]

THE FINAL PROOF

Another proof of the reality of the Resurrection resides in the fate of the first Christians. Stephen, a Hellenistic Jew, became the first Christian martyr, whose ranks came to include members of Jesus' own family. Within a generation, hundreds of men and women, mostly devout Jews, would suffer the most humiliating and painful deaths for proclaiming

---

24   Edwin M. Yamauchi, quoted in Ibid.

their belief that Jesus of Nazareth had risen from the dead. Some would be stoned; others would be torn to pieces by wild animals in a public arena, still others would be crucified in a grotesque manner.[25] Moreover, as Ian Wilson points out, they went to their deaths resolutely—even cheerfully—with no expectation of material gain or worldly acclaim for their outspokenness and self-sacrifice.[26]

The final proof of the Resurrection resides in their blood.

EASTER'S END

The Resurrection, however, is no longer central to Christian churches that have endorsed modern Gnosticism. For Marcion and his fellow Gnostics, Jesus came to the world from the realm of highest light and remained a pure spirit This Jesus never became immersed in the matter from which the God of the Old Testament fashioned the universe. Hence there was no Incarnation, no Passion, and no Resurrection.[27]

In keeping with this teaching, mainline Protestant denominations have eliminated all references to the blood of Christ from their hymns and all crosses from their sanctuaries.[28] The Gnostic Jesus whom they worship was neither the long-awaited Messiah who would restore the Kingdom of David nor the suffering servant who would atone for the sins of the world. He was and is a pure spirit who reminds people of the spark *(pneuma)* that remains within them and provides assurance that they will be reunited with the source of all light in the highest heaven.

Within this theology, there is no need of Penance and Holy Communion, let alone a cross and an empty tomb.

---

25   Ibid.

26   Ibid.

27   Frend, *The Early Church.*

28   Loren Davis, "Jesus and the Blood Have Been Removed from Most Contemporary Christian Music," Combine Harvesting International, 2013, www.lorendavis.com/news_articles_jesus_deleted_from_christian_music.html

19

JESUS: THE KINGDOM

Here considerable interest surrounds the identity of this mysterious James, who apparently had the authority to rule on matters of doctrine and adherence to traditional Jewish ways, even to the extent of overruling Peter . . . . What is quite astonishing to discuss is that this James was none other than Jesus' brother. This is attested by Josephus who, describing with genuine sadness James' unjust execution at the hands of a Sadducean high priest in 62 A. D., explicitly referred to him as "the brother of Jesus called the Christ." That this was no slip of the Josephus' pen is firmly corroborated by Paul who remarked of a trip he had made to Jerusalem. "I only saw James, the brother of the Lord" (Galatians 1:20). It is also corroborated in the writings of Hegesippus and Eusebius. And, in fact, the same information checks out with Mark's Gospel (which of course has no account of Jesus' "virgin" birth) in a passage in which the people of Nazareth say of Jesus: "This is the carpenter, the son of Mary, the brother of James and Joseph and Jude and Simon? His sisters, too, are they not with us? (Mark 6:3).

IAN WILSON, *JESUS: THE EVIDENCE*

IN HIS LETTER TO THE GALATIANS, Paul describes Peter as eating and drinking with uncircumcised Gentiles in Antioch until "certain men came from James" and ordered him to stay away from the "unclean" group (2:11-12). Paul, however, does not identify this mysterious James, who wielded such authority that Peter, who is revered as the first pope and the founder of the Roman Catholic Church, acquiesced to his demands without a whimper of protest. What's more, the word from

James was enough to make Barnabus, Paul's missionary companion, desert the disciple and abandon his work among the Gentiles.[1]

In the Book of Acts, James simply pops up without introduction or a remark from the narrator. This implies that the author of Acts assumed that every Christian would know James's identity, and the fact that he ruled the early Church as a monarch.

THE BROTHER OF JESUS

Who was James?

He was not James, the son of Zebedee, who became one of the twelve apostles, but rather the younger brother of Jesus. In the Gospel of Mark, the evangelist writes that the people of Nazareth questioned the identity of Jesus, after He spoke in the synagogue, by asking: "Isn't this the carpenter? Isn't this Mary's son, and the brother of James, Joseph, Judas and Simon? Aren't his sisters here with us?"[2]

The identity of James attracted widespread attention in 2002 when an ancient Middle-eastern ossuary (burial box) was found which bore this inscription: "James, son of Joseph, brother of Jesus." The find captured international headlines and caused a sensation in theological circles. If genuine (and that matter remains to be determined), the artifact would represent the first archaeological evidence, literally carved in stone, of the existence of Jesus and it would provide tell-tale proof that Jesus had siblings and that Mary was not a "perpetual virgin."[3]

Who was James?

The answer remains within the New Testament and early Christian documents.

---

1   Talib Morrison, "James, the Caliph of Christ," *Neurotherapy of Christian Brain,* May 12, 2012, neurotherapy-of-christian-brain.blogspot.com/2012/05/james-caliph-of-christ.html

2   Ian Wilson, *Jesus: The Evidence* (San Francisco: HarperCollins, 1996), p. 158.

3   Jeffrey J. Butz, *The Brother of Jesus and the Lost Teachings of Christianity* (Rochester, Vermont: Inner Traditions, 2005, p. 9.

THE RESURRECTION APPEARANCE

In his first letter to the Corinthians, Paul reports that Jesus made a Resurrection appearance to James (1 Cor. 15:8). Although this appearance is not recorded in any of the four gospels, the lost *Gospel to the Hebrews*, as cited by St. Jerome, contains this cryptic extract:

> But the Lord when He had given the shroud to the high priest's servant, went to James and appeared to him. For James had sworn that he would not eat bread from that hour when he had drunk the Lord's cup until he saw Him rising from those who sleep. . . . "Bring," says the Lord, "a table and bread." He took the bread and blessed it and broke it and gave it to James the Righteous, and said to him: "My brother, eat your bread, for the Son of Man has risen from those who sleep."[4]

THE AUTHORITY OF JAMES

In the Book of Acts, James, upon hearing the testimony of the two apostles, renders his verdict regarding the matter of sharing the Gospel with uncircumcised Gentiles by citing a passage from the prophet Amos:

> It is my judgment, therefore, that we should not make it difficult for the Gentiles who are turning to God. Instead we should write to them, telling them to abstain from food polluted by idols, from sexual immorality, from the meat of strangled animals and from blood. For the law of Moses has been preached in every city from the earliest times and is read in the synagogues on every Sabbath (15:19-21).

The Book of Acts further records that when Paul arrived in Jerusalem to deliver the money he raised for the Christian community, he was obliged to report to James, who insisted that Paul ritually cleanse himself at the Temple in order to prove his Jewish faith and to deny rumors of teaching contrary to the Torah. He further said that Paul, like James, should take the vow of a Nazarite. (Acts 2:17-26).

---

4   "Gospel of the Hebrews," quoted in Ian Wilson, *Jesus: The Evidence* (San Francisco: HarperCollins, 1996), p. 159.

JAMES AND JESUS

Those who took the vow of a Nazarite had to be willing to sacrifice certain aspects of their life for the duration of their pledge. They had to abstain entirely from wine or any fermented drink. They also were forbidden to eat grapes and any product made from them, including raisins. They could not cut their hair or trim their beards.[5] A Nazarite was not permitted to come near a corpse, even if it was from a close family member, so that they would not be rendered unclean.[6] He was to consecrate himself completely to the worship and will of God.

The fact that James, like his cousin John the Baptist, had taken the Nazarite vow sheds light on the possibility that Jesus, too, had assumed the vow and lived as an ascetic among His followers—shunning all earthly pleasures, include cotton attire, maintaining a strict regimen of prayer and fasting, and refusing to trim His hair and beard. New Testament scholar Jeffrey Butz writes: "He [James] knew the 'mind of the master' better than anyone. And if he did, Christians today are going to have to re-evaluate some of their most deeply held assumptions and beliefs about Jesus and his teaching."[7] Similarly, Prof. Barrie Wilson, a leading expert on first century Christianity adds: "As James, so Jesus. The best indicator of what Jesus of the 20s actually taught is likely to be James, his brother. James knew the man and what he stood for. He knew Jesus taught and practiced Torah, as they did....the example of James is the best clue we have today concerning the beliefs and practices of the Jesus of history."[8]

---

5   Michal Hunt, "The Vow of the Nazarite," *Agape Bible Study*, 2006, agapebiblestudy.com/documents/The%20Nazirite%20Vow.htm

6   "What is the Nazarite Vow?" *Bible Study. Org*, n. d., www.biblestudy.org/maturart/what-is-the-nazarite-vow.html

7   Butz, *The Brother of Jesus and the Lost Teachings of Christianity*, p. 186.

8   Barrie Wilson, *How Jesus Became Christian* (San Angelo, Texas: Phoenix Publishing, 2009), p. 98.

JAMES, THE RIGHTEOUS

Regarding James's asceticism, the early Christian apologist Hegesippus (AD 110–180) writes:

> He was holy from his mother's womb; and he drank no wine nor strong drink, nor did he eat flesh. No razor came upon his head; he did not anoint himself with oil, and he did not use the bath. He alone was permitted to enter into the holy place; for he wore not woolen but linen garments. And he was in the habit of entering alone into the temple and was frequently found upon his knees begging forgiveness for the people, so that his knees became hard like those of a camel, in consequence of his constantly bending them in his worship of God, and asking forgiveness for the people. Because of his exceeding great justice, he was called the Just, and Oblias, which signifies in Greek, 'Bulwark of the people' and 'Justice,' in accordance with what the prophets declare concerning him. Now some of the seven sects, which existed among the people and which have been mentioned by me in the Memoirs, asked him, 'What is the gate of Jesus?' and he replied that he was the Savior. On account of these words some believed that Jesus is the Christ. But the sects mentioned above did not believe either in a resurrection or in one's coming to give to every man according to his works. But as many as believed did so on account of James.[9]

The so-called Clementine Homilies, which date from first Christian century, contain a letter of the Apostle Peter to James, in which Peter addresses the brother of Jesus as "the lord, and the bishop of bishops, who rules Jerusalem, the holy church of the Hebrews, and the churches everywhere excellently founded by the providence of God, with the

---

9   Hegesippus, "Fragments from the Books of Commentary on the Acts of the Church," *Early Christian Writings*, www.earlychristianwritings.com/text/hegesippus.html

elders and deacons, and the rest of the brethren, peace be always."[10] The exalted position of James as the sole ruler of primitive Christianity is further upheld by the *Gospel of Thomas* which contains this passage: The disciples said to Jesus, 'We know that you will depart from us. Who is to be our leader?' Jesus said to them, 'Wherever you are, you are to go to James the righteous, for whose sake heaven and earth come into being.'"[11]

JOSEPHUS AND JAMES

Significantly, James, apart from Jesus and John the Baptist, is the only New Testament figure mentioned by Josephus (AD 37-100) in his seminal work *Jewish Antiquities*. James, according to Josephus, was a highly significant figure in first Century Jerusalem not only amongst his own community but also the "orthodox" Jews. He was, Josephus writes, the "most equitable of the citizens" who had garnered great admiration from the common people. Such popular support, Josephus continues, threatened the status of Ananias, the high priest, who arranged to drag James before a Jewish court on charges that he had violated the Mosaic law and should be stoned to death. Josephus says that the religiously observant Jews of Jerusalem were outraged at what they saw as a clear injustice and an invalid order of execution for one of their most pious citizens. According to this ancient historian, the Jews petitioned King Agrippa, who promptly removed Ananias from his position as the high priest at the Temple.[12]

The account is telling. Ananias had only been in the post for a few months and came from a highly influential family that had dominated the priesthood for the last sixty years. This indicates that James was an

---

10 "Epistle of Peter to James, *Clementine Homilies*, New Advent, www.newadvent.org/fathers/080800.htm

11 "The Gospel of Thomas, 12 (circa 40 AD – 140 AD), translated by Stephen Patterson and Marvin Meyer, *Nag Hammadi Library*, www.gnosis.org/naghamm/gosthom.html

12 Josephus, "Antiquities of the Jewish People," Book 20, Chapter 9, in *The Jewish Roman World of Jesus*, https://pages.uncc.edu/james-tabor/ancient-judaism/josephus-james/

important and revered figure with powerful advocates.[13] Some scholars, including John Dominic Crossan, have even postulated that James could have been in Jerusalem even before Jesus' ascension and might have been a respected Pharisaic leader, when His brother was proclaiming the message of the coming Kingdom.[14]

THE MARTYRDOM OF JAMES

According to Hegesippus, Ananus did not go quietly into the good night of sacerdotal retirement. His anger against James intensified into murderous rage. When James appeared at the parapet of the Temple at the start of the Sabbath and announced that the Son of Man was now "sitting at the right hand of God," Ananus and his henchmen cast him to the ground. Seeing that James was still alive after the precipitous fall, they stoned him and clubbed him to death with fuller clubs. Hegesippus recounts that James, with his dying breath, asked for divine forgiveness for his executioners by saying: "I beseech Thee, Lord God our Father, forgive them; for they know not what they do."[15] In this war, his final words echoed those of his brother.

THE CHRISTIAN CALIPHATE

The monarchial authority of James in the early church supports the claim of early 20th Century theologian Adolph Harnack that the followers of Jesus after His death sought to establish a caliphate along a Davidic bloodline.[16] James was assisted by the twelve disciples, who represented the twelve tribes of Israel.[17] As long as James lived, Jerusalem remained the center of the Christian movement, and the council over

---

13   Morrison, "James, the Caliph of Christ."

14   Ibid.

15   Hegesippus, "Fragments from the Books of Commentary on the Acts of the Church."

16   Adolph Harnarck. *Entstehung und Entwicklung der Kirchenverfassung und des Kirchenrechts in den zwei ersten Jahrhunderten.* (Leipzig: J. C. Hinrichs, 1910), p. 26.

17   W. H. C. Frend, *The Early Church* (Philadelphia: J P. Lippincott, 1966), p. 50.

which he presided served to leaven and guide the Jewish people in the short time that remained before the end of days.[18]

According to the Book of Acts (5:12-16), James' work among the Jews of Jerusalem bore abundant fruit. Many accepted the Good News that Jesus was the long-awaited Messiah, and this created a stir among the opponents of the early Christian movement. The New Testament, which is heavily slanted towards the missionary efforts of Paul, doesn't shine abundant light on the efforts of the Jerusalem Apostles and the reign of James.[19] Nevertheless, their success eventually brought about the martyrdom of Stephen and the Lord's younger brother.

THE JEWISHNESS OF JAMES

Although it is tucked away near the end of the New Testament, the Epistle of James, scholars now agree, bears the marks of authenticity and appears to have been written by James himself. British scholar John A. T. Robinson writes: "It shows no signs of developed Church or church order or of the arguments, such as mark the Epistles of Paul, about the terms on which Gentiles could be full members of the Church. . . . The Epistle is likely to have been written not long before, perhaps in about 47. It would then be the first finished piece of Christian writing to have survived."[20]

The dedication of James to the Old Testament and the Mosaic Law is evident in the following passage from his epistle:

> What good is it, my brothers and sisters, if you say you have faith but do not have works? Can faith save you? If a brother or sister is naked and lacks daily food, and one of you says to them, "Go in peace; keep warm and eat your fill," and yet you do not supply their bodily needs, what is the good of that? So faith by itself, if it has no works, is dead.

---

18   Ibid.

19   Morrison, "James, the Caliph of Christ."

20   John A. T. Robinson, *Can We Trust the New Testament?* (Grand Rapids: William B. Eerdmans Publishing Company, 1977), pp. 68-69.

But someone will say, "You have faith and I have works." Show me your faith apart from your works, and I by my works will show you my faith. You believe that God is one; you do well. Even the demons believe—and shudder. Do you want to be shown, you senseless person, that faith apart from works is barren? Was not our ancestor Abraham justified by works when he offered his son Isaac on the altar? You see that faith was active along with his works, and faith was brought to completion by the works. Thus the scripture was fulfilled that says, "Abraham believed God, and it was reckoned to him as righteousness," and he was called the friend of God. You see that a person is justified by works and not by faith alone (James 2:14-24).

Unlike the Epistles of Paul, James' letter mirrors the teachings of Jesus, including the Sermon on the Mount. The passage quoted above bears a striking similarity to Matthew 7:15-20 in which Jesus says:

Watch out for false prophets. They come to you in sheep's clothing, but inwardly they are ferocious wolves. By their fruit you will recognize them. Do people pick grapes from thorn bushes, or figs from thistles? Likewise, every good tree bears good fruit, but a bad tree bears bad fruit. A good tree cannot bear bad fruit, and a bad tree cannot bear good fruit. Every tree that does not bear good fruit is cut down and thrown into the fire. Thus, by their fruit you will recognize them.

AS JESUS, SO JAMES

The Epistle is grounded in obedience to dictates of the Torah. James writes: "If you really keep the royal law found in Scripture, 'Love your neighbor as yourself,' you are doing right. But if you show favoritism, you sin and are convicted by the law as lawbreakers. For whoever keeps the whole law and yet stumbles at just one point is guilty of breaking all of it. For he who said, 'You shall not commit adultery,' also said, 'You shall not murder.' If you do not commit adultery but do commit murder, you have become a lawbreaker" (2:8-11). This coincides with this teaching from the Sermon on the Mount:

Do not think that I have come to abolish the Law or the Prophets; I have not come to abolish them but to fulfill them. For truly I tell you, until heaven and earth disappear, not the smallest letter, not the least stroke of a pen, will by any means disappear from the Law until everything is accomplished. Therefore, anyone who sets aside one of the least of these commands and teaches others accordingly will be called least in the kingdom of heaven, but whoever practices and teaches these commands will be called great in the kingdom of heaven. For I tell you that unless your righteousness surpasses that of the Pharisees and the teachers of the law, you will certainly not enter the kingdom of heaven (Matt. 5:12-20).

James writes: "Religion that is pure and undefiled before God, the Father, is this: to care for orphans and widows in their distress, and to keep oneself unstained by the world" (James 1:27). This teaching reflects the following words of Jesus:

Be careful not to practice your righteousness in front of others to be seen by them. If you do, you will have no reward from your Father in heaven. So, when you give to the needy, do not announce it with trumpets, as the hypocrites do in the synagogues and on the streets, to be honored by others. Truly I tell you, they have received their reward in full. But when you give to the needy, do not let your left hand know what your right hand is doing, so that your giving may be in secret. Then your Father, who sees what is done in secret, will reward you (Matt. 6:1-4).

SIBLING SIMILARITIES

The parallels between the teachings of the brothers persist. James says: "My brothers and sisters, whenever you face trials of any kind, consider it nothing but joy, because you know that the testing of your faith produces endurance; and let endurance have its full effect, so that you may be mature and complete, lacking in nothing." This teaching appears to have been derived from the passage of the Sermon on the Mount in which Jesus says: "Blessed are you when people insult you, persecute you and falsely say all kinds of evil against you because of me. Rejoice and be glad, because great is your reward in heaven, for in the same way they persecuted the prophets who were before you" (Matt. 5:11).

James speaks of patience by writing: "Come now, you who say, 'Today or tomorrow we will go to such and such a town and spend a year there, doing business and making money.' Yet you do not even know what tomorrow will bring. What is your life? For you are a mist that appears for a little while and then vanishes. Instead you ought to say, 'If the Lord wishes, we will live and do this or that'" (4:13-15). He continues as follows: "The farmer waits for the precious crop from the earth, being patient with it until it receives the early and the late rains. You also must be patient. Strengthen your hearts, for the coming of the Lord is near" (5:7-8). The similarity between this teaching and the following passage from Sermon from the Mount remains striking:

> Therefore, I tell you, do not worry about your life, what you will eat or drink; or about your body, what you will wear. Is not life more than food, and the body more than clothes? Look at the birds of the air; they do not sow or reap or store away in barns, and yet your heavenly Father feeds them. Are you not much more valuable than they? Can any one of you by worrying add a single hour to your life? And why do you worry about clothes? See how the flowers of the field grow. They do not labor or spin. Yet I tell you that not even Solomon in all his splendor was dressed like one of these. If that is how God clothes the grass of the field, which is here today and tomorrow is thrown into the fire, will he not much more clothe you—you of little faith? So do not worry, saying, 'What shall we eat?' or 'What shall we drink?' or 'What shall we wear?' For the pagans run after all these things, and your heavenly Father knows that you need them. But seek first his kingdom and his righteousness, and all these things will be given to you as well. Therefore, do not worry about tomorrow, for tomorrow will worry about itself. Each day has enough trouble of its own (Matthew 6:25-34).

JAMES AND PAUL

As evidenced by his letter, James has a radically different understanding of the teachings of Jesus than Paul, who upholds the belief that man is saved by faith alone in Christ's work of Atonement and Resurrection. Many scholars have tried to reconcile the two apostles by overlooking the obvious contradiction between their views on faith and the Law. Others, realizing the futility of such an effort, opt to ignore the epistle from the Lord's brother for the sake of theological cohesion. There is an inherent danger in the doctrine of justification by faith that it may lead to a disregard for morality in general. Paul himself had to deal with such occurrences during his own lifetime and Christian communities have always struggled with trying to enforce and encourage morality whilst also preaching that man is saved by faith alone and that good works represent little more than "filthy rags." For this reason, the Epistle of James has played the vital role of serving as a check and balance against extreme Paulinism.[21]

Largely because of the theological cleft between James and Paul, several New Testament scholars have come to the conclusion that the beliefs of James and the Jerusalem Church stand in sharp contrast to normative Christianity. In *The Brother of Jesus and the Lost Teachings of Christianity,* Jeffrey Butz writes: "Everything points to the conclusion that the leaders of the so-called 'Jerusalem Church' were not Christians in any sense that would be intelligible to Christians of a later date."[22] Keith Akers came to a similar conclusion in his work *The Lost Religion of Jesus* by writing: "The books seeking to understand the Jewishness of Jesus are now legion. Yet almost no one wants to confront the problem of Jewish Christianity. The reason for this reluctance is not hard to find; the views of Jewish Christianity are not those of most Christians. The theology is of course unacceptable, being in essence a form of Jewish monotheism."[23]

---

21   Morrison, "James, the Caliph of Christ."

22   Jeffrey Butz, *The Brother of Jesus and the Lost Teachings of Christianity*, p. 151.

23   Keith Akers. *The Lost Religion of Jesus* (Myerstown, PA: Lantern Books, 2000), p. 226.

THE FIRST COUSIN

For James's successor as ruler of the early church, the Council at Jerusalem chose Simeon, whose father Cleophas was the first cousin of James and Jesus. Hegesippus writes: "And after James the Just had suffered martyrdom, as had the Lord also and on the same account, again Simeon the son of Cleophas, descended from *the Lord's* uncle, is made bishop, his election being promoted by all as being a kinsman of the Lord."[24]

At the time of the First Jewish-Roman War (AD 66–70), according to Eusebius (AD 263-339), the followers of James, under Simeon's leadership, relocated to Pella in Jordan.[25] They continued to observe the Hebrew Sabbath, the rite of circumcision, and the Jewish holy days. They preached in the synagogue and almost solely to Jews. The form, the ceremony, and the vestments of Hebrew worship, thanks to James, Simeon, and the church at Jerusalem, became incorporated into Christian worship. The Paschal lamb of sacrifice became the *Agnus Dei*, the expiatory "Lamb of God" whose vicarious death for mankind was offered on Christian altars. And appointment of elders *(presbyteri* or "priests") to govern the Christian congregations throughout the Greco-Roman world was modeled after the Jewish methods of administering the scattered synagogues.[26]

THE END OF THE LINE

During the reign of the Emperor Trajan (AD 93-110), according to Eusebius, Simeon and all blood relatives of Jesus were rounded up and put to death.[27] The martyrs came to include the grandsons of Judas, yet

---

24   Hegesippus, "Fragments from the Books of Commentary on the Acts of the Church."

25   Eusebius, *Church History*, Book III, translated by Arthur Cushman McGiffert, in *Nicene and Post Nicene Fathers* (Buffalo, NY: Christian Literature Publishing, 1890), www.newadvent.org/fathers/250103.htm

26   Will Durant, *Caesar and Christ, Volume III, The Story of Civilization* (New York: Simon and Schuster, 1944, pp. 578-579.

27   Hegesippus, "Fragments from the Books of Commentary on the Acts of the Church."

another brother of Jesus.[28] The temporal kingdom that the Church had sought to establish along the bloodlines of Jesus had come to an end. Trajan, to the end of his days, remained fearful that the Kingdom of David, once again, would rise from the deserts of Palestine. Hegesippus writes: "Up to that period the Church had remained like a virgin pure and uncorrupted: for, if there were any persons who were disposed to tamper with the wholesome rule of the preaching of salvation, they still lurked in some dark place of concealment or other. But, when the sacred band of apostles had in various ways closed their lives, and that generation of men to whom it had been vouchsafed to listen to the Godlike Wisdom with their own ears had passed away, then did the confederacy of godless error take its rise through the treachery of false teachers, who, seeing that none of the apostles any longer survived, at length attempted with bare and uplifted head to oppose the preaching of the truth by preaching 'knowledge falsely so called.'"

AQUINAS AND THE LAW

Throughout the Middle Ages, the Epistle of James remained venerated by Christians and no attempt was made to sever Christian doctrine from Mosaic law. This is evident from the following passage of the *Summa Theologiae* by Thomas Aquinas:

> The more a man is united to God, the better his state becomes: wherefore the more the Jewish people were bound to the worship of God, the greater their excellence over other peoples. Hence it is written in Deuteronomy 4:8, "What other nation is there so renowned that hath ceremonies and just judgments, and all the law?" In like manner, from this point of view, the state of clerics is better than that of the laity, and the state of religious than that of folk living in the world. . . .
>
> The Gentiles obtained salvation more perfectly and more securely under the observances of the Law than under the mere natural law:

---

28   Ibid.

and for this reason, they were admitted to them [the Christian congregations]. So too the laity are now admitted to the ranks of the clergy, and secular persons to those of the religious, although they can be saved without this.[29]

"AN EPISTLE OF STRAW"

This situation changed with the Protestant Reformation. Martin Luther, in espousing his teaching that man is justified by faith alone, realized that the principal stumbling block to his denial of the efficacy of good works was the Epistle of James, which he ripped from every Bible in his possession. Luther wrote: "In a word, St. John's Gospel and his first epistle, St. Paul's epistles, especially Romans, Galatians, and Ephesians, and St. Peter's first epistle are the books that show you Christ and teach you all that it is necessary and salvatory for you to know, even if you were never to see or hear any other book or doctrine. St. James' epistle is really an epistle of straw, compared to the others, for it has nothing of the nature of the gospel about it."[30]

Luther's reaction to the Epistle of James was compounded by his virulent ant-Semitism. In his diatribe against the Jews ("on the Jews and Their Lies"), he wrote:

What shall we Christians do with this rejected and condemned people, the Jews? Since they live among us, we dare not tolerate their conduct, now that we are aware of their lying and reviling and blaspheming. . . . I shall give you my sincere advice:

First to set fire to their synagogues or schools and to bury and cover with dirt whatever will not burn, so that no man will ever again see a stone or cinder of them. This is to be done in honor of our Lord and of Christendom, so that God might see that we are Christians,

---

29 Thomas Aquinas, *Summa Theologiae,* First Part of the Second Part, Question 98, Article 4, in New Advent.org, www.newadvent.org/summa/2098.htm

30 Martin Luther, *Luther's Works,* Vol. 35, *Word and Sacrament* (Philadelphia: Fortress Press, 1960), pp. 395-397.

and do not condone or knowingly tolerate such public lying, cursing, and blaspheming of his Son and of his Christians. . .

Second, I advise that their houses also be razed and destroyed. For they pursue in them the same aims as in their synagogues. Instead they might be lodged under a roof or in a barn, like the gypsies. . . .

Third, I advise that all their prayer books and Talmudic writings, in which such idolatry, lies, cursing and blasphemy are taught, be taken from them.[31]

Luther's hatred of the Jews led him to make a distinction between the *Deus Absconditus* ('the "hidden God") of the Old Testament and the *Deus Revelatus* (the "revealed God") of Jesus.[32] In this way, he forged a link with Marcion that led not only to the rise of the Third Reich but also to the widespread acceptance of Gnosticism by contemporary Christians.

The die had been cast.

31   Martin Luther, "On the Jews and Their Lies," 1543, extracts from the Jewish Virtual Library, www.preteristarchive.com/Books/1543_luther_jews.html

32   "Deus Absconditus, Deus Revelatus," The Lutheran Church, Missouri Synod, *Christian Cyclopedia*, edited by Erwin L. Lueker, Luther Poellot, and Paul Jackson, 2000, cyclopedia.lcms.org/display.asp?t1=D&word=DEUSABSCONDITUS.DEUSREVELATUS

20

JESUS: THE NEED FOR A SWORD

Nonviolence can be thought of as both a means and an end. It is an end in that it refers to the future world we long for—a world free from violence and war, free from hunger and poverty, free from injustice and oppression, and full of God's love and healing. Jesus called it "the kingdom of God"; Martin Luther King, Jr., called it "the beloved community"; and Walter Wink called it "the domination-free order." Nonviolence also can be thought of as a means in two ways: as a technique for engaging in conflict and as an ethic or philosophy for living one's life.

PRESBYTERIAN CHURCH (USA), "PEACE AND

DISCERNMENT INTERIM REPORT, 2012"

THE 2012 GENERAL ASSEMBLY of the Presbyterian Church (USA) issued a report on "Peace and Discernment Interim Report which maintained that the abstract concept of "nonviolence" was the central theme of the ministry of Jesus, even though nonviolence is a 20th Century term which was never used by Jesus or anyone else in the New Testament. The report maintains that Jesus lived "a prophetic and nonviolent life that threatened both the Roman and temple authorities."[1] It reduces Christ to an exponent of a "strategy that—rather than fight evil or flee—it resists evil through nonviolent means, an approach that outflanks and reverses aggression, sometimes by choosing to suffer." It downplays the "violent imagery" in Jesus' parables and other New Testament passages that show God's anger and determination to destroy Sin. The report excuses Jesus' attack on the moneychangers in the temple, stating, incorrectly, that "he stopped short of violence against persons."[2]

Old Testament instances in which God commanded Israel to wage war, according to the report, are products of a primitive mentality. In the manner of Gnosticism, it views the scriptures as "a progressive revelation leading from the initial wars in Canaan toward more profound models of faithfulness such as that of the 'suffering servant.'" The early Christians, the report states, beat their swords into ploughshares when it came to the matter of violence and self-defense, adding, "There is no affirmation of killing or war anywhere in the writings of the early church."[3]

This portrait of early Christians as Tibetan monks ignores the work of contemporary scholars. Peter Leithart, in his book *Defending Constantine*, explores the complexity of early Christian attitudes toward war. Long before Constantine, going back to the centurion Cornelius in Acts 10, there were Christians who served in the Roman army and were accepted in the Church. Leithart concludes, "The church was *never* united in an absolute opposition to Christian participation in war; the opposition that existed was in some measure circumstantial, based on the fact that the Roman army demanded sharing in religious liturgies that Christians refused; and once [after Constantine] military service could be pursued without participating in idolatry, many Christians found military service a legitimate life for a Christian disciple."[4]

---

1   "Peace and Discernment Interim Report," Presbyterian Church (USA), 2012, http://www.pcusa. org/media/uploads/peacemaking/pdf/peace-discernment-interim-report.pdf

2   Ibid.

3   Ibid.

4   Peter Leithart, *Defending Constantine* (Downers Grove, Illinois, 2010), p. 273.

JESUS: THE FLOWER CHILD

The position of the Presbyterian Church (USA) is mirrored by the pacifist statements of other denominations. In one of her sermons, Jane Florence, a United Methodist minister in Omaha, Nebraska, preached the following:

> When Jesus is accosted by a "large crowd with swords and clubs," they lay hands on him, and one of his followers pulls out a sword and slices off an ear of someone grabbing Jesus. It could have turned into a bloody mayhem—good guys against the bad. Jesus stops his follower who attempts to intervene with violence and says, "put your sword back—for all who take the sword will perish by it." As if to say, we won't become one of them by stooping to their violent ways. As if to say, retaliation is not the solution. As if to say, the sword is not God's Way. Jesus taught nonviolence—even in the face of his own imminent death, violence was not an appropriate response. Jesus lived and died a pacifist.[5]

Nowhere is the triumph of Gnosticism more telling than in this statement by a Methodist minister. Gone from this depiction of Jesus is the long-awaited Messiah, who said: "Do not suppose that I have come to bring peace on earth. I did not come to bring peace, but a sword" (Matt. 10:34). Gone is the teacher of righteousness who drove the money changers from the Temple with a whip he had made out of cords (John 2:16). Gone is the demanding Son of God, who maintained: "Not everyone who says to me, 'Lord, Lord,' will enter the kingdom of heaven, but only the one who does the will of my Father who is in heaven. Many will say to me on that day, 'Lord, Lord, did we not prophesy in your name and in your name drive out demons and in your name perform many miracles?' Then I will tell them plainly, 'I never knew you. Away from me, you evildoers!'" (Matt. 7:21-23). Gone, too,

---

5   Jane Florence, "Jesus, a Pacifist," First United Methodist Church, Omaha, Nebraska, February 28, 2016, http://fumcomaha.org/2016/02/28/jesus-a-pacifist/

is the long-awaited Son of David who surrounded himself with armed disciples and cursed the righteous leaders of His day with violent and vituperative language: "You snakes! You brood of vipers! How will you escape being condemned to hell?" (Matt. 23:33). What is left for the Rev. Florence and her flock is the clownish figure, depicted in *Godspell*, who performs magic tricks to the strains of "Day by Day."

THE ROD OF IRON

Jesus recognized that public officials were commissioned to protect and defend the common good, by force if necessary. When asked directly by Roman soldiers, "What shall we do?" Jesus does not tell them to lay down their arms, He instead warns them not to "extort money from anyone by threats or by false accusation" (Luke 3:14). Later in the Gospel of Luke, He gives unreserved praise to the Centurion for his faith, with no critique given regarding his profession (Luke 7:6). Jesus also endorsed the possession of lethal weapons when he urged his disciples to purchase swords, saying: "Then said he unto them, 'But now, he that hath a purse, let him take it, and likewise his scrip: and he that hath no sword, let him sell his garment, and buy one'" (Luke 22:36).

In Romans 13:4, Paul supported the use of force to uphold the law by writing, "For he is God's servant for your good. But if you do wrong, be afraid, for he does not bear the sword in vain." Similarly Peter wrote: "Submit yourselves for the Lord's sake to every human authority: whether to the emperor, as the supreme authority, or to governors, who are sent by him to punish those who do wrong and to commend those who do right" (1 Peter 2:13-14).

In the Book of Revelation, the sacrificial offering role that Jesus fulfilled on the cross is changed to the role of a judge who "rules with a rod of iron, as when earthen pots are broken into pieces" (Revelation 2:27). The word "rule" is translated from the Greek word *poimano*, which means to "shepherd" or "guard."[6] At the time of the Second Coming, Jesus' role will be to protect his children with violent force, with a "rod of iron." This is one more piece of evidence that the New Testament does not condemn the use of force or violence as inherently evil.

CHRISTIAN PACIFISM

In "Why I Am Not a Pacifist," C. S. Lewis wrote: "Does anyone suppose," he asks, "that our Lord's hearers understood him to mean that if a homicidal maniac, attempting to murder a third party, tried to knock me out of the way, I must stand aside and let him get his victim?"[7] He went on to write that the national use of force is often the only way to stop another invading nation. Viewing war as the "greater evil" implies a "materialist ethic, a belief that death and pain are the greatest evils." Lewis argued:

> It is arguable that a criminal can always be satisfactorily dealt with without the death penalty. It is certain that a whole nation cannot be prevented from taking what it wants except by war. It is almost equally certain that the absorption of certain societies by certain other societies is a great evil. The doctrine that war is always a greater evil seems to imply a materialist ethic, a belief that death and pain are the greatest evils. But I do not think they are. I think the suppression of a higher religion by a lower, or even a higher secular culture by a lower, a much greater evil.[8]

For Lewis, the "suppression of a higher religion by a lower or even a higher culture by a lower" is a much greater evil. At the time of his writing, Great Britain had just survived, at an extremely high cost of

---

6   The NAS New Testament Greek Lexicon, https://www.biblestudytools.com/lexicons/greek/nas/poimaino.html

7   C. S. Lewis, "Why I Am Not a Pacifist" in *The Weight of Glory: And Other Addresses* (New York: HarperCollins Publishers, 1940), p. 86.

8   Ibid., 77.

human life, the brutal attempt of Nazi Germany not only to dominate the British politically, but also to replace its Christian identity with one willing to use unlimited means to eliminate "non-Aryan" races. In his view, preventing the domination and potential eradication of Christian culture was an objective worth fighting and dying for.

DEFENSE AGAINST THE GOVERNMENT

Another aspect of self-defense to consider is defense against one's own government. The twentieth century provided ample evidence of what can happen when people replace faith in God with a secular ideology. The racial identity ideology adopted by the German National Socialist Workers Party, which took power in the 1930s, led to the deaths of 13-21 million human beings. Communist ideology led to the deaths of an estimated 150 million civilians. In the past century, six times more people died due to government-sponsored mass killings, democide, than died in combat in all the foreign and internal wars in the same period.[9]

NEW LIGHT ON JOHN'S GOSPEL

What remained most startling about the Dead Sea Scrolls was the fact that they contained the same language and imagery that had been dismissed as late Hellenistic in the Gospel of John. Like the Essenes, John makes persistent use of such phrases as "the spirit of truth," "the light of the world," "walking in darkness," and "the children of light." The similarities between the scrolls and the fourth gospel can be witnessed by a comparison of John's prologue with the opening of an Essene manuscript called the "Manual of Darkness."

He was with God in the beginning
Through Him all things came to be,
Not one thing had its being but through Him (John 1:2-3).

---

9   Rudolph J. Rummel, *Death by Government.* (New Brunswick, NJ: Transaction Publishers, 1994). Discussion at https://www.hawaii.edu/powerkills/NOTE1.HTM "IMPORTANT NOTE" states the "death by government" to be 262,000,000. Accessed March 30, 2019.

All things came to pass by His knowledge,
He establishes all things by His design
And without Him nothing is done (Manual 11:11).[10]

When speaking of the desire of government to remove unwanted members of the population, it does not help if those citizens are armed. There is a chilling pattern of gun confiscation and gun registration directly preceding outbreaks of mass murder, i.e. genocide. Here are some examples:[11]

- The Turkish government tightened gun control in advance of the Armenian genocide that began in 1915.

- Germany banned firearm sales to Jews in 1938. From 1939 to 1945 a total of 13 million[12] unarmed and disarmed Jews and other ethnic groups were sent to concentration camps and exterminated.

- The Soviet Union instituted gun control in 1929, confiscating weapons from a Soviet population that had always been heavily armed. From 1929 to 1953, about 20 million dissidents, now lacking any means for self-defense, were herded together and slaughtered.

- China's gun control program was launched by the Republic of China in 1938. From 1948 to 1952, 20 million political dissidents with no means of self-defense were massacred by the Communist government. An additional 53 million were killed through government policies that caused mass starvation.

---

10 Ian Wilson, *Jesus: The Evidence* (San Francisco: Harper Collins, 1996), pp. 33-34.

11 Further discussion of these 7 examples of democide can be read in the article "Gun Control and Genocide," posted 5/14/2016. https://archive.org/stream/FiveCasesOfGenocideInTheTwentiethCentury19151995101/Gun%20Control%20and%20Genocide%20-%20Mercyseat.net-16_djvu.txt

12 Scott Manning, "Communist Body Count," December 4, 2006. https://scottmanning.com/content/communist-body-count/

- Cambodia instituted gun control laws in 1956. From 1975 to 1977, over one million people who were considered to have been "contaminated" by education or contact with "bourgeois" Western values or culture were eliminated.

- Guatemala implemented gun control regulations in 1964, in advance of killing 100,000 Mayan Indians.

- Uganda launched its gun control program in 1970, just before an eight-year reign of terror put thousands of Christians to death.

Such horrors were deeply rooted in ideologies and political movements, which dehumanized members of different racial, religious, or class groups. As discussed in chapter 13, Nazism and Communism both viewed the state as the proper agent to control and eliminate the demonized. Unfortunately, mainstream media was often complicit with government-engineered mass murder. Journalists who already agreed with a national ideology or cause found a multitude of ways to portray their actions in a positive light.[13]

A 2018 report, which notably has received little attention in our mass media, warns:

Christians now face worse persecution than at any time in history. "Persecuted and Forgotten" warns that Christians in many countries will not survive if violence against them continues. The report highlighted "unspeakable atrocities" around the world including in North Korea where believers face "enforced starvation, abortion, and reports of faithful being hung on crosses over a fire and others being crushed under a steamroller.[14]

---

13 One example is Walter Duranty, writer for the *New York Times*, who was awarded the Pulitzer prize in 1932 for his articles praising the "progressive" leaders of the Soviet Union, even while the forced starvation of 4 million Ukrainians was taking place. See https://www.nytco.com/new-york-times-statement-about-1932-pulitzer-prize-awarded-to-walter-duranty/.

14 Persecution and Forgotten? A report of Christians Persecution and Oppression in the World 2015 – 2017. https://acnuk.org/country-profiles/

The report adds:

Not only are Christians more persecuted than any other faith group, but ever-increasing numbers are experiencing the very worst forms of persecution. As well as persecution in the Middle East at the hands of Islamic extremism, the report also outlines abuses in Nigeria where the Islamist ISIS-affiliate Boko Haram has displaced nearly 2 million people. . .

The pervasive nature of persecution—and evidence implicating regimes with whom the West has close trading and strategic links— means that it behooves our governments to use their influence to stand up for minorities, especially Christians. No longer should Christians be sacrificed on the altar of strategic expediency and economic advantage.[15]

"WE RECOGNIZE NO KING BUT JESUS"

In the political context the implications of Christian faith for real or potential tyrannies became crystal clear during the American War for Independence. As a British-appointed governor noted: "If you ask an American, who is his master? He will tell you he has none, nor any governor but Jesus Christ."[16] Likewise, when British Major Pitcairn shouted to an assembled regiment of Minutemen: "Disperse, ye villains, lay down your arms in the name of George the Sovereign King of England," Rev. Jonas Clark responded, "We recognize no Sovereign but God and no King but Jesus!"[17]

American Christians were well aware of scriptures that teach they should be meek and slow to anger, but when faced with government actions that violated Biblical teachings or attempted to smother out their

---

15   Ibid.

16   Peter Marshall and David Manuel, *The Light and the Glory* (Grand Rapids, Michigan, Revel, 2009), p. 324.

17   Ibid., 324.

"God-given" freedoms, many saw that it was their Christian responsibility to take up arms. Reverend John Peter Muhlenberg threw off his clerical garb at the end of his sermon to his Woodstock, Virginia congregation to reveal his military uniform, proclaiming, "There is a time to pray and a time to fight, and that time has now come!" Muhlenberg took part in the fighting at Charleston, Brandywine, Stony Point, and Yorktown, as well as in the winter at Valley Forge.[18]

After the victory of the militia at the Lexington Green and Concord in 1775, the British retaliated by seizing and obliterating colonial firearms: In Virginia, they seized twenty barrels of gunpowder from the public magazine in Williamsburg and removed the firing mechanisms in the guns, making them impossible to shoot.[19] By 1777, it appeared that the colonists would most likely be defeated. Colonial Undersecretary William Knox, anxious to prevent any further uprisings, ordered that the firearms of "all the People should be taken away" and the manufacture of arms should not be allowed in America.[20]

"TO DISARM THE PEOPLE IS TO ENSLAVE THEM"

Disarmament has often been seen as a crucial step to subjugate a population.[21] During debates about the proposed U.S. Constitution this issue was raised as an important reason for including the right to own firearms in the Bill of Rights. George Mason, referencing advice given to the British Parliament by Pennsylvania governor Sir William Keith,

18 John Peter Gabriel Muhlenberg, 1746 – 1807, University of Pennsylvania Archives and Records Center, https://archives.upenn.edu/exhibits/penn-people/biography/john-peter-gabriel-muhlenberg, accessed 2/24/19.

19 T. J. Martinell, "How the British Gun Program Precipitated the American Revolution," *Hidden History*, September 5, 2015, https://forum.308ar.com/topic/11816-how-the-british-gun-control-program-precipitated-the-american-revolution/

20 Ibid.

21 For an exhaustive discussion, see Rudolph J. Rummel, *Death by Government* (New Brunswick, New Jersey: Transaction Publishers, 1994).

stated: "To disarm the people...[i]s the most effectual way to enslave them."[22] Similarly, Noah Webster wrote in 1787: "Before a standing army can rule, the people must be disarmed, as they are in almost every country in Europe. The supreme power in America cannot enforce unjust laws by the sword; because the whole body of the people are armed, and constitute a force superior to any band of regular troops."[23] As Representative Elbridge Gerry of Massachusetts said before the Hall of Congress on August 17,1789: "What, Sir, is the use of a militia? It is to prevent the establishment of a standing army, the bane of liberty. . . . Whenever Governments mean to invade the rights and liberties of the people, they always attempt to destroy the militia, in order to raise an army upon their ruins."[24] In keeping with Gerry's statement, the Militia Act of 1792 made gun ownership and militia membership a legal obligation rather than a voluntary option.[25]

The Second Amendment was intended not to preserve Americans' right to engage in recreational hunting or sharpshooting competitions. It was intended to preserve their ability to resist a future potentially tyrannical government. But for faithful Christians the right to bear weapons for self-defense is not just an amendment enunciated in the Constitution's Bill of Rights, it is a fundamental, God-given right of all humanity.

22   George Mason, Addresses to the Virginia Ratifying Convention, June 14, 1788. Accessed on March 30, 2019 at https://en.wikiquote.org/wiki/George_Mason

23   Noah Webster, "An Examination into the Leading Principles of the Federal Constitution," 1787, a pamphlet aimed at swaying Pennsylvania toward ratification, in Paul Ford, ed., Pamphlets on the Constitution of the United States, at 56 (New York, 1888).

24   House of Representatives, Amendments to the Constitution 17, 20 Aug. 1789, *Annals 1:749-52, 766—67.* http://press-pubs.uchicago.edu/founders/documents/amendIIs6.html.

25   "The Militia Act of 1792," Constitution Society, http://www.constitution.org/mil/mil_act_1792.htm

THE LESSON OF FRANK BLAICHMAN

On December 27, 2018, a 96-year-old man died in Brooklyn, NY. Few of his neighbors who had passed this elderly man in the street could have known that Frank Blaichman was one of the leaders of the Jewish Partisan Army in Poland during the time when the Nazis were hunting down and exterminating Jews. Many of the pious Jews at the time thought it would be profane to take up arms to defend their lives, but not Frank Blaichman. In his early 20s he organized raids against the Nazis occupiers and their collaborators. He was most proud of the time he and other partisans captured 2,000 Nazi soldiers at a farm. As described in an obituary published in *The Economist*:

> Yet hiding was not his nature. When the Germans started to round up Kamionka's Jews he refused to be deported with them. He already laughed at the travel restrictions for Jews, racing out of town on his bicycle to trade stuff, leaving his white Star of David arm-band at home. Meanwhile, his fury mounted. When he saw Hasidim rifle-butted as they dug ditches, or heard that Uncle Moishe had been shot on the spot for having fresh meat in his house, he felt like fighting. Most of his neighbors said it was God's will. He did not agree.
>
> So he had run away. But what could he fight with? That autumn 80 of his companions were slaughtered at their wretched campsite in the forest. It was not enough to bury them, say Kaddish and vanish. Jews had to defend themselves, and also avenge the dead. Even the pretense of a rifle—old farm forks with their outer teeth knocked out, slung on a shoulder-strap—made him feel stronger. With proper firearms, they would make an army of resistance.[26]

---

26 "Obituary: Frank Blaichman Died on December 27th," *The Economist,* https://www.economist.com/obituary/2019/02/02/obituary-frank-blaichman-died-on-december-27th?frsc=dg%7Ce

21

THE PROBLEM WITH PAUL

In the history of our culture few individuals have been as influential as Paul, the First Century Jew who turned from being the most virulent persecutor of Christianity to become its most powerful advocate, its most effective interpreter and the leader of its triumphant march across the ancient world. Yet there is probably no one in that history with whom more of us have trouble coming to terms. We are not the first to find him perplexing, and, in a way, intractable. It has always been so. As a Jew, despite his claim to have been "extremely zealous" for the traditions of his fathers, he was almost certainly regarded with suspicion by his contemporaries—as he has undoubtedly been by later generations of Jews. Even as a Christian, he was not wholly accepted within the religious community to which he gave himself with such devotion.

JOHN KNOX, "THE VOICE OF CHRIST AMONG THE NATIONS," 1965

WHEN MARCION COMPILED his canon of scripture, he included the Gospel of Luke and Paul's epistles to the Romans, Ephesians, Colossians, Laodiceans (a letter now lost), Galatians, First and Second Corinthians, First and Second Thessalonians, Philemon, and Philippians.[1] Without Paul, the early Church would not have been plagued by the Gnostic

---

1   Steve Rudd, "The Canon of Marcion the Heretic," n. d., The Canon of the Bible, www.bible. ca/b-canon-canon-of-marcion.htm

272

heresy. In their article, "The Writings of St. Paul," John T. Fitzgerald and Wayne A. Meeks maintain:

> While the Valentinians and other Gnostics emphasized Paul, there was no one in the ancient church, either "heretic" or "orthodox," who made such serious and exclusive claims on Paul and Paul alone as did Marcion. Born some twenty or thirty years after Paul's death, Marcion became convinced that salvation by grace alone was the purest essence of the Christian gospel. But carried to its logical conclusion, he believed this would mean that the God of grace manifested in Jesus Christ was distinct from the God of the Old Testament. The creation and the law were the products of the God of justice, but humanity's hope lay in the God of pure love, unknown before Christ and totally unrelated to this world.[2]

PAUL'S GNOSTICISM

Marcion's love of Paul was rooted in the fact that the Apostle in his epistles often spoke like a Gnostic. To the Corinthians, he wrote: "Yet we do speak wisdom among those who are mature; a wisdom, however, not of this age nor of the rulers of this age, who are passing away; but we speak God's wisdom in a mystery, the hidden wisdom which God predestined before the ages to our glory; the wisdom which none of the rulers of this age has understood; for if they had understood it they would not have crucified the Lord of glory" (1 Cor. 2:6-8).

What's more, Paul intimated that he was about to reveal knowledge about a hidden God. In Acts 17:23, Paul said to an audience of Gentiles: "For as I walked around and looked carefully at your objects of worship, I even found an altar with this inscription: to an unknown god. So, you are ignorant of the very thing you worship—and this is what I am going to proclaim to you."

---

2   John T. Fitzgerald and Wayne A. Meeks, "The Writings of St. Paul ('The Only True Apostle: Marcion's Radical Paul, Excerpt')," Genius.com, n. d., https://genius.com/St-paul-the-writings-of-st-paul-the-only-true-apostle-marcions-radical-paul-excerpt-annotated

THE CURSE OF THE LAW

Above all, Paul endeared himself to Marcion and the Gnostics by his statements about the law. In 1 Corinthians 15:56, he wrote: "The sting of death is sin, and the power of sin is the law." In Galatians 3:10-13, he spoke of the law as a "curse" by writing:

> For all who rely on the works of the law are under a curse, as it is written: "Cursed is everyone who does not continue to do everything written in the Book of the Law." Clearly no one who relies on the law is justified before God, because "the righteous will live by faith." The law is not based on faith; on the contrary, it says, "The person who does these things will live by them." Christ redeemed us from the curse of the law by becoming a curse for us, for it is written: "Cursed is everyone who is hung on a pole."

By making such statements, Paul separated himself and his Christology from Judaism. For the true Jew, the law was God's gift to Israel, the very foundation of His covenant with His people.[3] Psalm 19 proclaims:

> The law of the LORD is PERFECT,
>   reviving the soul;
> the testimony of the LORD IS SURE,
>   making wise the simple;
> the precepts of the LORD ARE RIGHT,
>   rejoicing the heart;
> the commandment of the LORD IS PURE,
>   enlightening the eyes;
> the fear of the LORD IS CLEAN,
>   enduring forever;
> the rules[of the LORD ARE TRUE,
>   and righteous altogether.

---

3   John Knox, "The Voice of Christ among the Nations," *Life*, December 25, 1964.

More to be desired are they than gold,
> even much fine gold;
sweeter also than honey
> and drippings of the honeycomb.
Moreover, by them is your servant warned;
> in keeping them there is great reward (Psalm 7-11).

JESUS CHRIST

Paul's writings constitute more than a third of the New Testament and the core of contemporary Protestantism. Yet, within his letters, he speaks very little of the historical Jesus and makes scant reference to the Lord's instructions and admonitions. This is peculiar since Paul rubbed shoulders with several of the Twelve Apostles and would have been privy to information passed on to them by Jesus. Regarding Paul's strange silence about Jesus, Tom Harpur writes: "The earliest writings in the New Testament, which make up more than one-quarter of its total content, are the letters of the Apostle Paul. What is absolutely striking about them is their virtual silence on the whole subject of a historical Jesus of Nazareth."[4]

The experience of the resurrected Jesus remained for Paul the only matter of importance. He viewed the death of Jesus as an other-worldly matter, a part of a divine plan that had been drafted "before the eons," whereby the powers that rule the world crucified in ignorance "the Lord of glory" (1 Cor. 2:8).[5] What's more, instead of referring to Jesus as "the Christ," which would have been a correct interpretation of "Messiah" in Greek, he adopted the practice of calling Jesus "Christ," as if this was His proper name. Likewise, he referred to Jesus not as the apocryphal "Son of Man," but rather as the cosmic "Son of God."[6]

---

4   Tom Harpur, *The Pagan Christ: Is Blind Faith Killing Christianity?* (New York: Walker and Company, 2004), p. 166.

5   Ian Wilson, *Jesus: The Evidence* (San Francisco: Harper, 1996), p. 156.

6   Ibid.

A FIGURE OF SUSPICION

Moreover, Paul's relationship with James, the Lord's brother and ruler of the early Church, remained highly contentious and troublesome. In his account of Paul, David Wenham writes: "Today we may think of Paul as an important and influential figure. But all the evidence is that he was initially regarded by many of the Christians with suspicion. He spent little time in Jerusalem, and he had no part in the leadership of the church in the early days."[7]

Upon becoming a Christian, Paul preached at the synagogue in Damascus. The Jews, knowing that he had previously persecuted Christians, grew suspicious of him and made plans to kill him. Paul escaped with the help of his friends and made his way to Jerusalem to seek the guidance and support of James and the Jerusalem Council. But suspicions about Paul's intent remained and the Hellenistic Jews in Jerusalem also tried to put Paul to death before he headed off for his first great missionary journey.

THE APOSTOLIC DECREE

Paul traveled to Syria, Cilicia, Galatia, and Asia, where he spread the word that Jesus was the Christ—the "anointed one"—who had been long awaited by the Jews and the proponents of the various mystery religions that had spread throughout Asia Minor.

Upon reaching Ephesus, Paul and Barnabas, his faithful companion, were summoned back to Jerusalem to give a report of their activities. The meeting at Jerusalem centered on the question of circumcision. To the Christian Jews, circumcision was not only a ritual of health but also a holy symbol of their covenant with God.[8] It signified that they were a particular race of men who had been singled out to serve as God's chosen people. Paul, in proclaiming the Christian message to the Greek world, found that converts were ready to receive the "good news" that

---

7   David Wenham, *Did St. Paul Get Jesus Right?* (Oxford, England: Lion Books, 2010), pp. 48-49.

8   Will Durant, *Caesar and Christ* (New York: Simon and Schuster, 1944), p. 583.

Jesus was the Christ, but were reluctant to have the foreskin of their penises cut off with a sharp knife. The matter was of urgent concern, since circumcision represented the stumbling block to the universal acceptance of Christianity.

James rendered his ruling that became known as "the Apostolic Decree."⁹ It stated that pagan proselytes must "abstain from food polluted by idols, from sexual immorality, from the meat of strangled animals and from blood" (Acts 15; 20). The ruling only applied to those "turning to God" and not to converts seeking full church membership.

THE INCIDENT AT ANTIOCH

Paul now set off for his second missionary journey, which brought him to Antioch, where representatives from the Church of Jerusalem discovered Paul, Peter, and Barnabas eating with uncircumcised proselytes. The discovery was scandalous. Peter and Barnabas repented of their action and departed from Paul. Paul, on his part, was furious and wrote the following in his Letter to the Galatians: "And from those who were supposed to be acknowledged leaders (what they actually were makes no difference to me; God shows no partiality)—those leaders contributed nothing to me. . . . But when Cephas [Peter] came to Antioch, I opposed him to his face, because he stood self-condemned; for until certain people came from James, he used to eat with the Gentiles. But after they came, he drew back and kept himself separate for fear of the circumcision faction. And the other Jews joined him in this hypocrisy, so that even Barnabas was led astray by their hypocrisy" (Galatians 2:6-14).

Regarding this conflict, New Testament scholar Jeffrey Butz writes: "The Incident at Antioch starkly shows that the apostolic period was not a time of sweetness and light with the earliest followers of Jesus all living as one big happy family, as assumed by most Christians today;

---

9   Talib Morrison, "James, the Caliph of Christ," *Neurotherapy of Christian Brain,* May 12, 2012, neurotherapy-of-christian-brain.blogspot.com/2012/05/james-caliph-of-christ.html

on the contrary, it was a time of bitter rivalries as various parties and factions began to vie for supremacy."[10]

PAUL GROWS POMPOUS

Following the incident at Antioch, Paul started to see himself as an independent authority who was equal if not superior to James and the Apostles. He made this position clear in the following passage from his second letter to the Corinthians: "I think that I am not in the least inferior to these super-apostles" (2 Cor. 11:5). He now became defiant in his stance on circumcision of the law of Moses. He wrote to the Galatians as follows: "Listen! I, Paul, am telling you that if you let yourselves be circumcised, Christ will be of no benefit to you. . . . For in Christ Jesus neither circumcision nor uncircumcision counts for anything; the only thing that counts is faith working through love" (5:2-6).

From Antioch, Paul set out on his next missionary mission. He revisited the churches in Asia Minor before sailing to Macedonia, where he first set foot on European soil. From Macedonia, he went on to Thessalonica and Greece. During this period, he wrote his letter to the Romans in which he upheld his doctrine of justification by faith.[11] He wrote:

> For no human being will be justified in his sight by deeds prescribed by the law, for through the law comes the knowledge of sin. . . . For there is no distinction, since all have sinned and fall short of the glory of God; they are now justified by his grace as a gift, through the redemption that is in Christ Jesus, whom God put forward as a sacrifice of atonement by his blood, effective through faith. . . . For we hold that a person is justified by faith apart from works prescribed by the law. (Romans 3:20-28).

---

10 Jeffrey J. Butz, *The Brother of Jesus and the Lost Teachings of Christianity* (Rochester, Vermont: Inner Traditions, 2005, p. 99.

11 W. Sanday, "The Epistle to the Romans," *Ellicott's Commentary for English Readers,"* n. d., https://biblehub.com/commentaries/ellicott/romans/1.htm

THE FINAL CONFRONTATION

Shortly after his arrival in Corinth, Paul was summoned back to Jerusalem for another meeting with the church council. As soon as he appeared, James confronted Paul by saying: "You teach all the Jews living among the Gentiles to forsake Moses, and that you tell them not to circumcise their children or observe the customs. What then is to be done?" (Acts 21:21). James now ordered Paul to take the vow of a Nazarite, to undergo acts of purification, and to make an offering at the Temple. Surrounded by the church elders, Paul had no recourse except to comply.

Paul's appearance at the temple caused such outrage that Jews seized Paul from all directions, while crying out: "Fellow Israelites, help! This is the man who is teaching everyone everywhere against our people, our law, and this place" (Acts 21:28). The entire city, according to the author of Acts, became aroused and hauled Paul off to be stoned. Paul would have been killed if the Roman soldiers had not saved him from the irate mob by taking him into custody. Throughout his time of imprisonment, the Jewish people remained so outraged by Paul's abandonment of the law that they made plans to kill him. One group of Jews took an oath not to eat or drink until Paul was dead and buried (Acts 23:12).

PAUL THE PRISONER

As a Roman citizen, Paul managed to have his case heard before Felix, the Roman procurator at Caesarea. Festus dismissed Paul's accusers but kept him under house arrest for two years, hoping, perhaps, that the Apostle's fellow Christians would come up with a substantial bribe.[12] Not one Jewish Christian came to Paul's defense. Apparently, James, the church council, and the members of the primitive community, had washed their hands of the troublemaker.[13]

---

12   Durant, *Caesar and Christ*, p. 586.

13   Morrison, "James—Caliph of Christ."

Herod Agrippa, King of Judea, gave Paul another hearing, but the Apostle, fearing the hostile environment in Jerusalem, exercised his right as a Roman citizen and demanded a trial before the emperor in Rome.[14] In Rome, where he remained for the next ten years, Paul was treated leniently and allowed to live in a house of his own choosing. He invited the leading Jewish leaders of Rome to visit him, but when they heard his views of the law, they turned away from him.[15] He was also shunned by the Christian community, who practiced circumcision and upheld the Mosaic law.[16] During his imprisonment, Paul found solace in writing long letters to the churches he had helped to establish in distant lands. In his letter to the Ephesians, he upheld his view of the law by writing:

> Therefore remember that at one time you Gentiles in the flesh, called "the uncircumcision" by what is called the circumcision, which is made in the flesh by hands—remember that you were at that time separated from Christ, alienated from the commonwealth of Israel and strangers to the covenants of promise, having no hope and without God in the world. But now in Christ Jesus you who once were far off have been brought near by the blood of Christ. For he himself is our peace, who has made us both one and has broken down in his flesh the dividing wall of hostility by abolishing the law of commandments expressed in ordinances, that he might create in himself one new man in place of the two, so making peace, and might reconcile us both to God in one body through the cross, thereby killing the hostility (2:11-16).

PAUL'S AMBIGUITY

To the end of his life, Paul's view of the law remained ambiguous. Although he declares that the law is, indeed, holy, and the commandment is "holy and righteous and good" (Romans 7:12), he speaks of it

---

14   Ibid.

15   Durant, *Caesar and Christ*, p. v.

16   Ibid.

as one of the powers of evil that have set up their thrones within man's soul.[17] Although he claims to "uphold the law" (Rom. 3:31), Paul adds that no one can be made righteous by obeying the commandments, since they only serve to bring "wrath," adding "where there is no law, there is no transgression" (Rom. 4:15). While Paul insists that the law does not represent sin, he goes on to say: "I would not have known what sin was had it not been for the law. For I would not have known what coveting really was if the law had not said, 'You shall not covet.' But sin, seizing the opportunity afforded by the commandment, produced in me every kind of coveting. For apart from the law, sin was dead" (Rom. 7:7-8).

PECCA FORTITER, SIN BOLDLY

This ambiguity caused Marcion to conclude that since the "law" was a "curse" and a "source of evil," it must have been issued by a malevolent divine being. Marcion's belief that man must be freed from the law in order to come to terms with his true spiritual nature gave rise to Martin Luther's proclamation that sin was no longer of significance. The Protestant Reformer wrote: "Seek out the society of your boon companions, drink, play, talk bawdy, and amuse yourself. One must sometimes commit a sin out of hate and contempt for the Devil, so as not to give him the chance to make one scrupulous over mere nothings."[18] Similarly, Luther, in a letter to Philip Melanchthon, encouraged the commitment of bold sins:

> If you are a preacher of mercy, do not preach an imaginary but the true mercy. If the mercy is true, you must therefore bear the true, not an imaginary sin. God does not save those who are only imaginary sinners. Be a sinner, and let your sins be strong, but let your trust in Christ be stronger, and rejoice in Christ who is the victor over sin,

---

17   Knox, "The Voice of Christ among the Nations."

18   Martin Luther, *Werke,* Vol. XX (Weimar: Herman Bohlau, 1883), p. 58.

death, and the world. We will commit sins while we are here, for this life is not a place where justice resides. We, however, says Peter (2 Peter 3:13) are looking forward to a new heaven and a new earth where justice will reign. It suffices that through God's glory we have recognized the Lamb who takes away the sin of the world. No sin can separate us from Him, even if we were to kill or commit adultery thousands of times each day. Do you think such an exalted Lamb paid merely a small price with a meager sacrifice for our sins?[19]

CIRCUMCISION OF THE HEART

The ambiguity within the Pauline epistles was resolved by Paul himself, who maintained that Christians are not exempt from the law since they are obliged to receive a "circumcision of the heart." In his Letter to the Romans, he wrote: "A person is not a Jew who is one only outwardly, nor is circumcision merely outward and physical. No, a person is a Jew who is one inwardly; and circumcision is circumcision of the heart, by the Spirit, not by the written code. Such a person's praise is not from other people, but from God." In his Letter to the Colossians, Paul maintained that Christians obtain a circumcision of the heart when they submit to the sacrament of Baptism. He explained his position as follows:

> For in Christ all the fullness of the Deity lives in bodily form, and in Christ you have been brought to fullness. He is the head over every power and authority. In him you were also circumcised with a circumcision not performed by human hands. Your whole self ruled by the flesh was put off when you were circumcised by Christ, having been buried with him in baptism, in which you were also raised with him through your faith in the working of God, who raised him from

---

19   Martin Luther, "Letter to Philip Melanchthon," August 1, 1521. Translated by Erika Bullman Flores, from Dr. Martin Luther's Saemmtliche Schriften (St. Louis: Concordia Publishing, n. d.), www.projectwittenberg.org/pub/resources/text/wittenberg/luther/letsinsbe.txt

the dead. When you were dead in your sins and in the uncircumcision of your flesh, God made you alive with Christ. He forgave us all our sins, having canceled the charge of our legal indebtedness, which stood against us and condemned us; he has taken it away, nailing it to the cross (Colossians 2:9-14).

THE FORGIVENESS OF SINS

Baptism in the New Testament was the sole means by which believers could receive remission from sin so they could enter the Kingdom of Heaven. The concept of penance remained unknown.[20] For this reason, it was essential for every believer to be baptized. Jesus Himself had said: "Whoever believes and is baptized will be saved, but whoever does not believe will be condemned" (Mark 16:16).

The importance of baptism was stressed on the Day of Pentecost by the Apostle Peter, who delivered the following message to his fellow Jews: "Repent, and be baptized every one of you in the name of Jesus Christ for the remission of sins, and you shall receive the gift of the Holy Spirit" (Acts 2:38). Only by baptism, as Peter and Paul both believed, could believers partake of the death and resurrection of Jesus.[21]

AN EXACTING FAITH

After submitting to this rite, Christians were required to obey every letter of the law. Paul wrote the following in his first letter to the Corinthians: "Do you not know that wrongdoers will not inherit the kingdom of God? Do not be deceived: Neither the sexually immoral nor idolaters nor adulterers nor men who have sex with men, nor thieves nor the greedy nor drunkards nor slanderers nor swindlers will inherit the kingdom of God. And that is what some of you were. But you were washed, you were sanctified, you were justified in the name of the Lord Jesus

---

20 Paul Johnson, *A History of Christianity* (New York: Simon and Shuster, 1976), p. 80.

21 Jan Issac, "Baptism among the Early Christians," *Direction*, Spring 2004, https://directionjournal.org/33/1/baptism-among-early-christians.html

Christ and by the Spirit of our God (I Cor. 6:9-11). Through baptism, according to Paul and Peter, the body of believers became temples of the Holy Spirit. For this reason, Paul suffered at the thought of any baptized Christian having sex with a prostitute. He wrote:

> The body is not meant for sexual immorality but for the Lord, and the Lord for the body. By his power God raised the Lord from the dead, and he will raise us also. Do you not know that your bodies are members of Christ himself? Shall I then take the members of Christ and unite them with a prostitute? Never! Do you not know that he who unites himself with a prostitute is one with her in body? For it is said, "The two will become one flesh." But whoever is united with the Lord is one with him in spirit.
>
> Flee from sexual immorality. All other sins a person commits are outside the body, but whoever sins sexually, sins against their own body. Do you not know that your bodies are temples of the Holy Spirit, who is in you, whom you have received from God? You are not your own; you were bought at a price. Therefore, honor God with your bodies (1 Cor. 6:13-20).

THE THEOLOGICAL LYNCHPIN

Paul's insistence upon a circumcision of the heart constitutes the lynchpin that unites his writings to the Old and New Testaments, and the insistence that there is only one baptism for the forgiveness of sins made Christianity an even more demanding and rigorous faith than orthodox Judaism.

Since mortal sins committed after baptism could not be forgiven, the rite of baptism in the early church was administered only by bishops, who possessed the sacerdotal power to remit sins through their "vicarious ordination" as Christ's apostles.[22] Throughout the first three Christian

---

22   St. Cyprian, "Letter LXXIV," 16, translated by Ernest Wallis, in *Fathers of the Third Century*, Vol. V, *The Ante Nicene Fathers*, edited by Alexander Roberts and James Donaldson (Grand Rapids, Michigan: William B. Eerdmans Publishing Company, 1981), p. 394.

centuries, the words of Jesus to His disciples in John 20:22-23 ("Receive the Holy Spirit. If you forgive the sins of any, they are forgiven; if you retain the sins of any, they are retained") were interpreted in relation to baptism. St. Cyprian testified to this by writing:

> It is in baptism that we all of us receive the forgiveness of sins. Now the Lord proves this in His Gospel that sins can be remitted only through those who possess the Holy Spirit. For when He sent His disciples out after the Resurrection, He said this: "As the Father hath sent me, even so I send you." And when He said this, He breathed on them and saith unto them, "receive ye the Holy Ghost; whose sins ye remit, they shall be remitted unto him; whose sins ye retain, they shall be retained." This passage proves that only he who possesses the Holy Spirit can baptize.[23]

THE BODY OF CHRIST

Those who committed mortal sins after baptism were driven from the Church and handed over to Satan. This expulsion of sins was conducted in accordance with the teaching of Paul in his first letter to the Corinthians: "But now I am writing to you that you must not associate with anyone who claims to be a brother or sister, but is sexually immoral or greedy, an idolater or slanderer, a drunkard or swindler. Do not even eat with such people. What business is it of mine to judge those outside the church? Are you not to judge those inside? God will judge those outside. Expel the wicked person from among you" (1 Cor. 5:11-15). The Christian community as "the body of Christ" was to be kept "holy, blameless, and undefiled" (Heb. 7: 26).

During the first Christian centuries, those accused or suspected of committing a mortal sin were brought before bishops, who possessed the rabbinical power of binding and loosing sin (Matt. 16:19; John

---

23 St. Cyprian, "Letter 69," in *Early Latin Theology*, translated by S. L. Greenslade, Vol. V, *The Library of Christian Classics*, edited by John Baillie, John T. McNeill, and Henry Van Deusen (Philadelphia: Westminster Press, 1956), p. 157.

20:23). Those judged guilty of such sin were bound to their transgressions and excommunicated from the church. Those who were judged innocent were loosed from their transgressions and received back into the fellowship.[24] However, there was no way back through works of mercy or tears of regret for those who were bound.

24   David Brattston, "The Forgiveness of Post-Baptismal Sin in Ancient Christianity," *Churchman*, Vol. 105, No. 4, 1991, https://biblicalstudies.org.uk/pdf/churchman/105-04_332.pdf

22

MAKE CHRISTIANITY BRAVE AGAIN

We are becoming another people, and a post-Christian America appears to be our destiny well before the end of this century. Consider what has changed already. In the 19th century, blasphemy was a crime. In the Roaring '20s the "vices" of booze and gambling were outlawed. Now they are major sources of state revenue. Divorce was a rarity. Now half of all marriages are dissolved. After the sexual revolution of the '60s, births out of wedlock rocketed to where 40 percent of all children are born without a father in the home, as are half of Hispanics and 70 percent of all black children. Pornography, which used to bring a prison term, today dominates cable TV. Marijuana, once a social scourge, is the hot new product. And Sen. Kamala Harris wants prostitution legalized. In the lifetime of many Americans, homosexuality and abortion were still scandalous crimes. They are now cherished constitutional rights.

PATRICK BUCHANAN, "MAYOR PETE AND THE
CRACKUP OF CHRISTIANITY," APRIL 16, 2019

IF THE NEW TESTAMENT ended after the letters of St. Paul one would be left with the image of Jesus as the suffering Christ who offered himself as the sacrificial "lamb" taken to the slaughter on behalf of the human race. This is the Jesus who exemplifies God's unconditional love, sacrifice, and forgiveness.

The image of Jesus in Revelation is quite different. He returns as a judge and as a King to "make war against them with the sword of My mouth" (Rev 2:16). However, it is not just Christ Himself who comes as a judge and warrior. Believers are told that if they overcome all of the tribulations while holding fast to their faith in Christ, they will be given authority over nations. As is stated in Revelation 2:26-27: "To the one who is victorious and does my will to the end, I will give authority over the nations—that one 'will rule them with an iron scepter and will dash them to pieces like pottery'—just as I have received authority from my Father."

The implications of this co-authority for believers are worth considering. What if God asks His people to do more than watch His display of power and authority? Revelation 20 says that after Christ's return and reign of 1,000 years, there will be an attack against His Kingdom by Satanic forces numbering in the millions.

> Now when the thousand years have expired, Satan will be released from his prison and will go out to deceive the nations which are in the four corners of the earth, Gog and Magog, to gather them together to battle, whose number is as the sand of the sea. They went up on the breadth of the earth and surrounded the camp of the saints and the beloved city. Revelation 20:7-9

According to the Book of Revelation, God's Kingdom co-exists with other nations with varying periods of peace and threat. As discussed in chapter 14, while God is the ultimate source of power and protection, He also commands the faithful to be ready to defend their families and nation. Yet, as also discussed in chapter 14, churches with millions of followers openly oppose the use of force, even for self-defense. Would it really be virtuous to passively watch while Christians and other religious minorities are massacred? But this is not the only confusion afflicting today's body of Christ.

BELIEF IN RELATIVISM

While research shows that America is by far the most religious of the developed nations in the world,[1] it could also be said that relativism has become its predominant belief. A 2018 study found that 60% of Americans agree that "Religious belief is a matter of personal opinion; it is not about objective truth." Increasing numbers of Christians no longer agree that belief in God is needed to be moral. Two-thirds of white mainline Protestants, half of Catholics, and one-third of white Evangelicals reject the idea that religious conviction is tied to morality.[2]

A 2017 survey found that many practicing Christians agree with "New Spirituality" ideas that all religions are equivalent paths to God. More than half resonate with postmodern views that there is no objective truth. More than one third accept ideas associated with Marxism. Three in ten believe ideas rooted in secularism.[3]

THE RISE OF RELIGIOUS INDIFFERENTISM

Three in ten practicing Christians strongly agree that "all people pray to the same god or spirit."[4] One quarter (37% of those under age 45) strongly agree that "what is morally right or wrong depends on what an individual believes,"[5] rejecting the Biblical view that there is any objective morality defined by the Creator.

Three in ten practicing Christians under age 45 accept the postmodern idea that "if your beliefs offend someone or hurt their feelings,

1   Dalia Fahmy, "Americans Are Far More Religious than Adults in Other Wealthy Nations," Pew Research Center, July 31, 2018. https://www.pewresearch.org/fact-tank/2018/07/31/americans-are-far-more-religious-than-adults-in-other-wealthy-nations/

2   Gregory Smith, "A Growing Share of Americans Say It's Not Necessary to Believe in God to Be Moral," Pew Research Center, October 16, 2017. https://www.pewresearch.org/fact-tank/2017/10/16/a-growing-share-of-americans-say-its-not-necessary-to-believe-in-god-to-be-moral/

3   "Competing Worldviews Influence Today's Christians," https://www.barna.com/research/competing-worldviews-influence-todays-christians/ , May 9, 2017.

4   Ibid.

5   Ibid.

it is wrong," which would indicate they do not believe there is objective truth or that they consider feelings to be more important than truth.

THE NEW WORLDVIEW

Barna Research found that 36% of practicing Christians embraced one or more Marxist statements. One in five practicing Christian Millennials and Gen-Xers strongly agreed with the tenet that "private property encourages greed and envy."[6] One in four Black American Christians strongly agreed with the quasi-Marxist idea that "the government, rather than individuals, should control as much of the resources as necessary to ensure that everyone gets their fair share."[7]

The researchers concluded that there is an "ongoing shift away from Christianity as the basis for a shared worldview. We have observed and reported on increasing pluralism, relativism and moral decline among Americans and even in the Church. . . Only 17 percent of Christians who consider their faith important and attend church regularly actually have a biblical worldview."[8]

How did the most religiously active advanced Christian nation in the world come to have so many non-Christian views? Previous chapters have reviewed the unrelenting critique of the Bible in seminaries that train pastors and church leaders as well as the materialism that has come to dominate the understanding of the origins of life even when the scientific evidence for that has increasingly come into question. Such influences can be confronted as new evidence comes to light, but there is another force that inhibits not just freedom of thought, but also the freedom to publicly express deeply held religious convictions, and that is government.

---

6   Ibid.

7   Ibid.

8   Ibid.

THE WAR ON CHRISTIANITY

In his *Contribution to the Critique of Hegel's Philosophy of Right*, Karl Marx said, "Religious distress is at the same time the expression of real distress and also the protest against real distress. Religion is the sigh of the oppressed creature, the heart of a heartless world, just as it is the spirit of spiritless conditions. It is the opium of the people. To abolish religion as the illusory happiness of the people is to demand their real happiness."

When the Communist leaders in the Soviet Union had 95,000 Orthodox priests executed in the first two decades of the revolution,[9] they believed they were doing something good. Religion was a "drug" that distracted people from their oppression, so to eliminate religious leaders who were accessories to the oppressors and hindering the spread of Marxist "truths" was a good thing to do. As Marx had written several decades before, "To abolish religion as the illusory happiness of the people is to demand their real happiness."[10]

THE TEMPLE OF REASON

The Marxist bloodbath came one hundred and thirty years after the Jacobin leaders in France changed the Cathedral of Notre Dame into the "Temple of Reason." Then, in the name of "reason," they massa-cred tens of thousands of Catholic inhabitants of the Vendée region of west-central France. When it was over, French General Francois Joseph Westermann wrote a letter to the Committee of Public Safety stating: "There is no more Vendée. . . .According to the orders that you gave me, I crushed the children under the feet of the horses, massacred the women who, at least for these, will not give birth to any more brigands. I do not have a prisoner to reproach me. I have exterminated all."[11]

---

9   "Persecution of Christians in the Soviet Union," https://en.wikipedia.org/wiki/Persecution_of_Christians_in_the_Soviet_Union

10   Karl Marx, *Contribution to the Critique of Hegel's Philosophy of Right*, 1843. (Cambridge, UK: Cambridge University Press, 1970.)

11   Henry Samuel, "Vendée French call for revolution massacre to be termed 'genocide'," *The Telegraph*, December 26, 2008, London, UK.

THE AMERICAN REVOLUTION

Across the Atlantic the American revolutionaries had a profoundly different perspective. They did something unprecedented in history by limiting their own power. Despite a wide range of religious perspectives, they were united in their awareness of the human potential for evil. After all, most colonists had grown up with the *New England Primer* (1690), which began the study of the alphabet with "In Adam's fall, we sinned all."[12]

Alexander Hamilton wrote about the "folly and wickedness of mankind."[13] His pessimistic view of the human race was shared by John Jay, the third author of the *Federalist Papers*, who saw men as governed by "the dictates of personal interest" who will consequently "swerve from good faith and justice,"[14] Thomas Jefferson warned "in questions of power, let no more be heard of confidence in man but bind him down from mischief by the chains of the Constitution."[15] They intentionally sought to protect the free exercise of religious beliefs, which had often been harshly persecuted in England, in other European nations and even in some of the American colonies. The first amendment to the U.S. Constitution states that the federal government shall not impose a state religion and shall not inhibit the free exercise of religion. It reads: "Congress shall make no law respecting an establishment of religion, or prohibiting the free exercise thereof; or abridging the freedom of speech, or of the press; or the right of the people peaceably to assemble, and to petition the Government for a redress of grievances."

---

12   Crain, Patricia. *The Story of A: The Alphabetization of America from the* New England Primer *to* The Scarlet Letter. Stanford, Calif.: Stanford University Press, 2000.

13   Alexander Hamilton, Federalist, no. 78, 521—30, May 28, 1788, http://press-pubs.uchicago.edu/founders/documents/a3_1s11.html

14   Alexander Hamilton, John Jay, and James Madison, "Federalist No. 2. Concerning Dangers from Foreign Force and Influence," The Federalist Papers, October 27, 1787 (New York: The Independent Journal).

15   *The Works of Thomas Jefferson in Twelve Volumes*, Federal Edition, Vol. 9, edited by Paul Leicester Ford (New York: G. P. Putnam's Sons, 1904), pp. 470-1.

THE NEW SECULAR STATE

But, there are many in the U.S. who have been actively working to use the power of government to erase America's religious heritage and to establish a secular state sterilized of any references to our Creator. As pointed out by David Horowitz in *Dark Agenda: The War to Destroy Christian America,* when the U.S. Capitol Visitor Center opened in 2008 ". . .all references to God and faith had been carefully, deliberately edited out of its photos and historical displays." Horowitz writes:

> One panel in particular claimed that the national motto of the United States is E Pluribus Unum ("Out of Many, One"). In fact, the national motto, as established by an act of Congress in 1956, is "In God We Trust." A replica of the Speaker's rostrum of the House of Representatives omits the gold-lettered inscription "In God We Trust" above the chair. Photos of the actual Speaker's rostrum were cropped to hide the inscription. A protest by Senator Jim DeMint and other conservative lawmakers led to a rectification of this particular misrepresentation, but many others remained.
>
> The designers of the center had gone to great lengths to alter essential American history. An enlarged image of the Constitution was photoshopped to remove the words "in the Year of our Lord" above the signatures of the signers. The table on which President Lincoln placed his Bible during his second inauguration is on display—just the table, not the Bible.[16]

Horowitz argues that America was created as a secular republic with no official state religion in order to protect a lively, but diverse Protestant Christian culture:

> America was created as a secular republic precisely because of the Christian beliefs of its religious founders—specifically their Protestant Christian beliefs. Beginning with the Pilgrims who landed at Plymouth

---

16   David Horowitz, *Dark Agenda: The War to Destroy Christian America* (West Palm Beach Florida: Humanix Books, 2018), p. 37.

Rock in 1620, America's founders were mainly members of Protestant sects fleeing persecution by state-sanctioned rival denominations. . . . They were committed to the Protestant ideal of freedom of conscience and religious dissent. For these reasons too, it would have been unthinkable to found this new nation as a theocratic government with an official state religion. Creating a secular republic, then, was a necessary condition for their religious freedom."[17]

According to this analysis, America has freedom of speech and religion because of the Protestant identity and roots of its founders. Because Protestant Christianity affirms the individual right and responsibility of each person to relate directly to God with unmediated access to the words in scripture, it places the highest value on freedoms of religion and of speech. Even non-Christian agnostics, like Horowitz himself, would be wise to appreciate, or at least acknowledge, from where the roots of our constitutional freedoms arise.

THE OUTLAWING OF GOD

For leftist adherents of "reason," freedoms of speech and religion are simply tools of the ruling class to maintain and increase their privilege and power in society. These freedoms and religious "superstitions," which block the way to a more just and enlightened society, must be undermined and discredited. One of the most effective tools to do so has been litigation through the courts.

Due to a series of Supreme Court decisions that began more than five decades ago, the leftist agenda to drive any shred of recognition of the existence of God out of the public square has been remarkably successful. Consequently, many public-school teachers, administrators, and even school cafeteria workers, regard it as their responsibility to prevent school children from expressing any religious beliefs on school property.

---

17   Ibid. pp. 39 and 41.

ENGEL V. VITALE

In 1962, a landmark case involving religious liberty, known as *Engel v. Vitale*, was heard by the Supreme Court, which considered the constitutionality of a 23-word prayer in New York State. The prayer read: "Almighty God, we acknowledge our dependence upon Thee, and we beg Thy blessings upon us, our parents, our teachers and our country. Amen." The court ruled 6 to 1 that the prayer was a violation of the Constitution, rejecting the defense's claims that the prayer was voluntary and that it reflected no particular religion. The Court majority held that, because the prayer did not address the beliefs of atheists, it violated the Establishment Clause.[18]

As noted in *Original Intent: The Courts, The Constitution and Religion*, "For 170 years following the ratification of the Constitution and Bill of Rights, no Court had ever struck down any prayer, in any form, in any location."[19] Opponents of school prayer often cite Thomas Jefferson's January 1, 1802 letter to the Danbury Baptist Association of Connecticut because it speaks of a "wall of separation between Church and State."[20] Yet Jefferson himself invoked God and non-sectarian religious beliefs in the government documents he drafted, the most famous being in America's founding document, the Declaration of Independence, which states God the Creator is the source of our "inalienable rights."

As pointed out by Horowitz, "If the plaintiffs in *Engel v. Vitale* were interested in protecting their children from being offended by the Regent's prayer, they could have sought to remedy their concerns at the local or state level. . . . Instead they bypassed the democratic

---

18   Facts and Case Summary–*Engel v. Vitale*, 370 U.S. 421 (1962). https://www.uscourts.gov/educational-resources/educational-activities/facts-and-case-summary-engel-v-vitale, accessed April 4, 2019.

19   David Barton, *Original Intent: The Courts, The Constitution and Religion,* (Aledo, TX: Wallbuilder Press, 2011).

20   *Federalist,* No. 51.

channels and pursued a constitutional challenge in the courts. They did so because victory in this area would make their partisan view the new fundamental view of the land."[21]

Instead of making an accommodation for children of atheists who did not want their son or daughter to recite a prayer, now no child in an American public school would be allowed to pray.

NEITHER MEDITATION NOR PRAYER

Engel v. Vitale became the basis for other decisions that continued the attack on religious expressions. In *Wallace v. Jaffree* (1985), the Supreme Court ruled that an Alabama law permitting one minute for "meditation or voluntary prayer" was unconstitutional,[22] apparently assuming that atheists never take time for personal reflection.

In *Lee v. Weisman* (1992), the Supreme Court banned clergy-led prayer at middle school commencement ceremonies.[23] In 2000, the Supreme Court used the precedent of *Lee v. Weisman* as a basis to include all school-organized *student-led* prayer at high school football games.[24] Horowitz summarizes these trends as follows:

> In one despotic decision after another, the Supreme Court inflated the Establishment Clause while letting all the air out of the Free Exercise protection. Again and again, the High Court jammed its radical redefinition of the First Amendment down the throat of an unwilling, unready society.
>
> America came under the grip of a bizarre official hypocrisy. Both houses of Congress opened with prayer. The Supreme Court opened with the invocation, "God save the United States and this

---

21   David Horowitz, *Dark Agenda*, p. 53.

22   *Wallace v. Jaffree*, https://www.oyez.org/cases/1984/83-812, accessed on April 23, 2019.

23   *Lee v. Weisman*, https://www.oyez.org/cases/1991/90-1014, accessed April 23, 2019.

24   "Prayer and Religion in the Public Schools: What Is, and Is Not, Permitted," CRS Report for Congress, August 18, 2000. Congressional Research Service, The Library of Congress.

Honorable Court." The lunch money that jingled in the pockets of school children was stamped, "In God We Trust," but "God" could not be invoked in any public school in America. [25]

GOD GONE FROM HISTORY

In keeping with *Engel v. Vitale*, American history had to be filtered to erase any mention of the religious origins of American freedoms. Consequently, in 2002, the New Jersey Department of Education removed references to the Pilgrims and the Mayflower from its history standards for school textbooks. Brian Jones of the Education Leaders Council said: "The word pilgrim implies religion. It's getting more difficult to talk about the Bible and the Puritans." For this reason, schools described the Puritans as "early settlers," "newcomers," or "European colonizers."[26]

In 1986 NYU professor Paul Vitz reviewed sixty social studies textbooks used by 87 percent of public-school students. He concluded by writing:

> It is common in these books to treat Thanksgiving without explaining to whom the Pilgrims give thanks. . . . The Pilgrims are described entirely without any reference to religion. The Pueblo [Indians] can pray to Mother Earth—but Pilgrims can't be described as praying to God. And never are Christians described as praying to Jesus, either in the United States or elsewhere, in the present or even in the past. . . . There is not one story or article in all these books, in approximately nine to ten thousand pages, in which the central motivation or major content derives from Christianity or Judaism.[27]

---

25   Ibid. p. 55.

26   Ibid. p. 57.

27   Paul Vitz, *Censorship: Evidence of Bias in Our Children's Textbooks* (Ann Arbor, MI: Servant, 1986), pp. 18-19, 65.

PORTRAYING CHRISTIANS AS PERSECUTORS

But the re-education of current and future generations does not stop with erasing America's Christian roots. As documented in Michael Chapman's American Heritage Research site,[28] Christianity itself must be smeared. In one textbook for sixth graders, lessons on the Roman Empire, the Christians are portrayed as aggressors. In a textbook lesson on the Roman Coliseum, "persecution" is simply defined as "the act of being harassed for differing beliefs"[29] The lesson plan instructs the teacher to "Tell the students that *persecution* of Christians in the early days was occasional and local…" but makes no mention that Christians were tortured and martyred for their faith. Instead, students are to "discuss why *minorities*… face persecution in times of trouble." In the teacher's margin, "background information" helps make the discussion question "relevant" by identifying Christians as the true persecutors: "[In early times] Christians made fun of [rural people and their old beliefs in gods and goddesses] by calling them *pagani*, meaning 'country people' or 'hicks.' This is the origin of the word pagan."

In Michael Chapman's view, a social agenda can be seen: to build sympathy for politically favored groups today that might think they are under persecution *by Christians.*[30] The lesson ends with a Role-Playing exercise in which students are directed to "take the role of a traditional Roman disturbed by the rise of Christianity, and write a letter explaining why he or she is opposed to the new religion."[31]

"MUHAMMED IS THE LAST AND FINAL MESSENGER OF GOD"

In January, 2018 parents of students at Chatham Middle School in New

---

28   http://americanheritageresearch.com/

29   *Discover Our Heritage, Teachers Edition* (Boston: Houghton Mifflin, 1997). Sixth-grade textbook. All references to Christians in Rome, martyrdom, and persecution, are from page 245.

30   Michael Chapman, "Anti-Christian Bias in Education," http://americanheritageresearch. com/19/, accessed on May 9, 2019.

31   *Discover Our Heritage, Teachers Edition*, op cit., p. 245.

Jersey filed a lawsuit against the school, complaining that the school had shown two videos in 7th-grade classes designed to convert viewers to Islam. The first video, "Intro to Islam," is set to a musical version of a poem that describes "Christians and Jews as 'infidels' and prais[es] Muhammad in gruesome detail for slaughtering them." The parents complained that the five-minute assignment was "replete with biased, chastising statements encouraging the students … to follow the Quran and become Muslim" and declaring that "Muhammad (Peace be upon him) is the last & final Messenger of God."[32]

In addition to presenting the religious teachings of Islam as facts, one of the parents, Libby Hilsenrath, explained that the video includes a link where students can download "Qaseedah Burdah," the song with references to killing infidels. In the second video, an explanation of the five pillars of Islam, is a cartoon where a Muslim child explains the tenants of Islam to his non-Muslim friend, then ends with both boys walking off to "learn how to pray." A worksheet component of the assignment meanwhile focused on the shahada, what Hilsenrath described as "the Islamic conversion creed and prayer."

The Thomas More Law Center, which represented the parents, summarized, "Clearly, seventh graders were given a sugarcoated, false depiction of Islam. They were not informed of the kidnappings, beheadings, slave-trading, massacres, and persecution of non-Muslims, nor of the repression of women—all done in the name of Islam."[33]

CHRIST AND CHI ALPHA

The animus against expressions of faith are so widespread that even voluntary campus associations of Christians, which insist that their leaders actually believe in Christ, have been banned. In 2015, the

---

32 Nick Rummel, "Mom Says NJ School Assignment Recruited for Islam, " January 24, 2018, Courthouse New Service. https://www.courthousenews.com/mom-says-nj-school-assignment-recruited-for-islam/, accessed May 9, 2019.

33 Ibid.

California State University Stanislaus chapter of Chi Alpha, a Christian student organization, was deactivated because the group insisted that its leaders be Christians. The university said it would no longer recognize the group due to a non-discrimination executive order that prohibited student organizations from excluding anyone, including in leadership roles. "What they cannot be is faith-based where someone has to have a profession of faith to be that leader" said university vice president Tim Lynch.[34]

REVOKING NATURAL LAW

Chapter 10's discussion of "Natural Law" showed how newly enacted federal and state policies and laws ban the expression of Biblical views regarding homosexuality or even affirming the self-evident existence of two biological sexes. Such policies mandate radical medical treatments for children who express feelings of alienation from their biological sex, even when their parents are opposed. Transgender mandates require schools to allow boys unrestricted access to girl's bathrooms, locker rooms, dorm rooms, hotel rooms, showers, and sports teams if they claim to identify as girls. Mental health professionals are prevented from providing counseling that addresses deeper causes for children expressing such "gender dysphoria." Medical professionals are compelled to provide treatment to these children that includes suppression of puberty using powerful drugs followed by the use of cross-sex hormones—a combination that results in lifetime sterility.[35]

THE MATTER OF MAXINE

Those wishing for a dose of sanity to come from America's neighbor to the north were disappointed. In March, 2019 the Supreme Court of British Columbia, Canada ordered that a 14-year-old girl receive

---

34   2015 Report on Anti-Catholicism, Catholic League for Religious and Civil Rights, https://www. catholicleague.org/education-20/, accessed on April 4, 2019.

35   "Gender Dysphoria in Children," *American College of Pediatrics*, November, 2018.

testosterone injections without parental consent. The court also declared that if either of her parents referred to her using female pronouns or addressed her by her birth name, they would be considered guilty of family violence.[36]

Maxine had been encouraged by her school counselor in BC's Delta School District to identify as a boy while in seventh grade. When Maxine was 13 years old, despite her parents' reservations, Dr. Brenden Hursh and his colleagues at BC Children's Hospital decided that Maxine should begin taking testosterone injections in order to develop a more masculine appearance.

The court ruled as follows: "Attempting to persuade [Maxine] to abandon treatment for gender dysphoria; addressing [Maxine] by his birth name; referring to [Maxine] as a girl or with female pronouns whether to him directly or to third parties; shall be considered to be family violence under s. 38 of the *Family Law Act*."

Her father expressed his anguish as follows: "The government has taken over my parental rights," he said, "They're using [Maxine] like she's a guinea pig in an experiment … Is BC Children's Hospital going to be there in 5 years when she rejects [her male identity]? No they're not. They don't care. They want numbers."

THE ABNEGATION OF NORMALCY

Norms that were accepted as common sense even ten years ago are increasingly against the law in the United States and other Western nations. To have traditional values regarding marriage and the existence of two biological sexes, or parental rights and responsibilities to oversee the upbringing and education of children, exposes adults to ostracism, professional disbarment, loss of employment, and even imprisonment.

If this massive social experiment continues, people of faith will

---

36 Jeremiah Keenan, "Canadian Court Rules Parents Can't Stop 14-Year-Old From Taking Trans Hormones," *The Federalist*, March 1, 2019. https://thefederalist.com/2019/03/01/canadian-court-rules-parents-cant-stop-14-year-old-taking-trans-hormones/

have to choose whether to obey the State or to obey their conscience, regardless of the consequences. One would expect that the Christian community at large would be prepared to stand up and demand that their rights of religious freedom not be violated, but non-Biblical beliefs are widespread even among active Christians.

THE REVOCATION OF RIGHTS

As discussed in chapter 10, government–enforced transgenderism is just the latest episode in the imposition of a post-Christian, Gnostic religion on the population. It is authoritarian because it has to be, since nature and common sense oppose it. Its dictates have not been chosen by popular vote, but enforced by unconstitutional edicts from unelected judges and leftist bureaucrats in the U.S. Departments of Education and of Health and Human Services, with the support of angry LGBTQ mobs who will shame and intimidate those who dare to challenge their claims. Ultimately, its dictates are backed by the power of government to imprison and even to use lethal force.

Since the founders of America knew that government has the potential to misuse its authority and power, they enshrined the right to own lethal firearms in the Second Amendment to the Constitution. Thomas Jefferson, in a December 20, 1787 letter to James Madison, said that the purpose of civilian arms was to be a check on government. He wrote, "What country can preserve its liberties if their rulers are not warned from time to time that their people preserve the spirit of resistance. Let them take arms."[37]

But that right is increasingly under attack. In November, 2018, in Ferndale, Maryland, Gary Willis, a 61-year-old man was shot and killed by an officer trying to enforce the state's "red flag" law which allows the confiscation of firearms from gun owners who have not been convicted of any crime or lost their right by any due process. The "red

---

37   Thomas Jefferson to James Madison, Dec. 20, 1787, in Papers of Jefferson, https://founders. archives.gov/documents/Madison/01-10-02-0210 accessed on April 4, 2019.

flag" protective orders may be sought by family members, police, or others when the gun owner is perceived to be a danger to themselves or others. Willis' niece, Michelle Willis, said her uncle "likes to speak his mind. I'm just dumbfounded right now. My uncle wouldn't hurt anybody."[38] Apparently, being outspoken in one's political views in the presence of family members or others can lead to confiscation of one's firearms, without a diagnosis or due process.

Nearly two thousand years ago, the early Christians in Rome under the rule of Emperor Nero were martyred because of their unpopular beliefs. As described by the Roman historian Tacitus: "They were torn by dogs and perished, or were nailed to crosses, or were doomed to the flames and burnt, to serve as a nightly illumination, when daylight had expired."[39] If people of faith in America are intimidated into acquiescence, then where will persecuted Christians and members of other minority faiths find support and refuge? If the state continues to drive the acknowledgment of God and the practice of biblical Christianity from the public square, Christians will be faced with a choice, to be absorbed into the secular culture or to stand firm and suffer the consequences.

An anemic Christianity that rejects the God of the Old and New Testament while embracing an air-brushed, feminized Jesus is no match for the aggressive, militant atheism of our age, which leads to the torture and persecution of millions of Christians in Communist countries like North Korea[40] and China,[41] not to mention attacks by Islamists mur-

---

38   Colin Campbell, "Anne Arundel police say officers fatally shot armed man while serving protective order to remove guns," *Baltimore Sun,* November 5, 2018.

39   Tacitus, *Annals* XV, 44

40   "Total Denial: Violations of Freedom of Religion or Belief in North Korea" (*Christian Solidarity Worldwide*, September 2016), pp. 3, 16.

41   "China: Repression of Christian Churches Intensifies," December 13, 2018 (New York: Human Rights Watch) https://www.hrw.org/news/2018/12/13/china-repression-christian-church-intensifies.

dering thousands of Christians worshipping peacefully in their pews.[42]

Watching silently, while tens of thousands of fellow believers are tortured or massacred, is not an act of love; it is an act of cowardice. As during the times of Nehemiah, Christians are called to rebuild vibrant communities of faith with one hand, and a weapon ready to use, if needed, in the other. It is time for followers of Christ to be brave again.

---

42 Dawn Amenn, "Persecuted and Forgotten? 2015-2017: A Report on Christians Oppressed for their Faith 2015-17" Executive Summary, Aid to the Church in Need, Brooklyn, NY, https://www.churchinneed.org/persecution/

EPILOGUE

MARCION TRIUMPHANT

And Joseph went to Bethlehem. To be enrolled with Mary, his wife, who was then pregnant. And she brought forth her firstborn child. And her name was chosen to be Judith." [Luke 2:4-5, 7, 21]

And She bearing her cross, went forth into a place called the Place of a Skull, which is called in the Hebrew Golgotha; There they crucified her, and two others with her, on either side one, and Judith in the midst. [John 19:17-18]

Mary Magdalene and the other Mary came to see the tomb. But the angel said to the women, "Do not be afraid, for I know that you seek Judith who was crucified." . . . "She is not here; for She is risen." [Matthew 28:1, 5-6]

PASSAGES FROM *JUDITH OF NAZARETH*, LBI INSTITUTE, 2003

THE TRIUMPH OF MARCIONISM/GNOSTICISM over traditional Christianity is evidenced by the endorsement of gay rights, gun control, same-sex marriage, abortion, pacifism, and religious indifferentism by Christian denominations. It is verified by theological efforts to nullify or mollify much of the Torah and to sever the "mooring ropes" that tie human conduct to the Bible. It is witnessed by the statements of prominent feminist theologians, including Naomi Goldenberg, professor of religious studies at the University of Ottawa, who seek to "execute" the God of the Old Testament.[1] In her book *The Changing of the Gods,* Goldenberg writes: "The feminist movement in Western culture is engaged in the slow execution of Christ and Yahweh. . . It is likely that as we watch Christ and Yahweh tumble to the ground, we will completely outgrow the need for an external God."[2]

A COSMIC CHILD-ABUSER

In preparation for the new Gnostic age, Steve Chalke and Alan Mann in *The Lost Message of Jesus* have called for the removal of all crosses from Christian churches and the relegation of the doctrine of the Atonement to the trash heap of religious history. They write: "If the cross is a personal act of vengeance perpetrated by God toward mankind but borne by his son, then it makes a mockery of Jesus' own teaching to love your enemies and to refuse to repay evil with evil."[3] Explaining this passage, Chalke said: "In my view, the real problem with penal substitution (a theory rooted in violence and retributive notions of justice) is its incompatibility, at least as currently taught and understood with any authentically Christian understanding of the character of God or genuinely Christocentric worldview–given, for instance, Jesus' own non-violent, 'Do not return evil for evil,' approach to life. . . Hence my comment in *The Lost Message of Jesus*, about the tragedy of reducing

---

1   Douglas S. Winnall, "A Different Gospel?" *Tomorrow's World*, July-August 2000, https://www. tomorrowsworld.org/magazines/2000/july-august/a-different-gospel

2   Naomi Goldenberg, *Changing of the Gods: Feminism and the End of Traditional Religions* (Boston: Beacon Press, 1979), pp. 4 and 23.

3   Steve Chalke and Alan Mann, *The Lost Message of Jesus* (Grand Rapids, Michigan, 2004), pp. 182-183.

God to a 'cosmic child-abuser.'"[4]

Similarly, Alan Jones, an Episcopal priest, maintains that the substitutionary death of Christ to appease an angry God is a "vile doctrine!" He writes, "The Church's fixation on the death of Jesus as the universal saving act must end, and the place of the cross must be reimagined in Christian faith. Why? Because of the cult of suffering and the vindictive God behind it."[5]

PASTOR ANDY'S SERMON

As the Ten Commandments are removed from courthouses and crosses from churches, Gnosticism became embraced by the megachurches that sprouted up in America and throughout the world. Andy Stanley, the pastor of the North Point Community Church, the second largest church in the United States, delivered a sermon in which he said that contemporary Christianity must become unhitched from the Old Testament. "The Gospel of Jesus," he said, "is completely detached from everything that came before. . . . God has done something through the Jews for the world. But the 'through the Jews' part of the story is over, and now something new and better and inclusive has come." Stanley described the Old Testament as "violent," "disturbing," and a book that "offends our modern senses." He then went on to say:

> Many have lost faith because of something about the Bible or in the Bible, the Old Testament in particular... once they could no longer accept all the historicity of the Old Testament... suddenly their house of cards of faith came tumbling down because they were taught it's all true, it's all God's Word and if you find one part that's not true,

---

4   Steve Chalke, quoted in Don Boys, "Emergent Church Leaders Are Modern Gnostics," CST News, October 10, 2008, www.cstnews.com/bm/issues-facing-christians-today-common-sense-for-today/falling-standards-and-seeker-sensitive-churches/emergent-church-leaders-are-modern-gnostics.shtml

5   Alan Jones. *Reimagining Christianity* (Hoboken, New Jersey: Wiley, 2004), p. 132.

uh oh, the whole thing comes tumbling down.

Not Christianity. The Bible did not create Christianity. The resurrection of Jesus created and launched Christianity. Your whole house of Old Testament cards can come tumbling down.[6]

The same beliefs had been espoused in Rome 1,900 years earlier by Marcion, another charismatic preacher, whom the leaders of the early church had condemned as "the first born of Satan." According to Tertullian, "Marcion has laid down the position, that Christ who in the days of Tiberius was, by a previously unknown god, revealed for the salvation of all nations, is a different being from Him who was ordained by God the Creator for the restoration of the Jewish state, and who is yet to come."[7]

The Jesus of Marcion was not the Son of God, but a celestial being from the realm of light.

He was not the "suffering servant" foretold by the prophet Isaiah since He did not possess a human body and did not die on the cross.

He was not the Messiah, who would establish a Kingdom of God on earth.

And He will not come again to commit all those who have abandoned His teachings to eternal darkness.

In the belief that Christ will *not* return rests the only hope of all those who have embraced the first Christian heresy and thereby abandoned all that once was holy.

---

6   Andy Stanley, quoted in Stovan Zaimov, "Theologians Warn Andy Stanley's Message to 'Unhitch' Old Testament Is Heresy," *The Christian Post*, May 15, 2018, https://www. christianpost.com/news/theologians-warn-andy-stanleys-message-to-unhitch-old-testament-is-heresy.html

7   Tertullian. *Against Marcion*, Book IV, Chapter 6. excerpted from *Ante-Nicene Fathers*, Volume 3, edited by Philip Schaff, 1885. Online Edition, www.tertullian.org/anf/anf03/anf03-30. htm#P4763_1515567

SELECT BIBLIOGRAPHY

1. Akers, Keith. *The Lost Religion of Jesus*. Myerstown, PA: Lantern Books, 2000.
2. Alexander, Denis. *Creation or Evolution: Do We Have to Choose, 2nd ed.* Oxford and Grand Rapids, MI: Monarch, 2014.
3. Anderson, Hugh. *Jesus: Great Lives Observed*. Englewood Cliffs, New Jersey: Prentice Hall, 1967.
4. Anderson, Ryan T. *When Harry Became Sally: Responding to the Transgender Moment*. New York: Encounter Books, 2018.
5. Bayer, Ronald. *Homosexuality and American Psychiatry: The Politics of Diagnosis*. Princeton, NJ: Princeton University Press, 1987.
6. Behe, Michael J. *Darwin's Black Box: The Biochemical Challenge to Evolution*. New York: Free Press, 2006.
7. Bellegrandi, Franco. *Nikita Roncalli: Controvita di un Papa*. Rome: Eiles, 2009.
8. Berry, Jason. *Lead Us Not into Temptation: Catholic Priests and Sexual Abuse of Children*. Chicago: University of Illinois Press, 2000.
9. Black, Edwin. *War Against the Weak: Eugenics and America's Campaign to Create a Master Race*. Washington, DC: Dialog Press, 2012.
10. Bostaph, Samuel. *Andrew Carnegie: An Economic Biography*. New York: Rowman and Littlefield, 2015.
11. Bourke, Stephen. *The Middle East: The Cradle of Civilization Revealed*. Birmingham, Alabama: Sweetwater Press, 2018.
12. Bultmann, Rudolf. *Jesus and the Word*. New York: Scribner's, 1934.
13. Bultmann, Rudolf. *Kerygma and Myth*. New York: Harper Torchbooks, 1961.
14. Bultmann, Rudolph. *The Theology of the New Testament*, Volume I. New York: Scribner's, 1951.
15. Bultmann, Rudolf. "Die Bedeutung des Alten Testaments fur den Christlichen Glauben," in *Glauben und Verstehen* I, Seventh Edition. Tubingen: J. C. B. Mohr, 1972.
16. Butz, Jeffrey J. *The Brother of Jesus and the Lost Teachings of Christianity*. Rochester, Vermont: Inner Traditions, 2005.
17. Calvin, John. *Commentaries on the Four Last Books of Moses*. Ulan Press, San Bernardino, California, 2012.
18. Chadwick, Henry. *The Early Church*. Baltimore, Maryland: Penguin Books, 1969.
19. Chalke, Steve and Alan Mann. *The Lost Message of Jesus*. Grand Rapids, MI: Zondervan, 2004.
20. Chernow, Ron. *The House of Morgan: An American Banking Dynasty and the Rise of Modern Finance*. New York: Grove Press, 2001.
21. Clark, Elizabeth and Herbert Richardson, eds. *Women and Religion: A Feminist Sourcebook for Christian Thought*. New York: Harper and Row, 1977.

22. Colon, A.R. and P.A. Colon, *A History of Children: A Socio-Cultural Survey Across Millennia.* Westwood: Greenwood Press. 2001.

23. Coogan, Michael D. and Mark S. Smith. *Stories from Ancient Canaan.* Louisville, KY: Westminster John Knox Press, 2012.

24. Coxe, A. Cleveland, translator. *The Ante Nicene Fathers*, Volume I, Grand Rapids, Michigan: William B. Eerdmans Publishing Company, 1980.

25. Crain, Patricia. *The Story of A: The Alphabetization of America from the* New England Primer *to* The Scarlet Letter. Stanford: Stanford University Press, 2000.

26. Crooks, Robert and Karla Baur. *Our Sexuality.* Belmont, California: Wadsworth, 2008.

27. Darwin, Charles. *On the Origin of Species by Natural Selection or the Preservation of Favored Races in the Struggle for Life.* New York: D. Appleton and Company, 1861.

28. Darwin, Charles. *The Origin of the Species,* New York: D. Appleton & Co., 1881.

29. Dawkins, Richard. *The God Delusion.* Boston: Houghton Mifflin, 2006.

30. Denton, Michael. *Evolution: A Theory in Crisis.* Chevy Chase, MD: Adler & Adler; 3rd edition, 2002.

31. Doherty, Earl. *Challenging the Verdict: A Cross-Examination of Lee Strobel's "The Case for Christ."* Ottawa: Age of Reason Publications, 2001.

32. Durant, Will. *Our Oriental Heritage*, Volume I, *The Story of Civilization.* New York: Simon and Schuster, 1954.

33. Durant, Will. *Caesar and Christ,* Volume 3, *The Story of Civilization,* New York: Simon and Schuster, 1944.

34. Ehrman, Bart D. *How Jesus Became God: The Exaltation of a Jewish Prophet from Galilee.* New York: HarperOne, 2014.

35. Eusebius. *Church History*, Book III, translated by Arthur Cushman McGiffert, in *Nicene and Post Nicene Fathers.* Buffalo, NY: Christian Literature Publishing, 1890.

36. Ford, Paul Leicester, ed. *The Works of Thomas Jefferson in Twelve Volumes,* Federal Edition, Vol. 9. New York: G. P. Putnam's Sons, 1904.

37. Fosdick, Raymond E. *John D. Rockefeller, Jr.: A Portrait.* New York: Harper and Brothers, 1958.

38. Freke, Timothy, and Peter Gandy. *The Jesus Mysteries: Was the "Original Jesus" a Pagan God?* New York: Three Rivers Press, 1999.

39. Frend, W. H. C. *The Early Church.* Philadelphia: J. B. Lippincott, 1966.

40. Friedman, Richard Elliott. *The Bible with Sources Revealed.* New York: HarperOne, 2009.

41. Gardner, Laurence. *The Shadow of Solomon: The Lost Secret of the Freemasons Revealed.* London: HarperCollins, 2009.

42. Giberson, Karl and Francis Collins. *Language of Science and Faith.* Downers Grove, IL: InterVarsity, 2011.

43. Grant, Richard M. *The Early Christian Doctrine of God.* Charlottesville: The University of Virginia Press, 1966.

44. Greenberg, David. *The Construction of Homosexuality.* Chicago: University of Chicago Press, 1988.

45. Grimstad, Kirsten J. *The Modern Revival of Gnosticism and Thomas Mann's Doktor Faustus.* Rochester, New York: Camden House, 2002.

46. Harnack, Adolf von. *Marcion: Das Evangelium vom Fremden Gott,* Second Edition. Leipzig, Germany: J. C. Hinrichs, 1924.

47. Harpur, Tom. *The Pagan Christ: Is Blind Faith Killing Christianity?* New York: Walker and Company, 2004.

48. Hoffman, Paul. *Oh Vatican! A Slightly Wicked View of the Holy See.* New York: Congdon and Weed, 1984.

49. Homan, M.M. *To Your Tents, O Israel: The Terminology, Function, Form and Symbolism of Tents in the Hebrew Bible and the Ancient Near East.* Leiden: Brill, 2002.

50. Horowitz, David. *Dark Agenda: The War to Destroy Christian America.* West Palm Beach Florida: Humanix Books, 2018.

51. Hughes, Dennis D. *Human Sacrifice in Ancient Greece.* London: Routledge, 1991.

52. Irenaeus, *Against Heresies*, Book III, Chapter 3, in *Ante-Nicene Fathers*, Volume 1, edited by Alexander Roberts, et al. Buffalo, NY: Christian Literature Publishing Company, 1885.

53. Jefferson, Thomas. *The Papers of Thomas Jefferson*, Volume 2, edited by J. P. Boyd. Princeton: Princeton University Press, 1950.

54. Jones, Alan. *Reimagining Christianity.* Hoboken, NJ: Wiley, 2004.

55. Johnson, Paul. *A History of Christianity.* New York: Simon and Shuster, 1976.

56. Kaufmann, Walter. *Critique of Religion and Philosophy.* Princeton: Princeton University Press, 1978.

57. Koss, Peter. *Carnegie.* New York: John Wiley and Sons, 2002.

58. Keller, Werner. *The Bible as History*, translated from the German by William Neil, Second Edition. New York: William Morrow and Company, 1980.

59. Kirch, Jonathan. *Moses: A Life.* New York: Ballantine Books, 1998.

60. Kosnik, Anthony, and William Carroll, et al. *Human Sexuality: New Directions in American Catholic Thought.* New York: Paulist Press, 1977.

61. Koss, Peter. *Carnegie.* New York: John Wiley and Sons, 2002.

62. Lanfer, Peter Thatcher. *Remembering Eden: The Reception History of Genesis 3:22-24.* New York: Oxford University Press, 2012.

63. Laumann, Edward O., et al. *The Social Organization of Sexuality: Sexual Practices in the United States.* Chicago: The University of Chicago Press, 1994.

64. *Laws of the State of Delaware*, Revised Edition. Wilmington: R. Porter, 1829.

65. Leithart, Peter. *Defending Constantine.* Downers Grove, Illinois, 2010.

66. Lewis, C.S. *The Weight of Glory: And Other Addresses.* New York: HarperCollins Publishers, 1949.

67. Likoudis, Paul. *Amchurch Comes Out: The U.S. Bishops, Pedophile Scandals, and the Homosexual Agenda.* Petersburg, Illinois: Roman Catholic Faithful, 2002.

68. Lukas, Mary and Ellen Lukas, *Teilhard*, Doubleday & Co., Inc., Garden City, New York, 1977.

69. Luther, Martin. *Luther's Works*, Vol. 35, *Word and Sacrament.* Philadelphia: Fortress Press, 1960.

70. Luther, Martin. *Werke,* Vol. XX. Weimar: Herman Bohlau, 1883.

71. Leuker, Erwin L., et al., eds. Lutheran Church, Missouri Synod, *Christian Cyclopedia*, 2000.

72. Mackey, Albert G. *Encyclopedia of Freemasonry,* Volume 1. Chicago: Masonic History Company, 1924.

73. Malthus, Thomas R. *An Essay on the Principle of Population.* Cambridge University Press, 1992.

74. Marshall, Peter and David Manuel. *The Light and the Glory.* Grand Rapids, Michigan, Revel, 2009.

75. Marx, Karl. *Contribution to the Critique of Hegel's Philosophy of Right, 1843.* Cambridge, UK: Cambridge University Press, 1970.

76. Marx, Karl and Friedrich Engels, *Marx-Engels Collected Works*, vol. 40. Moscow: Progress Publishers, 1975.

77. Meyer, Stephen C. *Darwin's Doubt: The Explosive Origin of Animal Life and the Case for Intelligent Design.* San Francisco, HarperOne, 2014.

78. Michael, Robert T., John H. Gagnon, et al. *Sex in America: A Definitive Survey.* Boston: Little, Brown and Co., 1994.

79. Miller, Robert Moats. *Harry Emerson Fosdick: Preacher, Pastor, Prophet.* New York: Oxford University Press, 1985.

80. Moorhead Paul S. and Martin M. Kaplan, Eds. *Mathematical Challenges to the Neo-Darwinian Interpretation of Evolution.* Philadelphia, Wistar Institute Press, 1967.

81. Moreland, J.P. and Stephen C. Meyer, et al. *Theistic Evolution: A Scientific, Philosophical, and Theological Critique.* Wheaton, IL: Crossway, 2017.

82. Nasaw, David. *Andrew Carnegie.* New York: Penguin Press, 2006.

83. Neev, D. and K.O. Emery. *The Destruction of Sodom, Gomorrah, and Jericho: Geological, Climatological, and Archaeological Background.* New York: Oxford University Press, 1995.

84. Ortberg, John. *Who Is This Man?* Grand Rapids, Michigan: Zondervan, 2012.

85. Pagels, Elaine. *The Gnostic Gospels.* New York: Vintage Books, 1989.

86. Pike, Albert. *Morals and Dogma.* Charleston, South Carolina: Supreme Council of the Thirty-Third Degree of the Scottish Rite, 1871.

87. Plato. *The Laws.* Dutton, New York: Everyman's Library 1969.

88. Plutarch. *Complete Works of Plutarch*, Delphi Classics, 2013.

89. Posner. Gary. *God's Bankers: A History of Money and Power at the Vatican.* New York: Simon and Schuster, 2015.

90. Rohl, David M. *Exodus: Myth or History.* St. Louis, MN: Thinking Man Media, 2015.

91. Robinson, John A.T. *Can We Trust the New Testament?* Grand Rapids, Michigan: William B. Eerdmans Publishing Company, 1977.

92. Romer, Thomas. *Dark God: Cruelty, Sex, and Violence in the Old Testament.* New York: Paulist Press, 2013.

93. Rauschenbusch, Walter. *A Theology of the Social Gospel.* New York: Abington Press, 1918.

94. Rose, Michael S. *Goodbye, Good Men: How Liberals Brought Corruption into the Catholic Church.* Washington, DC: Regnery Publishing, 2002.

95. Robinson, John A.T. *Can We Trust the New Testament?* Grand Rapids, Michigan: William B. Eerdmans Publishing Company, 1977.

96. Rummel, Rudolph J. *Death by Government.* New Brunswick, NJ: Transaction Publishers, 1994.

97. Sanger, Margaret. *The Public Writings and Speeches of Margaret Sanger.* New York University, 1921.

98. Schonfield, Hugh J. *The Passover Plot.* New York: Disinformation Company, 2005.

99. Schoch, Robert. *Voyages of the Pyramid Builders.* New York: Putnam, 2003.

100. Schwager, Raymund. *Must There Be Scapegoats? Violence and Redemption in the Bible.* San Francisco: Harper, 1987.

101. Schweitzer, Albert. *The Quest of the Historical Jesus.* New York: Macmillan, 1968.

102. Semler, Johann Salomo. *Institutio as Doctrinam Christianam Liberaltier Discendam.* Regensburg, Germany: Halae Magdeburgicae, 1774.

103. Seters, John van. *Abraham in History and Tradition.* New Haven: Yale University Press, 1975.

104. Spencer, Robert. *The Politically Incorrect Guide to Islam and the Crusades.* Washington, DC: Regnery, 2005.

105. Strauss, David. *The Life of Jesus for the People,* Second Edition. London: Williams and Norgate, 1879.

106. Tannahill, Reay. *Sex in History.* New York: Stein and Day, 1981.

107. Templeton, Charles. *Farewell to God: My Reason for Rejecting the Christian Faith.* Toronto: McClelland and Stewart, 1996.

108. Thomas, Thomas L. *The Mythic Past: Biblical Archaeology and the Myth of Israel.* New York: Basic Books, 1999.

109. Vitz, Paul. *Censorship: Evidence of Bias in Our Children's Textbooks.* Ann Arbor, MI: Servant, 1986.

110. Wall, Joseph Frazier. *Andrew Carnegie.* Pittsburgh: The University of Pittsburgh Press, 1989.

111. Walton, John H. and J. Harvey Walton. *The Lost World of the Israelite Conquest.* Downers Grove, Illinois: Inter-Varsity Press, 2017.

112. Weiss, Johannes. *Earliest Christianity*, Volume I. New York: Harper and Row, 1959.

113. Wells, Jonathan. *Icons of Evolution: Science or Myth? Why Much of What We Teach about Evolution Is Wrong.* Washington, DC: Regnery Publishing, 2000.

114. Wenham, David. *Did St. Paul Get Jesus Right?* Oxford, England: Lion Books, 2010.

115. West, John G. *Darwin Day In America: How Our Politics and Culture Have Been Dehumanized in the Name of Science.* Wilmington, DE: Intercollegiate Studies Institute, 2007.

116. Wilkinson, Philip. *Myths and Legends: An Illustrated Guide to Their Origins and Meanings.* New York: DK Publishing, 2009.

117. Wilson, Ian. *Jesus: The Evidence.* San Francisco: HarperCollins, 1996.

118. Wormser, Rene. *Foundations: Their Power and Influence.* New York: Covenant House Books, 1993.

119. Yallop, David. *The Power and the Glory: Inside the Dark Heart of John Paul II's Vatican.* New York: Carroll and Graf, 2007.

120. Zagami, Leo and Brad Olsen, *Pope Francis: The Last Pope? Money, Masons, and Occultism in the Decline of the Catholic Church.* San Francisco, CA: CCC Publishing, 2015.

INDEX